CALLED

a memoir

MARK REDMOND

Thank you for reading my book!

Mark Redmond

ONION
RIVER

PRESS

BURLINGTON, VT

Onion River Press
191 Bank Street
Burlington, VT 05401

Publisher's Cataloging-in-Publication data

Names: Redmond, Mark, author.
Title: Called : a memoir / Mark Redmond.
Description: Burlington, VT: Onion River Press, 2021.
Identifiers: LCCN: 2021903707 | ISBN: 978-1-949066-66-1 (paperback) | 978-1-949066-76-0 (eBook) | 978-1-949066-77-7 (audio)
Subjects: LCSH Redmond, Mark. | Self-actualization (Psychology). | Conduct of life. | Self-realization. | Hope. | Homeless children--United States. | Homeless youth--United States. | BISAC BIOGRAPHY & AUTOBIOGRAPHY / Personal Memoirs | BODY, MIND & SPIRIT / General | FAMILY & RELATIONSHIPS / General
Classification: LCC BF575.H56 .R44 2021 | DDC 158.1/092--dc23

Dedicated to my parents

AIDEN & MARGARET REDMOND

AUTHOR'S NOTE

In this book I mention the names of certain people with whom I have interacted during my four decades of service. In most cases I did not use a last name and changed the first name to protect their privacy. When contact was possible, I sent them the text for their review and approval. In one case, their actual first and last names were used with their permission.

· *acknowledgments* ·

THERE ARE MANY PEOPLE TO THANK who made this book possible. I loved working with Onion River Press, in particular Rachel Fisher. If we're all into Buy Local, then you were the perfect fit. I am also so grateful to my editor, Virginia Simmon, and book designer, Lisa Cadieux. And thank you John LaSala for all the help on the audio book.

My readers were Julie Brooks, Bill Schubart, Mike Leach, David Mindich, Viki Zulkoski and Pete Cunningham. Thank you all, especially you, Pete, since this was the second one you've done for me.

While this book encapsulates my entire sixty-plus years of living, much of it is about my four decades helping homeless and at-risk youth, and the bulk of that has been at Spectrum Youth and Family Services in Vermont. The board members on that initial interviewing team took a big chance on me when offering me the job. I'm grateful to them, and to the others who have followed them on our board of directors over the years. Some executive directors complain about their boards of directors. I'm not one of them. And to the people on the Spectrum staff with whom I work: I am in awe of you, your compassion and dedication, and the patient way you work with the youth in our care.

Thank you to the editors of *Forbes, Huffington Post, The National Catholic Reporter,* and *The Washington Post* who published my columns. And I will forever be in debt to the wonderful people at The Moth who gave me my first break in the story-telling world.

And to my wife, Marybeth – I thank God every day that I met you, you fell in love with me, and that we have this wonderful life together.

· *introduction* ·

IT'S DECEMBER 30, the day before New Year's Eve. I'm at home, off from work at Spectrum Youth and Family Services, where I serve as executive director. I always take the week off between Christmas and New Year's, just to relax, unwind, and see family. My cell phone rings. I don't recognize the number, but I see it's an out-of-state area code and I have a feeling I know who it is. I suspect it's Rebecca, a former Spectrum youth, who we accepted into our shelter a few years earlier when she was alone, hungry, and homeless. She's probably calling me now because she needs help. Part of me doesn't want to pick up. It's my week off, and I just don't want to get into whatever Rebecca's issues are right now.

But I take the call. Guilt gets me every time.

"Rebecca?" I ask.

It's her.

"I know I'm not at Spectrum any longer," she said, "but I really need your advice."

"Go ahead," I said.

"In a few days I'm supposed to start a full-time job at a mental health nonprofit organization, but the job requires a car. I took mine to Girlington Garage, but it won't pass inspection. It needs new tires; you can actually see the metal wiring coming through the tires I have on there now. And it needs new struts. Girlington says they are not in a position to do these things for free, and even at cost it's over five hundred dollars; but I don't have that, and if I don't have that work done, my car won't pass inspection, and I can't start the job."

"Wait a minute," I said. "How about college? I thought you were going to college."

"I am. That starts in two weeks. I'm taking a full course load, eighteen credits. And I need the job so I can pay the tuition, which is why I need the car to pass inspection and be on the road."

Full-time college and full-time work. I always took on a lot, but I never had to do that.

"All I want is your advice," she said. "I don't know what to do."

"Here's my advice: Tell Girlington to do all the work and send me the bill. Spectrum will pay for this."

She paused. "But that's not why I called you. I didn't mean for you to do that. I just want your advice."

"Well that's my advice," I said. "Take it or leave it."

"Why are you doing this for me?"

"I'll tell you why. Do you remember that time a few years ago when Senator Leahy came to visit Spectrum, and we needed someone to welcome him, show him around, and say a few words to everyone present? You had only been with us for a few days, but you stepped forward and agreed to do it. Do you remember the time Spectrum was picked as the recipient of a large donation from the Clothes Exchange, and they asked that one of our youth stand up at the reception and say something, and you did it? And then the time Warren Buffett's sister gave us a big donation to build a new residence for homeless teenagers, and every reporter in town wanted to talk to one of our kids, and you volunteered to do it? Maybe you don't remember those things, but I do. I didn't forget. You helped us out then, so I want to help you now.

"And besides, even if you hadn't done those things, I would still be doing this."

"Why?" she asked.

"Because you're family to us, and this is what family does. Family looks out for one another and helps one another through the rough spots in life.

"But there is one catch. Very few things in life come absolutely free. There's almost always a quid pro quo, and there is with this. If I do this for you, you have to do something for me."

"What is it?" she asked. She sounded nervous.

"When are you graduating from college?" I asked.

"Not this May but the following one."

"Well I want to be invited. I want a ticket to that graduation. That's what you have to do for me if I do this now for you. Do we have a deal?"

She laughed and said, "It's a deal."

"Okay. I'm going to hang up the phone now and email the owner of Girlington Garage, whom I know really well, and tell her to do the work on your car so it passes inspection, and to send Spectrum the bill."

"Thank you," she said. "I mean it. Thank you."

I hung up the phone and turned to my wife, Marybeth, who had been sitting next to me throughout the conversation. She was in tears.

"Why are you crying?" I asked.

"Because you or I at age twenty-two or twenty-three had a multitude of people we could have called for help with something like that – parents, aunts, uncles, grandparents, friends with resources. These kids don't have that. They have you and your coworkers at Spectrum, and that's it. You really are their family."

I nodded in agreement.

This is the kind of work I do. I've done it for four decades. It's not how I ever expected my life to turn out, but it has.

It's hard work. Difficult. Frustrating. Dangerous at times. Wonderful at other times. Fulfilling. Amazing.

It's also why I believe I was put on this earth. I consider the work I do to be my true vocation. I get asked all the time, "How do you not get burnt out? How do you keep doing what you do in the face of so much pain and suffering?"

Depending on who is asking the question, I have various answers, all of which are true.

I have a loving and supportive wife by my side, and two wonderful sons.

It's a marathon, not a sprint, so I don't work crazy hours, and I take time to exercise and socialize with friends.

I pray and meditate daily and engage in other spiritual practices that sustain me.

But in the end, the main reason is that if you truly believe that the work you do is your calling, then that, more than anything else, is what sustains you through the difficult and even tragic moments.

This book is about my own journey to that realization, how I ended up on a path I never would have picked for myself, the circumstances that led me to it, and why I am so grateful that I am on it.

Mark Redmond
April 2020

. .

POSTSCRIPT

Rebecca got her car fixed, started the job,
took her eighteen college credits, and ended up
graduating right on schedule, the following May.
Today she works as a social worker here in Vermont.

· *one* ·

IF YOU TALK TO PEOPLE who do the kind of work I do and ask them about their personal backgrounds, they will almost always tell you one of two things: a) that they majored in psychology, counseling, social work, or something similar in college; or b) that they grew up in a family filled with poverty, substance abuse, and domestic violence, which led to a youth spent in foster care, the juvenile justice system, homeless on the streets, or in a gang.

None of this applies to me.

I grew up during the 1960s and '70s on Long Island, considered the suburbs to New York City, just fifty miles away. Born in 1930, my father is still a child of the Great Depression – a Coast Guard veteran who managed to miss both World War II and the Korean War. He went to college at night on the G.I. Bill when I was a baby and studied business administration. He was from Queens, my mother from Brooklyn. They met and married in 1954. In 1957 they had me and then four others, all within an eight-year span.

It was a typical middle class suburban upbringing for that time. My father was a businessman in New York City working in commercial real estate, buying and selling big buildings. He got up early each morning, my mother drove him to the train, he worked all day and at night the commute was reversed. My childhood days were set to the rhythm of the Long Island Rail Road. My mother didn't have paid employment, but she worked her tail off cooking and cleaning and making sure that homework was done, as well as the thousand other tasks inherent in raising five children. She was the one who went to all the parent-teacher conferences, drove us to Little League practices and games, broke up the constant fights we had with each other, made and packed our lunches every morning, washed and dried and folded our

FATHER'S DAY, 1968

clothing. It was endless for her, and when I look back at family pictures, she frequently looks exhausted, which she most likely was. She was always there for us.

We weren't rich, but we didn't want for anything, either. We went on nice vacations, but nothing extravagant. My dad eventually earned enough so we could join a beach and tennis club, but it wasn't anything over the top.

I loved working. I had a paper route as soon as I was old enough, in sixth grade. I loved being busy and productive. I still do.

I was athletic. I'd play sports year-round with the kids on our block. We'd transition from one sport to the other as the seasons passed: football, kickball, basketball, baseball, all out on the street or in a vacant lot behind one of the houses. I hated to be called in for dinner. I'd shove my meal in as fast as possible because I could hear my friends still out there, and I was dying to join them. "Slow down! We eat as a family!" my father would say. I joined Little League baseball the moment I was eligible, the same with Catholic Youth Organization basketball. I learned early on I was good at sports. I was athletic, although not as much as some other boys. But I figured out that if I worked harder than they did, I could make up for whatever I lacked in talent and keep pace.

I also figured out early on that I was smart. I wasn't necessarily the top student in class, but as with athletics, I learned that if I worked hard, I'd be right up there with the best. From the first report card in first grade at St. Mary's School, I earned all A's, with a few B-pluses. I loved reading; I won the reading award at the end of first grade. I'd walk to the public library next to St. Mary's every day after school and check out four books, the maximum number allowed. I'd go home, do my homework, then read the four books and do it over again the next day. I won an academic award for one subject or another almost every year of grade school.

In seventh grade, our teacher, Sister Lucille, announced that we were going to hold a vote for class president, something we had never done in any prior grade. She asked everyone to take out a piece of paper and write down their pick. Kids started pointing to me, and I was surprised by this. She collected the names. I won.

Later on that year she took me aside and said, "You have leadership abilities and it's important you know that about yourself for the rest of your life."

My parents made sure we attended Catholic Mass every Sunday morning, along with all the Holy Days of Obligation. They made us dress up, even though by the late sixties, we were the only ones. I'd protest, but my father would reply, "I want people to see the Redmonds all dressed up when we're at church." And we were always the last ones to go up to Communion. He'd wait until everyone else was in line, then he'd give us the signal to rise in unison and head toward the priest at the altar. I think he did this because he was proud of his family and wanted everyone to know it.

My father spent most of his childhood without a dad. His father died of a sudden heart attack when my dad was only eight years old, leaving my grandmother to raise five children in the middle of the Great Depression. This was before there were all kinds of publicly funded survivor benefits. From that point on it was a tough go for the family. My grandmother cleaned houses to earn money. Any clothes they got came from the St. Vincent de Paul Society run by the local parish. At fifteen, my father lied about his age and started doing manual labor for the Long Island Rail Road so he'd have money to give to his mother.

When I was only about eight years old, my parents would take me to upscale clothing stores to try on shirts, slacks, and suits. I hated it (I still do), and once, when my father was out of earshot, I turned to my mother and asked, "Why does Daddy make me try on clothes like this?"

She looked at me and said, "Because when he was your age, he got all his clothes second-hand from the church. He wants you to have these clothes now because he couldn't have them back then."

That shut me up.

Not that she had it all that much easier growing up. One day when she was just three years old, her mother went upstairs in their Brooklyn house and didn't come down. She had suffered a massive heart attack, in only her thirties. My mother had one sibling, a brother eleven years older, and not long afterward he

FIRST HOLY COMMUNION, MAY 1, 1965

was off fighting in World War II. My mother's father, a New York City fireman, then married an Irish immigrant, and the three of them eventually moved to a house near the beach on Long Island.

It's interesting to me that both parents suffered the loss of a parent, of their own gender, at such an early age. I'm guessing it's why they both wanted to have so many children of their own, although in the 1960s having five children was not such an extraordinary thing. Almost everyone did, especially if they were Catholic. "It's what was expected of us," my mother once told me.

From my earliest memories, I was a religious child. Making my First Holy Communion when I was in second grade was a profound experience. I still think about it every May 1, the anniversary. There were months of preparation at school. Parents had to purchase white dresses for their daughters and white suits with white ties and white bucks for their sons. The church was packed. Every parent had to get a ticket beforehand if they wanted to attend – two tickets per child, that was it, no other family members allowed. After the Mass, my parents held a big party at our house with dozens of relatives and friends there. People gave me cards stuffed with cash. After counting it at the end of the day, I and ran up to my father and said, "Dad, I have over forty dollars, can you believe that?!" He grinned and said, "Shhh, keep that quiet!" My grandmother gave me the largest crucifix I had ever seen, which hung above my bed for decades until I moved into my own apartment; it hangs in my parents' home today.

Someone gave me an illustrated children's version of *Lives of the Saints*. I thumbed through that book over and over. I longed for the day when I could be an altar boy, and it finally came in sixth grade. I was one of the first to sign up. I thought that was the ultimate: to dress up in the white stole, carry the big candle at a funeral, get the incense started for the priest. I loved it all. When Lent arrived that year, I committed to going to 6:30 a.m. Mass all forty days. I did it. I told people I wanted to become a priest when I grew up.

In those days, however, much of my catechism was fear-based. In first grade, for example, our teacher, Sister Christina Marie, went up to the blackboard and drew the outline of a human figure. She then took chalk and drew this dark mark in the middle of it.

"This is each of you when you were born," she said. "This is original sin. You got this because of what Adam and Eve did in the Garden of Eden."

I remember thinking, Life would be so much easier for me and all of us if those two had only obeyed God. We wouldn't even have to go to school.

And so began my steady diet of a shame-based version of Catholicism. My wife, though only six years younger than I, had a very different experience. The Second Vatican Council had already taken place by the time she entered her Catholic grade school. She tells me she was taught a religion based on love, forgiveness, compassion, and reconciliation. Mine was about following the rules and the punishment that followed if you did not.

None of my siblings were ever as into religion as I was, so I can't say this was anything overtly promoted by my parents. Religion, especially Catholicism, held a powerful fascination for me. When it was time to graduate from St. Mary's, we were given awards for math, science, English, and all other subjects. I won the religion award.

For all my accomplishments, I still had a lot of anxiety growing up. I had all kinds of physical tics. I pulled my hair out so much that I had a bald spot. (As an adult doing the kind of work I do I would discover the technical term for this condition: *trichotillomania*.) My parents took me to the doctor because I'd frequently make this noise with my nose and throat. His advice to my parents was, "Ask your son what he'd like you to give him, and give it to him it if he promises to stop making that noise." I heard this and said, "I want a dog." I didn't get the dog. I eventually stopped the nose and throat thing, but in second grade I had to ask to be excused from class to urinate so many times that the teacher finally took me aside and yelled at me. That ended but I then started stretching my jaw to the point that my Little League coach told my parents he thought I had the mumps. I was basically trading one tic for another, all of them anxiety-based. And even though I did well at school, when a teacher told us we were having a test or even just a quiz the next day, my stomach would be in knots until the moment the test was handed out. I'd then ace it, but that didn't matter: I'd go right through the whole process again next time around. When the school year ended, and I'd be given an almost-perfect report card, I'd fret over the summer that perhaps the next school year was the one in which I'd do poorly, and it'd finally be revealed that everything I'd done up to that point had been a façade – that I wasn't really that smart after all.

My siblings and I were surrounded by lots of family growing up. I've often thought we were lucky that way. It's so different now; my four siblings and I all live on different parts of the East Coast. We talk on the phone, but we don't see each other all that frequently. My father had four siblings, and three of them lived within a twenty-mile radius, each was married and had four or five children. My mother's one sibling also lived nearby, and he and his wife had five children. So we'd see one another all the time. Every holiday was aunts, uncles, cousins, cousins, and more cousins. And they were good people. My siblings and I were fortunate to be surrounded by good role models, what Tom Brokaw would later call "the greatest generation." They treated one another well and they treated us well. As kids we got to see in action how to speak to others in a respectful way. They modeled kindness. They modeled hard work and responsibility. They modeled loyalty: to their spouses, to their children, to their extended families, to their country. They modeled how to care about and for others. They weren't perfect. They weren't saints. We didn't need them to be. My siblings, cousins, and I needed them to be good role models, and they were.

Now my grandmother – my father's mother, Nana Kelly – she was different. She was a saint. She is the one whose husband had died suddenly and left her a widow with five children all under the age of ten. She was pure light, that's all I can say. Pure light; pure love. If I close my eyes, I can picture the time I was sitting by her in a chair in the living room of our house when I was probably only four or five years old. She was holding me, and I could literally feel her love. It was almost like an electric current. Her love for you had a physical feeling, it wasn't just emotional. All the grandkids were crazy for her. You just wanted to see her and be around her. She had had a tough life. Her mother had died when she was little. When she was in her early twenties she married my grandfather. A widower, he had grown children, was, I think, in his fifties, and had emigrated from Ireland in the late 1800s. When he died it was very difficult for her and her children. They scraped by. Years later when she remarried, my father was a teenager and walked her down the aisle. But that husband passed away, too, when I was a baby.

Nana was very religious, always going on retreats. There were all kinds of religious paintings and cards in her room. "Pray to the Holy Spirit," she'd advise her grandkids. But she wasn't judgmental. It was what religion is supposed to be: unconditional love, forgiveness, and acceptance.

By the time I was in my early twenties, she started having blackout spells. It would look like she was gone, and then she'd pop back to life. I bought her a book that had recently come out about "near death" experiences and gave it to her, but first I asked, "Do you ever remember anything when you wake up from one of those spells? What it was like when you were out?" She went on to tell me something that corresponded exactly with what was in the book. I was blown away. It was as if she had read the book first and then made up something to correlate with it, but she hadn't. She told me that once, when she was on retreat and had been praying a novena to St. Joseph, she blacked out, and met him. He had the long robe and the wooden staff and a beard. She felt this incredible peace and told him she did not want to go back to earth. She said St. Joseph told her, "You have to go back; it's not your time yet," and she argued with him, but next thing she knew, the priest from the retreat was slapping her cheek, saying, "Wake up Ellen, wake up."

Her health declined in the nineties, and she had to move to a nursing home. We had a big reunion there for all the relatives to see her, but she just sat in the middle of the room in a wheelchair, head slumped down. It was really sad. Not long after, she stopped eating and drinking and passed away.

I presume Saint Joseph was there to greet her on the other side.

My aunt and uncle had taken care of Nana for decades, and after her death they offered each grandchild one object that had been in her room. Mine was a small maroon vase; I keep it on a shelf in my office at work. I also had a funny experience in a HomeGoods store a few years ago: I spotted a deep blue piece of glassware and immediately thought of Nana Kelly. I wondered why that particular item had triggered her memory for me, and then realized that it was the same color as the jar of the Vicks VapoRub that she would rub on my chest, lying in bed when I had a cold.

Every morning when I say my prayers, there are a couple of people to whom I pray, asking them for help and guidance in my life. Nana Kelly is on the top of that list.

AS GRADE SCHOOL CAME TO AN END, I had to decide where I wanted to go to high school. There wasn't even a question about my going to the public school; it was a choice between the two Catholic ones. I picked the smaller one, Seton Hall High School, after going to visit it. I'd take the bus every morning along with some of my former grade school classmates.

I was small for my age, so my parents had not let me play football up until that point, but now that I was in high school, I asked if I could try out for the team. They said yes and I was delighted. There were about fifty guys trying out for twenty-two spots, and I was one of the last ones picked. I got in for six plays in the last minutes of the first game, because we were up by over forty points. Then I sat on the bench all the ensuing games.

But I went to every practice after school, and on Saturday mornings, in what was called the Mud Bowl. It was aptly named. I didn't miss a single practice. I was put on defense and trampled over time and again by the bigger players. Then one day I figured out that if I dived low and torpedoed my head, shoulders, and body into a runner's legs, even if he was much bigger than I was, he'd go right down. That's what I started doing, and the coach started noticing.

"He's gonna put you in the next game, Redmond," the other subs told me.

But it didn't happen until the very last seconds of the very last game. We were losing, the other team had the ball, and our coach turned around and said to me, "Redmond, get in there." I ran as fast as I could. (My mother was in the stands and later told me that some man next to her said, "Look at that kid! That's the kind of attitude this team needs.") Their quarterback called a play at the line of scrimmage, handed the ball off to a running back heading right in my direction, I lowered my head, slammed him in the legs and tackled him.

The ref blew the whistle. Game over. Season over. I ran to the sidelines and one of my fellow subs came up to me and yelled, "Redmond, you did it! You made the tackle!"

That one play was all I needed to motivate me further. I thought about it over, and over, and over, month after month. I would go down to my basement every night and lift weights. I got taller, I got bigger, stronger, faster. The next year I tried out for the junior varsity team. I made it, was selected as the starting linebacker, and at the end of the season, the school newspaper named me the best player on the team.

This experience taught me that hard work and motivation pay off. And because of sports I was getting popular, and that was important to me. I enjoyed being known. But more than anything I wanted a girlfriend.

Seton Hall had dances, and for most of them you had to invite a date. For the Christmas one, I managed to screw up my courage and ask a girl to be my date. She told me no. I didn't tell a soul, and I hoped she wouldn't either. The next dance was for St. Patrick's Day. I asked a different girl. She looked surprised, hesitated, and said, "Uhm, I have to babysit that night. Sorry." I believed her, but when I told my friends, they laughed and said, "Redmond, the dance is weeks away, you really think she has to babysit that night? She blew you off man, admit it!"

They were probably right, but a few months later, she invited me to the Sadie Hawkins dance held every spring, in which the female had to invite the male. I said yes. I finally had my first date. We didn't go out again, but, hey, I was encouraged, and at least I finally felt like I was in the romance game.

My third year I made the varsity football team and started almost every game as a linebacker. I discovered that one of the cheerleaders liked me. I was thrilled. We started dating and were soon inseparable.

Then the nuns who ran the school announced they were out of money and the school would be closing at the end of the year. I was devastated. I loved it there and didn't want to be away from my girlfriend.

My parents gave me the option of attending public school my senior year or enrolling in the other Catholic school, St. John the Baptist. I was intimidated by the thought of going to public school, so I picked St. John's. It was a much bigger school, and in terms of sports, was a completely different and higher level of play.

I tried out for the football team. I had a cousin one year older who had played there and was then on a full scholarship at a Big Ten college team. He'd eventually make it to the NFL. I knew I'd be lucky to even make the team, much less actually get in a game.

But my new coach liked me. He could see I had drive and that I was a fighter, even if I lacked the physical size. I made the team but as a third-stringer. Before I knew it, a few players became injured, and I was on the field.

I played really well, surprising even myself. I give Coach Byrne Gamble the credit. He didn't yell at me when I made a mistake; he encouraged me. He believed in me and communicated that belief, and because he believed in me, I started to believe in me.

I have carried this lesson through the decades of my work with teenagers and young adults. Yelling and punishing have limited results, if not the opposite of what is intended. Encouraging, promoting, teaching – these are what help people to reach their potential.

And this coach recognized that sports was just a minor part of life. The first time I met him, he didn't ask my speed in the forty-yard dash. He asked me about my SAT scores. He was impressed and told me that. In fact, on the first day of tryouts, he gathered all the players in a classroom, went up to the blackboard, and wrote in big print:

1170

My first thought was that it was the name of some play we'd be running that season. Instead, he turned to the dozens of guys there and said, "That is the SAT score of one of our new players, Mark Redmond. That is what is really important in life. Academics. Football is secondary."

I sat there and didn't know what to say. I didn't know any of these players, or what they now thought of me, but I knew I now had a coach who valued me for what I could do on and off the field.

We did not have a very good season, but I personally played well. I was suddenly the focus of a lot of attention, especially from the females at the school. The temptation to start dating others was great, and I broke up with my girlfriend.

Besides sports, I learned something else important about myself that last year of high school: that I was a good writer. I took a creative writing class taught by a nun, and one of our assignments during the semester was to write an autobiography. She was impressed enough with mine to pass it along to another English teacher – someone who actually taught my younger brother, not me. He stopped me in the cafeteria and said, "I read your autobiography. You're a good writer. You need to know that, and no matter what field you go into in life, you should use that."

He said something else I would always remember: "Make sure that whatever career you go into, it's something you enjoy. You don't want to be the person who is in their forties and realizes you don't even like what you've been doing, and you still have twenty years of it ahead of you."

I started looking at colleges early in senior year. There was no question in our household that we were all going to college – a good one. At one point I said to my father, "Why don't I just go to community college for two years to save money and then transfer somewhere?" (This was actually my ploy to stay connected to a girl I was dating.)

"No way in hell," he said. He and my mother were determined we'd all go to the best college we could get into.

I was inducted into the National Honor Society; my football coach thought I had the grades to get into an Ivy League school and he was promoting that. My parents drove me up and down the East Coast looking at several. I applied to, and was rejected by, Dartmouth, Yale, Princeton, Brown, Hamilton, and Williams. Fortunately I had visited Villanova University, where my cousin was a freshman, and liked it. That was my backup, which turned out to be a good thing when all the thin envelopes starting arriving in my last semester of high school.

When it was time to send Villanova my acceptance notice along with payment for the first semester, I saw that I had to check a box signifying my major, the options being: arts and sciences; nursing; engineering; business administration. I turned to my father and asked, "Which box should I check?"

He, in turn, asked me, "What do you want to do with your life?"

Being seventeen, I responded, "I have no idea."

"Then put down business," he said.

It made sense. He loved being a commercial real estate broker, and it enabled him to provide a very good life for his family to the point that all five of us would end up going to private colleges without so much as a dime in loans to repay.

So I went to Villanova and majored in business administration. I knew I wasn't capable of playing football on the collegiate level, so I played rugby instead. I loved it. I made close friends on the team, and at Villanova in general. It was a college that attracted quality people with good values. I was completely at home there.

I did very well academically at Nova, ending up with close to a 4.0 GPA. I was elected president of the Finance Society and was inducted into the business honor fraternity. There was nothing indicating that I was headed to anything other than a successful career in the business world, whereupon I would make a lot of money.

Unlike some of my peers, who grew up Catholic and went to Catholic high schools but once they were out of parental control on a college campus stopped going to church on Sundays, I always went. I don't know if it was out of guilt or obligation or still following the Catholic rules. I might have even been hung over from a rugby party the night before, but I always went. (It earned me the nickname "Father Redmond," which, even now, my classmates call me.)

But that was the extent of my faith life during college: going to Mass on Sundays and Holy Days. I didn't pray. I didn't think about faith or spirituality and what role it might have in my life. I didn't step foot in the Campus Ministry office. I don't think I even knew where it was. I basically went to class, studied, worked a part-time job in the library, played rugby, partied with my friends, and chased girls. We all did.

Still, going to Sunday Mass would have a deep impact on me in ways I never could have predicted. In my third year at Villanova, there was a 9 p.m. Mass in our dormitory. I went one Sunday, and the celebrant was a Glenmary priest. They are an order of priests and brothers who work in Appalachia, one of the poorest sections of America. During the homily, he talked about the desperate conditions there and that he was looking for students who would spend spring break in Kentucky helping to rebuild homes and farms. But he went beyond that. He talked about dedicating your life to helping those who were in need. "I'm not necessarily asking you to become a priest," he said, "but I am asking you to think about having the courage to ask God what you should do with your life, and being open to the idea that it has to do something with helping the poor and impoverished of our world."

I was transfixed. It moved me, and I kept talking about his homily with my friends, to the point that one said, "What are you going to do Redmond, move to Appalachia for the rest of your life?"

I didn't know about that, but I knew I wanted to at least go there on spring break. This priest had said that he'd be outside of the main campus cafeteria the next day in case anyone had questions. I went and spotted him standing alone behind a table with brochures and other information spread out. I so wanted to go up to him and tell him that what he said had affected me deeply, but I lacked the courage to do so, and instead shuffled up, took a brochure, mumbled thanks, and walked away.

I actually intended to go to Appalachia that spring break. I really did. I started to try recruiting some rugby friends to go with me. Word got around, and one of them stopped me outside a classroom and asked, "You're thinking of doing what? Going where?" These kinds of service trips are popular today among college students, but they weren't back then. This was truly doing something out of the ordinary.

So I went to Fort Lauderdale instead. That's right: I got talked into driving down to Fort Lauderdale with a bunch of my friends, where we sat on the beach all day and partied all night.

After we returned a week later, I ran into someone I knew who did go to Appalachia. As he described his time there and what they did, I had an immediate feeling that I had made the wrong choice, and that he had had a much better week there than I had in Florida.

Junior year ended, and I started getting serious with a Villanova female classmate. We traveled back and forth all summer between my home on Long Island and hers outside of Philadelphia. Senior year began, and I knew I had to start thinking about what I'd be doing after college. Villanova had lined up recruiters from all kinds of corporations to conduct on-campus interviews, and I signed up for as many as possible.

I rarely read the local paper, the *Philadelphia Inquirer*, but for some reason, I picked it up one fall day, and there was a story about a young man from the area, Edward Fischer, who had been working in Guatemala, helping to rebuild after a terrible earthquake had devastated much of the country. The article was about how he was walking from there to Philadelphia to raise money for his projects in that Central American country. "That is one long walk," I thought.

A few weeks later we had our annual last-Saturday-in-October rugby game against Georgetown. The Hoyas were our big rival, and we had beaten them every year I played, so it was a big deal to us. We traveled to D.C. on a Friday night, partied on M Street all night long, somehow took to the field the next morning, lost by a very close score, partied all Saturday night, and assembled Sunday morning in front of the statue at the main campus gate. (We always called him Father Georgetown, but it's actually Archbishop John Carroll, the founder of the university.) As I sat there on the lawn waiting for all of my teammates to arrive, I noticed a van with a group of children nearby and a young man with them. For some reason he came over to talk to us. He was very friendly and asked who we were. When we told him rugby players from Villanova, he laughed and said he had played for the Georgetown squad several years earlier. Talking to him I began to realize that this was Edward Fischer, the person I had read about in the newspaper, having made it all the way to D.C., and the van and the kids were part of this section of his walk. It was a pretty weird coincidence.

A few Sundays later, I was at the 6 p.m. Mass at the main Villanova chapel. This Mass was very popular and usually packed with students. When it came time for the homily, instead of the celebrant priest's speaking, it was none other than Mr. Fischer. He talked about the work he was doing in Guatemala. He showed pictures of the devastation there, and how he was trying to help them rebuild. He talked about his decision to walk over three thousand miles, and why he was doing it.

I wish what he said had been recorded, but this is what I remember:

"I look out at all of you and I see myself at your age. I had everything in front of me in terms of financial security, job security. But now I have very little money of my own.

*I have spent hours and days walking in the pouring rain,
cold and shivering. But I'm telling you, I could not be
happier. I felt joy even when I felt physically miserable. I
would not trade the life I have now, and what I am doing,
for anything else."*

After Mass, as everyone filed out of the pews, most toward the
campus library to study, I stood there in that pew. I felt like yelling
out to everyone leaving, Hey! Didn't you hear what he said?
Didn't you listen to him? How can we all just get up and go about
our business and our lives, as if nothing was different? Where are
you all going?

I also desperately wanted to go up to him and tell this Edward
Fischer how much he had affected me, how much I wanted to be
doing with my life what he was doing with his. But as with the
Glenmary priest the year before, I lacked the courage.

Eventually I was just standing in the pew alone. Only a few
people remained in the chapel, chatting with their friends. So I
just wandered out, carrying my business books, walked into the
library, found a desk, and started studying about interest rates,
stocks, and bonds; but then, more than ever, the focus of my
studies felt so futile, so useless, so not me. In light of all that I had
just heard, a paradigm shift had taken place.

That night I lay in bed, unable to go to sleep. I stared at the ceiling
as I envisioned the life ahead of me. It flashed through my mind
like a movie, scenes of my graduating in a few months, probably
landing a job on Wall Street, getting married – perhaps to this
woman I was then dating – having children, getting promotions,
making more money, buying a house, then a bigger house, a boat,
joining a country club. And then one day I'd die. My life would be
over. And what had I really done with that life? What impact had I
made on the world? How had my existence on the planet changed
things in any way for the millions of people in the world who went
hungry every night or had no home in which to live?

It chilled me to the bone to even think about this.

Later that week I went to the college career center to see if any new corporations were scheduled to do interviews. Spots were always limited, so I'd need to sign up quickly if there were. And this time I noticed there was a new one: the Peace Corps. Very few people had signed up for that; there were plenty of spots left to interview there.

I put my name down. No harm in at least checking it out, I thought to myself.

I go back to Villanova every five years for my class reunion. The most recent one was our fortieth in 2019. Each time, I make sure to stop at the campus chapel, and I always sit where I was that day in the fall of 1978, on the left side, near the back. I say a prayer of gratitude.

And each time, I think to myself, This is where it all began.

· *two* ·

ON THE APPOINTED DAY, I went for my Peace Corps interview, hoping none of my classmates would find out, because I'd be embarrassed beyond belief if any of them knew I was even half-considering this. I sat and met with a representative of the Peace Corps; I can't remember in which country he had served. He filled me in on the basics, that they were looking for volunteers with a variety of skills, including health care, teachers, engineers, and yes, those with a financial and accounting background, which, of course, meant me. It was a two-year commitment, and there were volunteers across the globe.

"Do you have a preference where you would like to go?" he asked me. "Any particular country in mind?"

"I don't," I replied, and it was true. I probably wasn't going to do this anyway, but even if I did, it didn't matter to me where I ended up.

He gave me the application to fill out, and I left. I hadn't made any promises. No harm, no foul, just a chance to learn more.

The first semester of senior year drew to a close. I went home for the Christmas break. One night, sitting at home in our living room watching a hockey game on television with my father, I blurted out, "What would you think of my joining the Peace Corps?"

I thought he'd go ballistic, but he surprised me.

"I actually think that's a good idea," he said. "It would probably help you in the long-term as far as your career goes, to have that under your belt."

So I filled out the application. I also found out that one of my Villanova friends, Tim Clarke, was applying too. We met and I learned that he was much more serious about doing it than I was. In my mind this was still a flight of fancy that I was mostly sure I was not really going to pursue. In fact, I was still going on all of my corporate interviews.

A few months later I heard back from the Peace Corps. I was accepted, and the country where I would be placed in was Guatemala.

My first thought was, That's where that guy Edward Fischer was.

My next thought was to head to the reference room at the campus library to pull out a World Almanac so I could see exactly where Guatemala was. All I knew was that it was south of Mexico somewhere.

And there it was, wedged among Mexico, Belize, El Salvador, and Honduras.

My friend Tim got his letter the same day as well.

"Where are they sending you?" I asked him.

"Some place called Guatemala," he replied.

I cannot now pinpoint when I decided I was going to do this, but I did. Job offers from various corporations and companies started to come in, and I started turning them down.

I wrote to the Peace Corps telling them I was accepting. They gave me start dates, the first of which was only one month after my Villanova graduation, June 10, 1979, which I chose, and coincidentally, again, Tim had too. We would both join the Peace Corps, serve in the same country, and start on the same day.

As the end of senior year drew to a close, it was common for my classmates to sit around a table and ask who was going where or doing what after graduation. Their hard work had paid off in lucrative job placements. I was still embarrassed to say what I was doing, that they'd think it was hippie-dippie.

"I'm going to work for Chase Bank in New York City."

"I've got offers from Citibank and Manufacturers Hanover; I'm still trying to decide which to take."

"Three pharmaceutical manufacturers have offered me jobs, and I think I'm going with SmithKline."

"I'm going to law school."

"I'm joining the Peace Corps in Guatemala."

But my classmates surprised me. They thought this was pretty good. This was different. They admired me for the choice I was making.

And I began to really enjoy that attention. In a short while I couldn't wait for someone to ask me what I was doing post-graduation.

I also relished turning down the various job offers coming in. Most were done by phone.

"We're pleased to offer you this job Mr. Redmond."

"That's fine but I've decided to pursue another option."

And when the person asked, "And what is that?" I knew they were expecting me to tell them some other company to which I had committed.

"The Peace Corps," I'd reply. "I'm joining the Peace Corps. I leave for Guatemala in a month."

A stunned silence would follow on the other end.

My family remained supportive of my decision. I don't think they were thrilled I was doing this, but they didn't try to stop me or talk me out of it.

Graduation was a fun weekend with all of them there. I packed up my dorm room and drove home to spend a month saying goodbye to friends. I headed back to Pennsylvania once, to say goodbye to my girlfriend, who didn't think this was such a great idea after all, and looking back, I cannot say I blame her. My family threw a good-bye party for me at our house, inviting all our relatives over.

And on Sunday, June 10, they drove me to JFK Airport, where we had a tear-filled goodbye. The last thing my father said to me was, "If it's not for you, if you don't like it down there, just come back."

I shook my head and said, "That's not going to happen, Dad, I'll be fine." And it's true, the very notion, the idea, that I would not fulfill the two-year Peace Corps commitment was completely anathema to me.

I boarded the plane.

And exactly nine days later I was back at JFK.

· *three* ·

THE FLIGHT FROM JFK was not to Guatemala, but to Miami. Over forty volunteers and I would spend two days in a hotel there getting to know one another, learn the ground rules, fill out more paperwork, and get an orientation. Tim was there when I arrived, and it felt really good to have someone with me I already knew. I considered myself lucky in that respect.

Two days later we boarded another plane to head to Guatemala City, but before we did, someone from the Peace Corps announced that three of our group had decided not to proceed and were heading home.

For a brief second I could feel myself wishing that I was among them, that I was going home too. I surprised myself by even having that reaction, and I don't know why I felt that way. No one had said or done anything to dissuade me from proceeding as planned, but I had this strong sense of wishing that I was heading back to New York instead of Guatemala. But I ignored it and got on the plane.

After we landed in Guatemala, we went by bus to a hotel in the countryside, where we'd have another two-day orientation. At the initial gathering of all of us in one room, the head of the Peace Corps in Guatemala gave a rousing and inspiring talk, telling us how proud he was of America for producing people like us who would want to go to a third world country to help improve things for the people there.

That quickly shifted into a kind of what I term a *scared-straight approach*. They did individual meetings with each volunteer and hit us with these realities:

"We'll teach you Spanish for the next three months, but there are almost two dozen Mayan languages spoken that are entirely different from one another, as well as other indigenous languages where you will be living, so the Spanish may not actually do you much good."

"We don't place Peace Corps volunteers in groups, you each go one-by-one to different locations, and travel between locations is difficult. You may be able to see other volunteers every few weeks or so, but don't count on it."

"You're likely to get sick. Everyone does. American bodies are not used to the various bacterial infections prevalent in a third world country like this."

That last part turned out to be very true, and right away. We later learned that the cooks in the hotel had not boiled or purified the water they used to prepare our meals. People were dropping like flies, running to the bathroom constantly. Tim was one of the first, and in fact, ended up going to the hospital with dysentery. I was one of the last, but when it hit, it hit big.

The scared-straight approach worked on me. I was now officially freaked out. I was thinking of heading back home.

In retrospect, I wondered if the Peace Corps personnel in the United States had told me all these things back when I was applying. They probably had, and they likely did so again when they accepted me and told me I was going to Guatemala. It was likely that I was so swept up in the idea of the whole thing that I wasn't paying attention to the warnings being issued. Besides, that was my whole modus operandi, that no matter what people told me I couldn't do, whether in sports, academics, dating, whatever, I never paid attention and barreled ahead anyway, figuring out I'd make my way through determination and smarts.

I managed to buck myself up and board the bus to the town where we each would live with a host family for the next three months while we attended Spanish school. I was taken to a small house where a young mother lived with her mother and a five-year-old boy named Oscar. I had my own room and access to an outhouse, which I would learn was frequently populated by chickens. There was a shower but no hot water.

The next day, I walked the mile to the school along with some of the other volunteers who lived nearby. We were all constantly running to the bathroom during the day. That night I did the same. I think I was up every other hour.

The second day of school, I sat in a Spanish class, and the teacher was pointing to a bottle and having us recite the Spanish word for it. "Botella." I still remember the moment. And then I just stood. The teacher smiled, presuming that I was once again headed for the bathroom.

But instead I walked past the bathroom and down the hallway where I presumed the Peace Corps staff would be. I found the woman who was the assistant director for Guatemala. She had seemed friendly when we had arrived a few days before, although I had never talked with her. "Can we go for a walk?" I asked.

"Of course," she said.

We walked and walked, and walked and talked, and it all just poured out of me.

"I don't know why I'm here. ... I thought this was a good idea, but now I don't. ... I'm afraid of being all alone in some village where I don't even know the language. ... I miss my family. ... I miss my friends. ... I miss my girlfriend. ... I didn't think it would be like this. ... I don't like being constantly sick. ... The friend I came down here with is in the hospital."

She didn't say anything. She just listened, and when I finally stopped, she stood there and said, "It sounds to me like you want to go home."

And I said, "Yeah, I think I do."

The next few days I probably changed my mind fifty times, but when June 19 arrived, I boarded the plane to head back to JFK. I had called my family ahead to tell them I was returning. My mother and siblings picked me up when I arrived, and we met my father at the train station. I can't even remember how they reacted to my return. They were probably confused as to what had transpired in so short a time and what I was going to do next.

One thing I do remember, which is that I felt like a total idiot, a failure, a quitter. Part of me was glad to be back. I was still running to the bathroom twenty times a day, and it was sure better to be in an American bathroom than an outhouse with a chicken in it. But once that was over, and my body was back to normal, I was lost and confused.

I didn't know what to do.

My first thought was to call the various corporations that had offered me jobs which I had turned down the previous spring, to see if any position was still available. It was a ridiculous notion, and I quickly learned the jobs had all been filled by other recent grads. So that was a dead end.

I bought a book that listed all the corporations and financial firms in the country and started writing to the ones in New York City, attaching my résumé. This was before home computers and laptops, so I had to painstakingly use my Smith Corona typewriter and type each individual letter. But I did it. I sat in our family dining room and typed those letters and put them in the mail, although I still knew it was a long shot. It was summer, most of the hiring had already taken place, and people who might do the interviewing were on vacation.

I did get one callback from a bank that had offered me a job months earlier, which of course, I had turned down. They would agree to meet with me. I put on a three-piece suit, took the train in, then the subway, and met with a woman there. She was nice, but it was hard to explain away the whole Peace Corps thing in any logical way, and I left there with no job offer, no nothing. I took the train back to Long Island, fell asleep, and managed to miss my stop. I got off at the next one and walked, in the steaming summer heat, the few miles to my parents' house. I quickly became drenched in sweat. Stopping for a breather at one point, I thought, How did this happen? How did I get myself in this situation? How did I screw up so badly? It was a low point.

I felt like I had quit; had failed; had given up. My college friend Tim was still down there. He had gotten sick, worse than me and ended up in the hospital, but he had recovered and was still in the Peace Corps. Why couldn't I hack it? It ate away at me. Not that I was the only one who had left early. I found out that, of the original forty-plus volunteers, a good dozen, including myself, had left within the first three months. At times I wondered if any of them were giving themselves the psychic lashing the way I was. Friends would tell me, "Hey, at least you tried. Most people don't even try. ... It just wasn't the right thing for you. ... Let it go." None of that helped. I felt like I wanted to hide in my basement and come out after two years to fool people that I had actually been in the Peace Corps that entire time.

Eventually the application letters to corporations paid off. A woman from the Metropolitan Life Insurance Company called me in late July. She told me there was still a spot left in a training program they had started recently. It was composed of ten people; most were recent college graduates, although some had their Masters in Business Administration. Did I want to interview for it?

I told her yes. I interviewed, did not even mention the fact that I had been in the Peace Corps in Guatemala a few weeks earlier, and did well enough that they offered me the spot.

I started the Tuesday after Labor Day 1979, eleven weeks to the day from when I had flown back from Guatemala. It was almost as if it hadn't even happened. I was right back in my stride, this time jettisoning any notions about doing anything other than what I was supposed to do – work for a big firm, to be a success in the business world.

It was a two-year training program, and for the first year I was assigned to offices on Long Island, which suited me fine. I lived at home, bought a used car, saved money, and traveled on weekends to see my girlfriend in Pennsylvania. On some weekends I'd drive into New York City and party with my Villanova friends, many of whom were working for corporations there and living in the city. For a while it felt like college had never ended, except this time it was better, because we actually had money to spend.

Despite the outward appearances of success, though, I was still profoundly unhappy. I also did not enjoy, or find interesting in any way, the work I was doing at the insurance company. It was deadly dull, and I think the people in charge of the training program didn't know what to do with us. Heading into the city on weekends to party with my college friends grew old pretty fast. I

METROPOLITAN LIFE INSURANCE COMPANY, 1979

tried playing for a Long Island rugby club; it wasn't the same. I broke up with my college girlfriend; she was hinting about getting married, and I knew I wasn't even close to that.

I was fundamentally lost. I should have been happy: I had what would have made most of my peers content. But I felt empty inside. At one point my sister said to me, "You have what everyone else wants – a good job, a future ahead of you. Why aren't you happy?"

"I feel like there's this hole inside of me," I replied. "I feel empty."

I began to feel the familiar pull toward faith, toward religion. I had never abandoned my Catholic faith; remember, at Villanova I was Father Redmond. But in reality my spiritual life in college consisted of going to Mass once a week, and that was it. I was going to Mass every Sunday at St. Mary's, the parish where I had grown up. It was at this time that a new pastor arrived – Monsignor Peter Chiara. It was obvious that St. Mary's desperately needed new leadership. The place was languishing. When I heard the homily at his first Mass, and his plea for people to come forward to help get the parish going again, I was stirred enough to write to him offering any help I could offer. He contacted me and we met. We hit it off right away, and I got involved with teenagers in the parish's youth ministry.

For the first time in my life, I started reading the Bible, doing so every morning. I'd go to evening prayer services at St. Mary's. I started praying daily on my own. The only time I had ever prayed in college was when I had an exam coming up. Someone told me about the Trappist monk Thomas Merton, and I started reading his books. One day I ran into a fellow employee on the subway platform, and he spotted Merton's *New Seeds of Contemplation* in my hand.

"You're reading *that*?" he asked.

After one year on Long Island, my employer moved my work site into the city. I dreaded taking the ninety-minute train ride back and forth each day, so I found a sublet for a studio apartment on East Sixty-second Street between Park and Lexington avenues. One of my rugby friends moved in; it was crazy – one of us on a bed, one on a couch – but we didn't mind. The place had an outdoor porch with a barbecue; it was ideal. We'd have parties out there with college and work friends every Thursday night.

I found a Catholic church a few blocks away, St. Vincent Ferrer on Lexington Avenue. I joined the faith formation group that met there one night a week. The church also held periodic retreat days on weekends, which is where I first learned about, and started practicing, a form of meditation known as "centering prayer."

It was around this time that I went back to Villanova to see a college friend who still lived near the university, and she persuaded me to attend a Volunteer Day event organized by campus ministry. There were several organizations represented at this event, including Maryknoll Lay Missioners, the Jesuit Volunteer Corps, and Covenant House, a shelter for homeless and runaway teenagers in Times Square. A representative from each organization did a short presentation, and most showed a film, with the idea that those of us in the audience would sign up to volunteer in some capacity.

I knew of Covenant House; a friend of my cousin's worked there in an administrative capacity. When it was time for its presentation, the person who walked to the front of the auditorium looked like a suburban grandmother: perfectly coiffed white hair, Lily Pulitzer pants, and Pappagallo shoes. Her name was Marge Crawford, and I guessed she was in her seventies. I pictured her on an upscale country club golf course rather than at some shelter for homeless kids, but she surprised me and gave an inspiring talk about the work they were doing there.

After her presentation I went up and introduced myself, telling her that I lived in Manhattan and would like to come and visit sometime because I was interested in volunteering. We exchanged phone numbers, and a week or so later I called her. We set a date for me to come by and have a firsthand look at the work they were doing.

When I arrived at Covenant House, I told her that I'd be interested in volunteering one evening a week after work and help in whatever way needed.

"That'd be fine," she said, "we can set you up for that, but what I really think you should consider is becoming part of the Faith Community here. There are about forty of us who live at Covenant House and have made a one-year commitment to work full-time helping homeless kids. The pay is twelve dollars a week. But to join us, you first have to come on a one-week orientation." She pulled a calendar off her desk and said, "I have an opening this coming May. I will put you down for that."

As she was saying this I could feel myself breaking into a sweat, panicking, and thinking, Whoa, whoa, whoa! Wait a minute, lady, wait a minute! What are you talking about here? This is *definitely not* in the Mark Redmond life plan!

I mean, really, there was a world of difference between my volunteering at Covenant House one night a week to hand out snacks compared to quitting my job and giving up my apartment and my lifestyle and my future.

But I calmed myself down, thinking, Just keep cool, let her put your name in her little calendar there, humor the nice lady, you can always fix this with just one phone call and cancel this some-time between now and May. Easy peasy, no problem.

I did, however, start to volunteer one night a week. Every Tuesday evening, upon leaving my Madison Avenue job, rather than take the number 4, 5 or 6 subway to the Upper East Side, I would take the R train and get off at the Times Square stop. Today, Times Square is all about the Disney store and the Hard Rock Café, but it definitely was not like that in 1981. *Rolling Stone* magazine that year declared it, "The sleaziest block in America." As one of my brothers said recently, "In the 1980s you ran through Times Square." It was disgusting, raunchy, violent, and the center of the prostitution and pornography industries. (One time I ran into one of my corporate co-workers on that subway, and when I told him I was going to Times Square, he raised his eyebrows, smirked, and muttered something along the lines of, "Have a good time.") It was also where homeless and runaway kids congregated, which is why Covenant House was there.

Every Tuesday night I'd walk (briskly) from the Times Square subway stop over to Covenant House. Once there, I'd duck into a bathroom, change out of my business suit and into the jeans, t-shirt, and sneakers I had stuffed into a gym bag. I'd spend the next few hours serving meals, giving out snacks, and playing basketball in the gym with the kids. When I started, I was petrified. The kids were primarily African American and Hispanic, from the most poverty-stricken and crime-ridden neighborhoods of New York City. I'd had absolutely no exposure to this segment of society in my twenty-three years of living. It was challenging for me, to say the least. But I stuck with it, going to Covenant House week after week, doing what I could to help out.

Then something happened I didn't really expect: I began to enjoy it. I liked the kids, and I liked being there. I also met a few members of the Faith Community that Marge Crawford had tried

TIMES SQUARE, 1981

to talk me into joining. They invited me over one night for dinner, and I went, expecting to meet a collection of fanatical holy rollers. They were not. They seemed normal – nice, friendly people of all ages and backgrounds who had made a decision to do something extra-ordinary for one year. I began to think, You know? This is something I could see myself doing in a few years, after my career is established, after I've saved up a lot of money.

I decided I would not call Marge and cancel the May orientation. In fact, when she let me know they had an opening in the March orientation group, I accepted. Again, I was still thinking this was something I might consider doing at some distant time in the future, but it occurred to me that it wouldn't hurt if I checked things out. So I lied to my employer and said I was going on vacation somewhere, but instead I spent the week at Covenant House.

Even now, decades later, it's hard to explain what happened to me during that week, but by the end of it, I knew that this was my path. I didn't want to be on the corporate ladder. I wanted to be among the homeless, the poor, the broken, the despised, the addicted, the prostitute, those without family, those who felt unloved. Following the Gospel was no longer solely about going to Mass on Sunday and praying. It was a way to live your life, and for me, a completely different way than the path I was on. After the five days living at the Faith Community and being at Covenant House, I didn't have a shred of doubt that I was going to do this, and it felt different from the decision to join the Peace Corps. This wasn't about a two-year commitment to something that might or might not look good on my résumé later on; this was a commitment to live my life in a completely different and deeper way.

I did have to go back to work after that week, and I remember being in some big gathering where one of the top-tier vice-presidents spoke to us about how, "We now have assets totaling X billion, and it's your mission to make sure that by the end of the decade we're at Y billion. That's what all of you should be working toward; that is your goal." I just sat there thinking, That is not my goal. It may be somebody else's goal. I'm not saying it's wrong. I'm not saying it's evil. It's just that it's not my goal, not what I want to dedicate my life to. Mine is something else.

I traveled back to Long Island one weekend to see Monsignor Chiara. We sat across from one another in the rectory, and I told him I had decided to leave my corporate job to become a full-time volunteer helping homeless teens.

"A lot of people think I'm crazy doing this," I told him, "but I believe that if I do this, God is going to take care of me. I don't know if I am going to do this for one year or for the rest of my life, but I do believe God is calling me to this, and when I am done, God will be there for me. God will not let me down."

His face lit up and he exclaimed, "What faith you have! What faith!"

I was so surprised by his reaction. I mean, he was a priest. He had dedicated his entire life to God. What I was doing seemed like so much less.

But it didn't to him. He was so happy and supportive. That conversation left a real mark on me, and I took it as a sign that I was going in the right direction in my life.

A few weeks later I gave notice at work, gave up the Park Avenue apartment, donated my suits to Goodwill, gave my car to my brother, and became a member of the Covenant House Faith Community, moving into dirty, sleazy Times Square, across the street from the infamous Show World with "Live Sex Acts" emblazoned on its marquee – into a hovel of a room in a roach-infested tenement at Forty-third Street and Eighth Avenue. I was thrilled. Once the crowds of theater-goers departed the area at the end of each evening's performance, sex workers congregated around every street corner. To my friends and corporate co-workers it seemed like an absolutely crazy thing to do. (One of my friends, whom I had known since first grade, came by to see me and kept saying, "I can't believe you live here. What are you doing here?") I am sure they all thought I had gone insane.

But to me, this seemed like the most sane thing I had ever done in my life.

· _four_ ·

IT WAS A RADICAL CHANGE, a case of on one day wearing a Brooks Brothers suit, walking down Madison Avenue, entering the stately international headquarters of the venerable Metropolitan Life Insurance Company, attending to meetings about types of insurance policies and pension plans, and a few days later wearing jeans, sneakers, and a t-shirt, walking past porn places and strip clubs to enter Covenant House, where I'd be helping homeless teenagers.

But it didn't bother me one bit. I fit right in. I felt I was finally where I belonged.

I was one of about forty people who were part of the Covenant House Faith Community. It was an interesting mix. Some were older, had recently retired, and wanted to do this instead of watching the grass grow in a senior center. Others had recently graduated from college and wanted to do a year of service before going on to graduate school. One was an alum of Harvard Law School, another from Georgetown Law.

We lived like little monks there. We started the day with one hour of praying together in our chapel at 7 a.m. The work-day then began, and we gathered again for Mass at 5:30. We were all together one more time at nine o'clock for evening prayer, and we were expected to pray privately for half an hour each day.

This is roughly the same schedule that contemplative Trappists monks follow; I was told that someone from the Faith Community had visited them a few years earlier and come back with this daily routine. I followed it dutifully and grew to appreciate it, for it provided a certain rhythm to the day. I felt like it helped me to grow spiritually. It had worked for over a century for the Trappists, so who was I to question it?

Because I had already been volunteering one night a week for several months, I was immediately assigned to a unit with forty teenage boys. My job was pretty clear: help keep order there; get them to and from the cafeteria three times a day; help kids to find a job; help them find a place to live. And this all had to be accomplished within thirty days, because that was the maximum stay.

That was unrealistic, given the demographics of the youth at Covenant House. Ninety-nine percent of them came from the poorest sections of the city, had a limited education, and no job skills. Their family backgrounds contained drug abuse, alcoholism, physical abuse, sexual abuse and domestic violence. Many of the kids had spent their lives in the foster care system, having been removed from their parents due to abuse or neglect. They had bounced around from foster home to foster home to group homes to institutions. Now they were on their own, and Covenant House was their only respite from the streets.

None of this dissuaded me. I jumped right in, learning as much as I could from the veteran staff there. I worked daytime, evenings, some weekend shifts. I was ready to serve, whenever needed.

Covenant House was founded and run by a Franciscan priest named Father Bruce Ritter. I was only there about two months when someone in the Faith Community told him about me. He asked me to come see him. When I did, he told me that the person who was serving as his "ombudsman" was moving on from Covenant House. Would I take that position?

"What's an ombudsman?" I asked.

It turned out that at Covenant House the ombudsman was Father Ritter's hand-picked person from the Faith Community who served as his "eyes and ears" to oversee everything going on there, since he was frequently on the road fundraising. (As one Covenant House board member would later tell me, "You're Father Bruce's CIA.") The ombudsman had complete veto power over any decision made by any staff member there, up to and including the Franciscan nun who had been running the place for several years.

I'm an executive director now, and I can tell you with all confidence that there is no place for a position like this in any nonprofit organization. You hire the best people you can to fulfill a certain role, and then you learn to trust them – or not – and if the latter, they either need more training or they have to go. But this idea that I'd have an ombudsman on staff who'd give me the inside scoop as to what is going on, and who also has the ability to overturn decisions made by the leaders officially in charge? No. Full-stop no.

But I said yes. Father Ritter was the most famous priest in America at the time. President Reagan had mentioned him in the State of the Union address. *Newsweek* magazine had profiled him. He was on a lot of talk shows. Mother Theresa had stopped by to see him only a month before I arrived. And now I was going to report directly to him? Looking back, I wish I had turned it down. I had only been there a few weeks. I was in the absolute infancy of my initiation into working with homeless teens. There were others in the Faith Community with far more experience than mine who were better suited to this role. The problem was that they were female, and Father Ritter was sexist. It had to be a male. Today I am ashamed I agreed to accept this new role.

I stayed in that role for the remainder of my one-year commitment. It was a difficult job. There was a constant stream of kids protesting that they were being wrongly treated, that they should not have been discharged from Covenant House for some infraction, and they wanted back in. I was always being asked to overturn a decision that had been made by an administrator. And these were frequently administrators with years of experience in this field, with Masters degrees in social work or counseling. They resented that some kid who had just left Madison Avenue was now in the position of overruling their calls, and I don't blame them. I did the best I could, and I learned a valuable lesson, that the backbiting and careerism I witnessed in the corporate world could be just as bad in the nonprofit world, even in a faith-based organization. At one point I said to a priest I knew, "I've got to get better at politics in the workplace," and without a moment's hesitation he said, "Don't do that. Always stick to the truth."

That advice has remained with me.

That first year at Covenant House was life-changing in many respects. The basics were covered for those of us in the Faith Community. Each of us had a tiny room in which to live. Meals were provided to us. There was a physician on the Covenant House board of directors to whom we could go free of charge if we became ill. (For dental care, people would go to the free clinic staffed by students at the Columbia University College of Dental Medicine; I declined and didn't see a dentist for another few years, at which point I was told I had a half-dozen cavities and needed a root canal.) I learned to live very simply on twelve dollars a week pay. A luxury was when several of us pooled our cash and bought a pint of Ben and Jerry's to share. I came to appreciate things like that – things that, before, I had very much taken for granted. Going to a movie was a luxury. We were smack dab in the middle of all the Broadway theaters, and if you volunteered to be an usher for one night, you had a shot at seeing a show.

My family was only a ninety-minute train ride away, and my father and two of my siblings worked in New York City, so I could see all of them frequently. I kept in touch with college friends, though I didn't have the money to go to restaurants and bars as I had before.

As year one at Covenant House ended, I wasn't sure if I wanted to stay on. I'd had enough of the ombudsman job. I knew I didn't want to do that any longer, but I loved being in the Faith Community, so I was torn. Then Father Ritter asked me to take over Covenant House's outreach to high schools and colleges. I'd be in charge of a team of people speaking at gatherings of students, telling them about the work of Covenant House and about the Faith Community. That sounded right up my alley, so I said yes and signed on for another year.

I didn't stay in that role very long either. Covenant House was expanding rapidly in the Western Hemisphere, opening sites in Toronto, Houston, and – wait for it – Guatemala. There were plans for Los Angeles in the works too. At each site there was to be a small Faith Community, based on the New York model.

With all this growth taking place, it was decided that a new position would be created to oversee all the locales. By this time, the Faith Community in New York City had grown to about seventy people, and every day there were new applicants. A vote was to be held among the members to select the new director. I took my name off the ballot, as I had only recently taken over the outreach to high schools and colleges, but I got elected anyway. At that point I felt I didn't have any other choice but to accept.

Now I was tasked with travelling to the various cities in which Covenant House had located and meet with the Faith Community members there. This included Guatemala. I flew there and could tell as soon as I entered the airport that conditions were very different. The country was in an all-out civil war at this point. I was not alone on this trip, and the military pulled our vehicle over on the highway as we drove to our destination. They made us exit the car and went through the interior of the vehicle and all our belongings. Three Catholic sisters and a lay missionary had been killed in neighboring El Salvador not long before in a similar scenario, so to say this ordeal was unnerving would be an understatement.

Eventually we made it to the Covenant House site, which, incredibly enough, was located in the very city where I had briefly been while in the Peace Corps four years earlier. The Covenant House program was basically an orphanage for children, many of whom had lost parents in the civil war. I spent a week there, and even got to visit the family that had hosted me during my short Peace Corps stint. I was disappointed to learn that Oscar was gone; his mother told me she had sent him to live in California. But overall it felt good, as if I had come full circle and was now on the path I was supposed to be following.

I enjoyed the job of director of the Faith Community. I liked going around to the different sites, and so many people were applying to become full-time volunteers. I think half my efforts went to looking for expanded housing so we could accommodate everyone. But as twelve months came to an end, I knew it was time to leave Covenant House. It had been twenty-seven months since

I joined, well past the original one-year commitment, and those volunteers I served with had all moved on, as had most of the group after them. I began to have this feeling of, Okay, so why am I the only one still hanging around?

I did know that I absolutely wanted to keep doing some version of the work I had come to love. I think my old friends were hoping that I had "gotten this out of my system" and that I would be heading back to the corporate world, but I had zero interest in doing that; so I sought out people inside and outside of Covenant House who had years of experience and asked them for advice. One theme emerged: I needed to go to graduate school if I wanted to keep doing this kind of work.

I considered several options, including a master's in social work, master's in counseling, or a doctorate in psychology, but landed on a master's in public administration. Nearby New York University had an MPA program. I applied, was accepted, and was even awarded a full scholarship.

Something else very important happened during my last year at Covenant House: I fell in love with one of the other volunteers, Rosanne Haggerty. There were a lot of marriages coming from people who had met at the Faith Community, and so did ours. We married in August 1984, just as I started at NYU.

Rosanne left the Faith Community around the same time I did, and she found a job developing low-income housing at Brooklyn Catholic Charities. I worked part time at the Catholic Charities in Manhattan while taking my master's courses. Charities had just opened a new office to deal specifically with the burgeoning homelessness crisis in the city, and I was assigned there.

That's how I met Father Bill McNichols.

One afternoon I was in the Charities office and the phone rang. I happened to pick up, and the caller introduced himself as a Jesuit priest living in New York City; he wanted our assistance in opening up a residence for homeless men diagnosed with AIDS.

Little was understood about AIDS at that time, except that it was tantamount to a death sentence. Father McNichols was ministering to men afflicted with it, many of whom had been banished from households out of fear, ignorance, and prejudice. They were, literally, dying in the streets.

A facility was needed where he could minister to the sick and dying, and he had a location in mind.

"There is a rectory at St. Veronica's church on Christopher Street that would be perfect," he said.

I asked why he thought it was so ideal, fully expecting he'd mention such details as the proper zoning and permitting of the site.

"Because St. Veronica was the one who wiped the face of Jesus on his way to Calvary," he replied. "She comforted him. That's what I want to do for these men."

That told me everything I needed to know about the holiness and spirituality of Father McNichols and why this project was so important.

He then introduced me to one of the nuns he'd met while caring for AIDS patients at nearby St. Vincent's Hospital. She and her companion sisters also desperately wanted this residence to be opened.

I wrote a detailed proposal and sent it to the monsignor who was the head of Catholic Charities. A few weeks went by and I did not hear back from him. When I then ran into him at a meeting and asked about the project, he assured me he was looking into it.

A few months after I graduated from New York University and left Charities, I was watching the local news on television. Before the commercial break, the news anchor said, "Stay tuned, after the break, Catholic Charities announces it's opening the first shelter in the city for homeless men with AIDS."

Sure enough, it was a statement by that very monsignor about Charities opening up a residence at the St. Veronica's rectory called the Gift of Love Hospice, to be run by the Missionaries of Charity. There was no mention of Father McNichols, nothing about the nuns from St. Vincent's Hospital.

I called Father McNichols. He confirmed what I had just heard: Catholic Charities took our idea, ran with it, and gave it to someone else.

I was livid and sent a harsh letter to the monsignor. I never heard back.

Two years later, I was with my father and three brothers at Inis Fada, a Jesuit retreat house on Long Island, for the weekend. At some point during the two days, I happened to spot Father McNichols there. I went over and we re-connected, delighted to see each other.

That evening the retreat master went door to door to spend some individual time with each person, and when he came to my room I told him how glad I was to see Father McNichols. He asked how we knew each other, and I told him, including the story about the AIDS residence and my take on what Catholic Charities had done.

He could easily pick up my anger at what had transpired, and asked, "Did the residence open?"

"Yes," I replied.

"So men with AIDS are being cared for and have a decent place to live?" he asked.

"Yes."

"So why are you upset?" he asked.

I hesitated and then finally sputtered, "Uhm ... because ... we didn't get ... the credit."

He looked at me with a wry grin and asked, "Credit? What's credit?"

I just sat there, speechless, stunned really.

"What's credit?" hung there in the air in the room.

I don't think I said anything. I may have just changed the subject, or he did, or he politely excused himself and moved on to the next retreatant. I can't remember.

That was over three decades ago.

That retreat leader has passed away, as has the monsignor from Charities.

Inis Fada was closed and sold off.

Even St. Veronica's church, on Christopher Street in New York City, is closed.

But some things haven't changed.

I'm still in contact with Father McNichols.

ST. VERONICA'S CONVENT, GREENWICH VILLAGE

And I never forgot "What's credit?" Those words have crossed my mind many times in the ensuing decades, whenever I am tempted to seek recognition for something, whenever I feel jealousy over an award or accomplishment earned by a peer, or when I feel resentment.

Most important of all, the Gift of Love Hospice at St. Veronica's is still open, still run by the Missionaries of Charity, still doing the work of God.

· *five* ·

IN 1986 ROSANNE AND I HAD A BABY BOY, Aiden. We rented an apartment in Brooklyn, and I started working for another nonprofit organization helping homeless teenagers and young adults. Called My Brother's Place, it was run by a Catholic priest named Father Jim MacDonald. I had been introduced to him a few years earlier when I was at Covenant House. He had an idea about opening a series of houses for young men with no place to live, and that rather than make them leave after thirty days, they could stay for up to eighteen months, a concept I liked.

We stayed in loose contact and he reached out to me just as I was leaving graduate school. He told me he had been able to open one house in Brooklyn and one in the South Bronx, but he needed someone besides himself to organize the nonprofit and help it grow, and his religious order was willing to pay for such a person. He asked me if I would do it, and I said yes.

My Brother's Place was really a shoestring operation. I don't think it had so much as a photocopier when I got there. Father Jim gave me a mailing list of people to whom he sent appeals, but it was disorganized and I found that half the addresses were incorrect. He was running his two houses completely on volunteers, people with no experience whatsoever in this type of work. And the kids were difficult. They were like the kids at Covenant House – in fact many of them came from Covenant House – and the two houses were in very dangerous neighborhoods. Crack cocaine was devastating the poorest sections of New York City at that time. Overdoses and homicides were skyrocketing. Crime was at one of the highest levels ever recorded in the city, and our residences were at the epicenter.

But none of that deterred me. I was ready to jump in and take the organization to the next level because I believed the mission of My Brother's Place was worthwhile. These boys really did need help; they needed some place to live and someone to guide them in their lives, including going back to school and finding employment. And I knew thirty days wasn't going to do it; if they had a year or so of stability, perhaps they could move ahead in a career and move into permanent housing.

The problem was that Father MacDonald under-estimated just how dangerous young men who had been living on the street could be. They easily bamboozled him. One evening Rosanne and I had a dinner party at our house and we invited him along with about a dozen of our other friends. He brought along a young man he had been helping, telling me, "He is thinking of studying for the priesthood." The boy ended up lifting a wallet from the coat pocket of one of our friends that night. While I was busy trying to get these kids into rehab for abusing crack cocaine or heroin, Father MacDonald was lamenting that we didn't even have "one young man preparing for the sacrament of Confirmation." Then we had an incident in the South Bronx house, when criminals burst in in broad daylight and threatened to shoot and kill one of our staff, who managed to escape execution only by hiding in the bathroom.

I should have felt relieved that we had escaped certain tragedy in the face of such violence. But I didn't. A sense of foreboding clung to me that a tragedy was in the making. Turned out I was right.

January 25, 1987 was Super Bowl Sunday. I was thrilled because the team I had been following my entire life, the New York Giants, had finally made it to the championship. Rosanne and I traveled with three-month-old Aiden to a friend's house in New Jersey to watch the game that night. We knew this person from Covenant House, and a lot of our friends from there were with us.

About mid-way through the game, a feeling that I can only describe as melancholy, or a deeply felt sadness, slowly descended upon me. I had never experienced anything like it. It was such a strange sensation, that I suddenly shook myself and thought, Hey Mark, you're surrounded by your friends and your team is ahead and finally going to win the Super Bowl. Snap out of it!

I did, and the Giants won. We drove home, and I watched the local news reports about the game on television. I was on Cloud Nine.

Then around 10 p.m., the phone rang. It was one of the men volunteering at the My Brother's Place house in the South Bronx. His voice was shaking.

"Mark, you've got to get up to the house immediately. Sister Virginia is dead. She's been murdered."

I was shocked. Stunned. When you do this kind of work, in the back of your mind you know something like this could happen, but you reassure yourself it never will. Now it had.

"Are you sure?" I practically screamed into the phone. "Are you sure she's dead?"

"Well, maybe she's not," he said. "Maybe she's just been stabbed." But then two seconds later he said, "No, she's dead, I'm sure of it. You need to come up here now."

I rushed back to our bedroom to tell Rosanne. She was holding Aiden. She asked if they should come as well.

"No," I told her, "you stay here with the baby. Please."

I then called Father MacDonald, who lived not far from us in Brooklyn. I told him what had happened and that I was picking him up.

The trip to the South Bronx usually took about forty minutes, but this time I did it in twenty-five. I'll never forget crossing over the Willis Avenue Bridge and spotting what looked like thirty police cars, all with lights going, in front of My Brother's Place.

I parked the car, we got out, and an African American female police officer greeted us at the door. We explained who we were and she motioned for us to go inside. Before I went in, though, I asked her, "Is every boy who was in this house sometime today in the house right now?"

"Yes," she said, but then she talked into her radio, asked a question, got a response, turned to me and said, "Actually, one is missing. There is one person who was here earlier today who is not in there now."

"And who is that?" I asked.

"Wilfredo Jones."

"Then that's who you want to find."

Wilfredo Jones was a nineteen-year-old boy who had been living at My Brother's Place for a few weeks. He had stowed aboard a plane from Puerto Rico several years earlier, living on the streets of New York City and staying at Covenant House. We then accepted him at My Brother's Place. He had a job, but our experience had made it easy to figure out he was addicted to crack cocaine. We had been urging him to go to rehab, but he refused. He carried a Bible around and insisted that was all he needed to overcome his addiction.

Two days earlier I had been at a meeting with our South Bronx staff, and we decided that we would give Wilfredo one more chance to agree to go to rehab. If he refused, he'd be discharged. I would not be at that meeting, which was to take place the following day, Saturday. I called that day to find out what had transpired, and the person on duty told me they had met with Wilfredo, given him the ultimatum, and he refused.

"How did he take it?" I asked.

"He was fine," he responded. "He knew what was coming. He was respectful, didn't give us a hard time or anything. He just packed up his stuff and left."

That was the day before Super Bowl Sunday. Now Sister Virginia was dead, Wilfredo had somehow been in the house that day, and he was now missing. None of it made sense, but I was focused on going inside the house to see the boys and the volunteers.

I went in, and all nine boys sat on the couch, staring at the ground. They looked petrified, all their hard-won street bravado stripped away. I went downstairs, where, I was told, the murder had occurred. Sister Virginia's body had already been removed. I stared into the small office she often used, now roped off with yellow tape as a crime scene. I could see files on the desk and a coffee mug, ordinary kinds of things, but also drying blood caked all over the floor. It was a ghastly scene.

Sister Virginia had come to volunteer at My Brother's Place

about four months earlier. She was sixty-five and a member of the Good Shepherd Sisters in Pennsylvania. She had read about My Brother's Place in a Catholic magazine and wrote to us, asking if she could be a full-time volunteer and live there. I interviewed her and she was as kind a human being as anyone could imagine. She had a heart of gold and loved the boys in the house.

She volunteered to be the business manager for that house, which put her in charge of money. She had apparently been in that basement office, counting petty cash during the game, while everyone else was upstairs, and someone had gone down there and stabbed her.

I stayed for a few hours, but I can't remember what I did or who I spoke to. The place was crawling with police officers and detectives, and before I left, I sought out the lieutenant in charge, naively asking him, "Do you think the media will hear about this and cover this tomorrow?"

He looked at me and said, "Son, your life as you know it is about to drastically change a few hours from now."

Was he ever right. Once the police released the information about the murder of a Catholic nun, reporters from every New York City radio and television station and newspaper descended upon our South Bronx house. We told the kids and the staff, "Just say no comment," but all of us were chased and descended upon whenever we entered or exited the house. It was front page news, and everyone in New York City was looking for Wilfredo Jones. Everyone.

The next day I pieced together what had happened. Wilfredo had indeed been discharged as planned that Saturday. The next day, Father MacDonald came up to fulfill his long-standing tradition of saying Sunday Mass at the house. Former residents could come into the house for Mass and then stay for dinner. Wilfredo, discharged just a day earlier, knew that and did so. After dinner he turned to Father MacDonald and told him he had nowhere to go.

Father MacDonald always felt sorry for those boys we had to discharge for whatever reason, including drug abuse, and frequently offered to put them up for a night or two at the YMCA in Manhattan. I didn't agree with this policy – I thought it was just softening the inevitable – but he was in charge so I reluctantly agreed. We did have a firm policy, though, on how this was done, and Father MacDonald knew it. The boy was never just given the money for the Y. You took him down to the Y yourself, and gave the money to the staff there directly. We all knew that if we gave a young man money it'd likely be diverted to something else. Like drugs.

Father MacDonald broke the rule. He gave Wilfredo money. Father MacDonald left the house; Wilfredo left the house. He didn't go to the Y, he smoked up that money, returned to the house, where the boys let him back in, and he sat down to watch the Super Bowl. They later reported that they could see he was high. After a few minutes he said he was going downstairs, came back up, and walked out the door.

The game ended a few hours later and one of the boys went down to see Sister Virginia for something, but the door was locked. He banged on the door, but no one answered, so he grabbed a few of the other boys to go to the front of the house, on the sidewalk, where there was a window into that office. Although the curtains were drawn, they could see the silhouette of her body slumped over the desk. They banged furiously on the bars of the window to awaken her, but it was too late. They went upstairs and called the police. When they arrived, they broke into the office and found her there, dead.

The manhunt for Wilfredo was over in two days. He actually showed up at his job to pick up his paycheck and a detective was there waiting for him. The picture of him in handcuffs was plastered all over the papers and on TV.

I went to visit Wilfredo at Riker's Island prison. He was in seclusion. Prison officials rightly figured that if he was put in general population, he'd be quickly killed. I didn't know Wilfredo all that well – I had probably only talked to him once or twice during his time at My Brother's Place. They let me in to see him, and I asked him point blank, "Did you kill Sister Virginia?"

"I was so high on crack that night, I don't even remember," he answered.

There was a trial a year later. He pled innocent and had a court-appointed lawyer defend him. Father MacDonald went, but I didn't. He was found guilty of second degree murder.

I have many times thought back to that Super Bowl, when, during the middle of the game, I felt an inexplicable sense of melancholy and sadness. Piecing together when Wilfredo went back to the house, and when he went downstairs and took Sister Virginia's life, it was during that same time period. I believe it was her tragic murder that I was feeling at that moment, even though it'd be hours later when I found out. It's proof to me that we are connected to one another on more than a physical plane in this world.

That night I learned, first-hand, how true this is.

· *six* ·

AFTER SISTER VIRGINIA'S DEATH, I stayed at My Brother's Place for about a year, but I limped through it, pondering almost the entire time where to go and what to do next. I had lost faith in Father MacDonald's judgment and ability to responsibly head up the organization. I knew it was his failure to abide by our own safety procedures that had led to her murder. He continued to underestimate just how dangerous young men who had been living on the street and addicted to drugs could be.

I started actively looking around the New York City nonprofit world and was introduced to Bob McMahon, the executive director of a large Catholic organization called St. Christopher-Ottilie (now called SCO Family of Services). A Notre Dame grad who then became a religious brother, Bob eventually left his order, married, and had three daughters. In two decades' time, he took St. Christopher's from being a small, one-site residence for foster youth on Long Island into a sprawling organization with programs in some of the most poverty-stricken neighborhoods of Brooklyn and Queens. I liked him right away and sensed the feeling was mutual. He told me that the organization had recently expanded its site in downtown Brooklyn and was adding dozens of social workers in response to the crack epidemic that was causing thousands of children to go into foster homes. He told me an administrative position was opening there, and that he'd set up an interview for me.

I interviewed for the job and learned that it had absolutely zero contact with children or teenagers. It was a big change from my previous jobs, but that was perfectly fine with me. It was a job that entailed making sure the right papers were filed, background checks were completed on prospective employees, the agency automobiles were functional, and the mechanics of the building were in order. After seven years on the front lines interacting with teenagers with addiction and mental health issues, who also tended toward violence, and after what had happened with Sister Virginia, I relished the idea of a purely administrative role.

Right up until the time I didn't. I got bored quickly. It became just a job, not a calling. My dissatisfaction led me to question my career choice. I began to think that this whole idea of working with the poor, of helping people who were homeless and on the margins, had been a mistake. In high school, I had heard about what a physical therapist does, and it interested me, so I started to research what it would take to return to school to become a certified physical therapist. I also toyed with the idea of taking my business degree and finally using it for something that would create more financial security for my family. Aiden was age four by then, and Rosanne was in graduate school, while also working at Catholic Charities. Money was tight. What was so bad about finding a job on Wall Street or selling computers or something like that? I had plenty of college friends in that field, as were my three brothers. They all seemed to be making money hand over fist. This was the age of the yuppie and New York was their mecca. One phone call could probably land me a job and I'd be set.

All of this was rumbling through my mind when Bob hired a new senior vice president at St. Chris's, who had, until then, been one of the top people in the New York City mayor's administration in charge of the foster care system. Turns out I knew him; even in New York City, the nonprofit world was fairly small. Poul Jensen had been a supervisor at Covenant House nine years earlier when I was there. His tenure and mine had overlapped by only a few months, but we had developed a rapport at that time, which made reconnecting at St. Chris's easy.

He sat in my office that first time in downtown Brooklyn, and when I described the role I had there, he asked, "How did you manage to screw up your career so much?" That was characteristic Poul – brutally honest. I winced when he asked. I wasn't even sure how to respond. And then I said, "I'm really not happy here at all. I'm looking around. I may even leave nonprofits completely."

"Don't rush," he responded. "I'll find a good role for you in this organization. There aren't that many competent, capable people in this field, and I consider you to be one of the few. Don't go anywhere just yet. Hang in there."

I appreciated the compliment, but internally I shrugged. I had my doubts Poul would come through with something that sparked my interest.

A few weeks later he called me.

"You know the Epiphany Youth Hostel we have in Williamsburg, Brooklyn?" he asked.

Epiphany was a twenty-bed residence for homeless young men that St. Christopher's ran. A friend of mine had worked there a few years earlier, and I had visited once. I had also met the director of the program a few times.

"Yes, I know it," I replied.

"Well the director there is doing a terrible job. The place is a mess. I'm going to fire him, and I think you should take over."

I didn't even hesitate. I turned him down.

"No thanks Poul. I know the kinds of kids who go there, they're like the ones who were at My Brother's Place, and one of them killed somebody I cared about. I don't think they want to be helped. I don't even think they can be helped."

"No, that's not true," he replied. "There is a way to help them, and I know how, and if you will allow me to, I will teach you."

"I am flattered you asked me," I said, "but the answer is no."

Poul is not someone to take no for an answer.

He kept calling.

I kept saying no.

He kept calling.

I said maybe.

He kept calling.

I said yes.

Looking back, I think I said yes because I had to admit there was something still in me that felt called to try and help young people who, for whatever reason, found themselves without a home, without a family. That's why I had left Madison Avenue and that whole lifestyle nine years earlier. Maybe there was a way to work successfully with kids like this, and maybe Poul did know the way, and maybe he could teach me. I decided to give it one more shot.

Word started to spread around St. Chris's that I would be taking over Epiphany. One of the senior managers whom I knew pretty well, a former priest, called me and asked, "Why are you going to that God-forsaken place?"

I knew what he was talking about. He wasn't referencing Epiphany specifically. He was referencing Williamsburg. There were many dangerous parts of New York City in 1990, and Williamsburg was right up there with the worst of them. There were entire blocks of rubble where apartment buildings had once been. Torched-out husks of cars lined the sidewalks and empty lots. It was not uncommon to hear gunfire at night. It was, in a word, a war zone.

WILLIAMSBURG, BROOKLYN, 1990

Coincidentally, around that same time I received a call from the human resources director of another nonprofit in upstate New York, inviting me up to see his place, a residential treatment center for about a hundred teenagers who had arrest records and behavioral difficulties. It was gorgeous. Rolling hills. Landscaped. Really nice dormitories where they lived, and a new school building.

"You know, we need a new operations director here," he said.

I wasn't expecting a job offer while on this visit, but then again, I figured he had invited me up there for some reason.

"Thanks," I replied, "but I am actually about to start a new job in Williamsburg."

His look was incredulous. He didn't even have to say what I knew he was thinking: "You mean you'd give up *this* in order to go to *Williamsburg?*"

I was scheduled to start at Epiphany the day after Labor Day, but four days before, on Friday, Poul and Bob called me and said, "We're sending you a fax right now. Read it and call us back."

This was before email, and faxes back then came out like toilet paper, all rolled up. I unfurled it as it came off the machine, read it, and my heart sank.

It was a petition to Bob and Poul, signed by every staff member at Epiphany, with two demands:

We want our old director reinstated.

We don't know who this Mark Redmond is, but whoever he is, we don't want him as our new director.

As I dialed Bob and Poul back, I thought for sure they would say something along the lines of, "Let's slow this down. Don't go there on Tuesday. Let us go and hear the staff out first."

Not only was I sure they would say that, I was *hoping* they'd say that.

When I got them on the phone, the first person who spoke was Bob.

"Screw them!" he said.

"That's right!" echoed Poul. "You go there on Tuesday just like you are supposed to. We have your back!"

"Okay," I squeaked.

I went to Epiphany the day after Labor Day just like I was scheduled to. Epiphany got its name from the Epiphany Catholic Church, which was right across the street. The hostel had once been a convent. St. Christopher's had bought it and reconditioned it to be a residence for homeless young men ages eighteen to twenty-one. It was four stories high, containing five large rooms with four beds to a room. On the first floor there was a kitchen, living room, dining room, and three offices, one of which would be mine.

It was a warm, sunny day when I arrived. A few of the staff were sitting out front on the stoop. I introduced myself and they took me inside.

I learned a lot that first day. As I toured the building, it was impossible not to notice what a wreck the place was. Dirty. Dumpy. There was not enough furniture, and what was there was in bad shape. Nothing on the walls to liven it up or make it look homey. The whole place needed a paint job. Really a mess.

Then I asked to see a census count. Only ten boys were living there of out a capacity of twenty. "How can this be?" I wondered. This was New York City in 1990. There were *thousands* of homeless young men in the city at that time. It seemed *impossible* to me that only half the beds were filled, and of the few who were there, only one or two held jobs or were attending school. Most slept until noon every day.

Epiphany was funded by the New York City Division for Youth, and the next day a team from there showed up unexpectedly. They did a walk-through and then perused the files we had for those living there. They asked to see a schedule of activities and clinical groups, but of course there were none because nothing remotely like that took place at Epiphany.

After a few hours they left, but before they did, the woman supervising the team came into my office. "This place is a disaster," she told me. "You have ninety days to clean it up and get it in order or we are pulling your funding."

I knew she wasn't joking.

Unbelievably, things got worse. On my third day a steady stream of staffers came to my office, all muttering about the food. "It's too bad about the food." "I can't believe what happened about the food." "I don't want to be blamed for the food situation."

I could not understand what they were talking about, so I went in to see our part-time cook. Margaret was in her sixties, from Trinidad-Tobago, with a low-key personality, and who seemed to rarely speak to the staff or the boys. Her job was to prepare dinner each day. "What's all this about the food?" I asked.

She shrugged and said, "We got a big shipment of food here yesterday. You need a lot to feed all these boys, and when I left here last night it was here in our freezers and refrigerator. Now only about half of it is left."

"What?" I asked. "Where did it go? Where is it now?"

She just shrugged again and walked away, saying, "This has happened many times before."

That night I called a friend who had worked with me at My Brother's Place and then gone on to Epiphany. She was the one I had visited there years earlier, but was retired now and living in Illinois. She had no idea I was director at Epiphany, and when I told her she was thrilled.

But when I told her about the missing food, she wasn't surprised at all. She told me there were four or five male staff at Epiphany who routinely pulled their cars up at night and emptied the freezers of food.

"You could walk right down the block to the bodega and see the same side of beef there that was at Epiphany only a few hours before," she said.

She also said it was widely suspected they were dealing drugs to the kids in the house and were even having drug parties in there late at night.

"Why hasn't anyone done anything?" I asked.

"The other staff there are good, but they are afraid," she replied.

She went on to give me the names of who the likely culprits were.

"How about Darrell?" I asked her. "He keeps telling me how glad he is that I am there and what a good job he thinks I am doing."

She almost leapt through the phone.

"Darrell is the ringleader!" she exclaimed. "He was probably the one who pulled his car up last night and emptied the freezers. *Do not trust Darrell!*"

I thanked her profusely for all this information. Before I hung up she said something I will never forget.

"Epiphany has the potential to be a great place for homeless young men. God has led you there Mark. God will be with you."

I began to confront the suspected staffers. I told them I knew what they were up to, and that it needed to stop. My rationale was, "If I tell them I know what they are doing, and give them a chance to stop, they will." But I discovered something important, which is that they had a very different justification: "We've had a good thing going here at Epiphany. We don't want it to stop, and we're not letting this Redmond guy get in the way."

Darrell approached me in my office and said, "Mark, I think I know who's stealing the food."

"I do too," I said.

"Really?" he replied. "Who do you think it is?"

"You," I said.

He went nuts – I mean nuts – screaming and yelling, and from that point on it became a pitched battle. I'd arrive in the morning and find unsigned threatening notes slipped under the door. I still have one:

Mark,
This is to inform you of your future.
I'm going to disgrace you, humiliate you,
and destroy your career in court.
You're finished!
You'll wish you never stepped foot in Epiphany.
This I promise!

Another time I arrived to find my office had been broken into and ransacked.

Then Poul called me and said, "I'm going to ask you a simple question. Did you give a boy at Epiphany named Raul twenty-five dollars?"

"No," I answered.

"Did you give any kid there twenty five dollars?" he asked.

Now I was annoyed. "No! What is this about?"

He then read me a letter he had received from Raul, stating, "Mark Redmond offered me twenty-five dollars if I would write a letter to you saying that he is doing a good job at Epiphany."

A few days later Poul called because he had received a similar letter from another young man at Epiphany, except now it was up to forty dollars.

Not surprisingly, the corrupt staffers at Epiphany were giving these boys money to write the letters.

I was mad at these kids for doing this, but I didn't want to put them in the middle of this mess any more than they already were. They had been, by and large, short-changed by the adults all their lives. Now it was happening to them again.

There were some good, decent people working at Epiphany, and at one point I asked one of them, "You can see what's happening, what these men are doing, why won't you help me?"

"This is between them and you," she replied. She was afraid.

The cook, Margaret, grew to like me, recognizing that I was trying to improve things. Poul was visiting Epiphany one day and she took him aside, pointed at me when I wasn't looking, and said to him, "That man, he is good." One night I was working late at Epiphany, and she slipped a tray of food onto my desk, leaned over, and whispered, "People talk in front of the cook as if I am not even there, but I hear what they say. You had better be careful. These men are now talking about harming you physically."

That was not a blind threat. A few months earlier the finance director of a nonprofit in the city had uncovered corruption, was about to report it, and the staff had her killed, knifed right on the street. People were shot and stabbed in Williamsburg all the time back then. It could happen to me walking to the subway or on my way to buy a soda at the bodega. It would be so easy for these men to do it themselves or pay one of their friends to do it, and no one would ever know. It would just be another murder in Brooklyn in 1990.

I was scared – really scared. My stomach was in a perpetual knot. Walking into Epiphany every day felt like walking into a booby trap, like walking through a gantlet. Many times I wondered, "How did Oscar Romero do it? Martin Luther King? Veronica Guerin? Malcolm X? How did Jesus do it? How do you go about your work, your mission, knowing in the back of your mind that someone is out to get you, and you don't know when it will happen, or where, or even who, but it's coming."

That is a very, very difficult way to live.

I asked Bob if the agency could provide me with a car on a temporary basis, since I was taking the subway to and from Williamsburg, and it was about a ten-block walk to Epiphany. He got me one right away. I called Poul and told him the warning Margaret had given me.

"What do we do now?" I asked him.

"I don't know," he replied, which felt oddly reassuring to me. If this was new territory for Poul, and even with his decades of experience he did not know what to do, in a way it gave me the okay not to have the answers. It was a good lesson in leadership – one I have held onto in the intervening decades – that in a difficult moment it is okay for the person in charge to acknowledge they don't have all the answers, they don't know what to do in the moment, but we'll figure it out together.

Poul and Bob received constant letters from these men, accusing me of all kinds of things, including using the "S word" toward those of them who were Hispanic. I kept waiting for the accusation that I was sexually abusing the boys in the house; I was sure that was next. But one day Bob called and said, "The grammar and spelling in these letters are awful. You sure they each have a high school diploma?" I knew that was a Division for Youth requirement, and that they had each stated they had a diploma or GED on their respective résumés.

Bob had someone from the St. Christopher's administration check with the State Board of Education. A few days later Poul called me.

"We just hit a home run!" he said. Four of the men did not have diplomas or GED's, including Darrell. We let them go immediately for falsification of their résumés and for failure to meet the educational requirement.

That was a huge win, but two men who had been followers of Darrell and part of the corruption remained. Without their leader, however, they floundered and managed to trip themselves up a number of times. It was easy to show them the door.

Shortly after they were gone, Poul came in to address the remaining staff. Pointing to me he said, "No more standing on the sidelines. This is your supervisor and you get behind him or leave, because we have a ton of work to do to get this place in shape."

One of them looked at me and said, "We've talked. You have our loyalty."

And they did.

We filled the empty beds and helped kids find jobs and/or get into training programs, finish their high school education, or go on to community college. No one slept till noon any more.

We painted Epiphany, put artwork up around the house, and hung curtains. When my grandmother on Long Island passed away, I went to her house with a van and one of the Epiphany kids, and whatever furniture wasn't nailed to the ground we hauled back to Williamsburg. Epiphany had a backyard that was mostly dirt, and I persuaded a local contractor to donate sod so we could have a nice lawn. We even built horseshoe pits and had horseshoe tournaments back there.

We worked hard and made Epiphany feel more like a home.

We started individual and group therapy for those in the house and had a part-time addiction counselor on staff.

Recreation became key. We formed a touch football team that I coached, and we played against other kids in Brooklyn. We had weekly bingo nights in the house. It was a funny sight, twenty rough teenage guys, some of whom had been gang members, others former prison inmates, all in our living room waiting for their cards to be filled so they could yell Bingo! and win a gift certificate to Dunkin' Donuts. They were totally into it. It was hysterical.

We started a speaker series. Most of the youth living at Epiphany were black or Hispanic, so for speakers we invited in people of color who had grown up in places like Williamsburg but had managed to obtain an education or training and gone on to successful careers in a number of fields. The youth at Epiphany ate it up. They loved hearing stories like this because it inspired them and gave them hope.

The longer I was at Epiphany and interacted with the young men there, the more I understood how deeply they mistrusted adults. In one group session, I listened as one of them asked his peers, "How do you learn to trust others? I've trusted people and have been burnt, time and time again. How do I honestly know who I can trust?" Another time I listened in as one of our staff asked a young man, "How do you like your new social worker?"

"A lot," he replied.

"Can you trust him?" the staff member asked.

"Oh no," was the answer. "He's a nice guy but you can't expect us to trust an adult after all they have done to us."

This was going to be our biggest challenge at Epiphany. Poul brought in one of the foremost experts in our field, Dr. Howard Polsky of Columbia University, to train the staff.

"Kids like these have a very hard protective shield they wear because of all that's happened to them," Polsky told us. "Your job is to somehow bore through that in order to reach the human being inside. That requires you to come through if you promise them something, if you say you will do something for them. If you don't, they will view you as untrustworthy and unreliable as all the other adults they have encountered. And you won't get that opportunity back from them."

We made tremendous progress at Epiphany. The same city officials from the Division for Youth who were ready to close us down ended up declaring Epiphany a model program for homeless youth in New York City. They later funded four others like it.

The success at Epiphany altered my life in important ways. For one thing, I didn't become a physical therapist or start selling stocks and bonds. I stayed in the field of caring for homeless youth, and twenty-nine years later am still at it. It turns out I had been right all along: This was my destiny. This was what I was put on earth to do.

The things that Poul taught me back then I still use today in my work – how to create an environment within a program that holds kids accountable for their actions while also making them feel like they are respected, heard, and cared about; the importance of the physical environment, and that it be kept clean and orderly; how to recruit staff who are not only intelligent but also compassionate and kind; how to integrate the clinical elements of therapy into a program and why that is essential.

Just as important, he taught me how to be a leader: how to listen to your staff and get their input on an issue, but in the end be able to make a decision and live with it; how to spot when someone is lying to you and just sucking up; how to set the standards of excellence and help people live up to them. Poul is retired now; so is Bob McMahon, and I am still in contact with both. I will always be grateful to them, because as they said at the outset, they would have my back, and they did.

The other person I will always be grateful to is Margaret, the cook. She went out of her way, at personal risk, to help me when no one else would, and I will be indebted to her for the rest of my life.

· *seven* ·

I LOVED WORKING AT EPIPHANY and seeing the positive changes we were making. It was as if it had rejuvenated me. After a year, Poul asked me if I'd also take over a program run by St. Christopher's that was about twenty minutes away, in Bushwick, another crime-ridden section of Brooklyn. It was an eight-bed group home for boys as young as nine years old coming out of "QCPC," the Queens Children's Psychiatric Center. It was a step-down program, with the idea that they would leave the psychiatric center, stabilize at the Bushwick house for a few months, and then go back home.

I said, "Sure, why not?" After all, a bunch of nine-year-old boys? I was used to dealing with twenty very tough young men at Epiphany, ages eighteen to twenty-one, some of whom had been gang members and former prison inmates. How difficult could a bunch of middle school kids be?

Turns out, very.

I went to the Bushwick house before my start date for an evening meal to meet the staff and the kids. I sat there in the living room, and without so much as a hint of warning, one of the boys picked up a folding chair, held it over his head, and aimed it at me. I literally dove out of my chair and leapt for cover behind a couch. The chair barely missed me, and the staff on duty immediately physically restrained the boy.

"How often does this kind of thing happen?" I asked one of the staff.

"Often," she answered.

I went home shaking and said to Rosanne, "I think I've made a mistake. This is more than I can handle."

"That's what you said about Epiphany, remember?" she said.

It was true, I had.

I kept going back to the Bushwick house, splitting my time between there and Epiphany. My office was on the second floor with a window facing out onto Central Avenue, the main street. One afternoon I heard a couple of the boys out front coming back from school. It was winter, with a buildup of snow on my window ledge. I quietly opened the window, scooped up some snow and flung a snowball in their direction. That started it. They all followed suit and ran in the house, snowballs in hand, chasing me around the building, floor to floor. Really funny and a reminder of how the little things can make such a big difference.

I brought in a camera and took photos of each individual boy, which I blew up into a framed eight-by-ten, with each boy's name written under his photo. I hung them up on one wall with "Central Avenue All Stars" printed beneath them. Let me tell you, those boys were frequently doing physical damage to that house, but that one wall? It was sacred to them. No one touched it.

In short order I enjoyed being there as much as at Epiphany. And I was learning a lot about childrens' psychiatric disorders and what they required to heal and make progress in their lives.

But I wasn't feeling so great about Brooklyn in general. After renting an apartment there for a year, we had saved up enough to purchase a small attached row house in a neighborhood known as Borough Park.

It's fascinating for me to see Brooklyn now. I visited there a few years ago and found it hard to believe that areas that were blighted and bombed out thirty years ago are now filled with Starbucks, hipsters, and high-priced condos. It wasn't that way in the late eighties. I was once thrown to the ground in broad daylight on the corner of Flatbush and Fulton while some teenagers rifled through my pockets searching for my wallet. (I fought back; they didn't succeed.) I had a hand-printed sign taped to the side of my car window, "Radio already stolen, please don't break glass." I carried something called The Club in my vehicle, a bright red metal bar that could be locked into place on the steering wheel so that when thieves (inevitably) broke in, they would be unable to turn the wheel and travel any distance.

Borough Park was considered safer than most Brooklyn neighborhoods; our house was broken into only once in the five years we lived there, so our friends viewed us as fortunate. People on our block were friendly. They'd stop by and chat on their way to or from home. We had a small front yard where other children would come down to play with Aiden.

Borough Park was also white. Very white. I cannot remember a homeowner or éven a renter who was a person of color in our neighborhood. I can't even remember seeing a person of color walking down our block. And there was a terrible racial incident less than a mile away. In 1989 a sixteen-year-old black male, Yusef Hawkins, traveled to this part of Brooklyn with three of his friends in order to buy a used car that had been advertised. For that simple act they were chased by dozens of white youth, and Yusef was shot and killed. This technically took place in the adjacent neighborhood, Bensonhurst, but it was very close to where we lived.

Borough Park, when we moved there, was a curious mix of Italian Catholics and Hasidic Jews, and there was this palpable unease that existed between the two populations. It never became physical, but it was there, this general distrust. It wasn't hard to detect that the two groups were at odds with each other. Although Catholic, Rosanne and I were of Irish descent, so in a way, we were outsiders to both groups.

That distrust evaporated, however, or at least was put on hiatus, when word got out that a nonprofit organization, the Catholic Guardian Society, had purchased one of the houses at the end of our block, and they planned to use it as a group home for adults with developmental disabilities. While the Italian Catholics and Hasidic Jews could not agree on much, they were in total alignment on the idea that this group home had to be stopped.

I couldn't understand why. A home for adults on the autism spectrum, or with Downs Syndrome? So what? Opposition meetings started taking place almost weekly, in VFW halls, American Legions, and other places. My neighbors attended them. It was all anyone talked about, that this group home had to be halted.

I finally decided to go to one of the meetings with Rosanne. I think it was in a church basement. The room was filled to capacity. People kept talking about their property values going down because of this group home, how bad it would be, how it was the wrong location, why couldn't the nonprofit go find another location?

Again, none of it made sense to me, until an elderly man spoke up.

"We can't let that home open, because what if they put blacks in there?"

There was immediately an awkward silence. People looked at the floor, and I thought, Now I see. This is it. This is what it's all about. This is why no one wants this home to open, because there could be people of color living in it.

At this gathering several people mentioned an upcoming City Council meeting. I decided that I would attend, and I would speak.

It took place a few weeks later, at night, in a school auditorium. This was not the City Council for the entire city of New York, but for that part of Brooklyn. When I entered, there was a sign-up sheet, and I wrote my name on it. Rosanne and I sat down. I spotted some of our neighbors in the audience, and we waved hello to a few.

The meeting began, the council went through several pro forma agenda items, and then there was the discussion and official vote on the group home. The council chair took the microphone and announced to the audience, "This is now the part of the meeting for public comment. Only one person has signed up to speak. Is Mark Redmond here?"

I froze. I just froze. I felt an immediate lump in my throat. I could not believe this. All these meetings, all these gatherings, everyone talking incessantly about this group home, and I was the only one going on record to speak?

And since I hadn't said anything at the church basement meeting, nor had I expressed my sentiments to neighbors, no one there except Rosanne even knew my stance on the issue.

For a brief second I considered not going up. But my conscience wouldn't let me. I had to do it. I left my seat and walked toward the front of the auditorium, my neighbors all watching me, probably wondering, What's he doing? Why is he going up there?

I stood on stage and walked up to the microphone. I still remember what I was wearing – jeans, sneakers, and a gray sweatshirt.

"I live on the block where they want to put this group home," I said. "I also work in the nonprofit world, and I know the organization that wants to open it, the Catholic Guardian Society. They have an excellent reputation, and I trust them to do a good job.

"This is a nice neighborhood. My wife and I like it here. People are friendly. They look out for one another. It's safe. It's clean.

"If I had a relative with a developmental disability – an aunt, an uncle, a brother, a sister – and they didn't have a place to live, I'd want them to live on this street. So I have no problem at all with this group home opening up here. I'm for it, and in fact I hope that you, the members of the City Council, vote in favor of it."

That was it. I stepped away from the microphone and walked back to my seat. I didn't have to look at my neighbors; I could just feel the stares of hatred. I really could. I knew what they were thinking, and how they despised what I had just said.

As I walked up the side aisle toward my seat, a female City Council member reached over to me as I passed and whispered, "That was so beautiful, so moving."

The chair of the council then announced, "Call to vote. All in favor of the proposed siting of the group home on Fifty-fourth Street, say aye."

No one responded.

"Nay?" he asked.

All hands went up, including the woman who had just commended me.

I guess it wasn't that beautiful and moving, I mused.

Despite the vote, the group home opened. There was a law in New York State called the Padavan Law, which stipulated that in order to stop a social service program from opening, it had to be proven that that part of the city was already overburdened with similar services. Since it was impossible for the opponents to prove that, the home opened.

After that meeting, none of our neighbors said anything to us. In fact, none of them spoke to us again. At all. At any time. Ever. People drove or walked by without acknowledging us. Their children no longer came down to play with Aiden in our front yard.

We were personae non grata.

So that was one good reason to start looking to live elsewhere. Another was that Aiden was five and attending a public magnet school in Manhattan, near where Rosanne worked. They took the subway together once, having to change trains along the way. It was hot, crowded, and chaotic, and they ended up arriving late. So that was it for the subway school commute. From then on, we resorted to all of us piling into our car, and I'd fight the traffic through Brooklyn, into the Brooklyn Battery Tunnel, up the West Side Highway in Manhattan, drop them off, fight my way across town, drive over the Williamsburg Bridge, and go to Epiphany, then on to Bushwick. At night, I'd reverse it. It was getting to be a drain.

I started perusing the Help Wanted section of *The New York Times* every Sunday, when it had a special section for health care and social service jobs. One Sunday I spotted this ad:

DIRECTOR
RESIDENTIAL TREATMENT CENTER
ST. CHRISTOPHER'S – JENNIE CLARKSON
DOBBS FERRY, NEW YORK
HOUSING INCLUDED

My first reaction was, "You mean there's more than one St. Christopher's around?" There was. The official name of the one I was then employed by was St. Christopher – Ottilie. This other one, St. Christopher's – Jennie Clarkson, was completely different. I had to look up where Dobbs Ferry was. It turned out to be in

Westchester County, just a short distance north of the city, but a world away.

I cut the ad out and left it on my bureau for a week. I was about to throw it away when I thought, What the heck, they've probably already hired someone, but I'll send in a resume.

I did, and the Human Resources director called and asked me to come in for an interview.

I had yet to tell Poul or any of my staff about this, but the day before the interview, Poul stopped by Epiphany and I handed him the ad.

He read it and said, "Crap."

I laughed, and he said, "That job is a big leap up for you, but if I was in charge there, I'd hire you. You'll make mistakes, but you will do well."

I told him I didn't want Bob McMahon to know I was applying. He promised me he'd keep it between us.

I drove up to Dobbs Ferry the next day for the interview. I met with the Human Resources director and two others. They described the Residential Treatment Center as being an eighty-four-bed facility for teenage boys and girls, most of whom were from the New York City foster care system. Some were in the juvenile justice system for having committed crimes, and St. Christopher's was where they were now placed. They lived in seven cottages on the eighteen-acre campus, which was situated on the banks of the Hudson River. There was a high school on the campus, although that was run by a separate entity and staff.

They explained that the campus director was retiring after being there for eleven years. I later found out he had been fired. They let me know that there was an active "Close St. Christopher's" movement organized by local citizens, and there were many problems at the program, including kids wandering off into town and robbing stores and breaking into homes. And they talked about riots.

At the end of the interview I said to the three participants, "My direct supervisor knows I am here today on this interview, but the executive director, Bob McMahon does not, and I prefer to keep it that way, at least for now." They agreed to this, thanked me for coming, and said that if I was selected for the next round, it would be with the executive director, Luis Medina.

I got back home that night and there was a voice message from Poul Jensen on our answering machine.

"Bob McMahon knows you were on the interview today," he said. "Call me."

I was mad, because I had explicitly told the people in Dobbs Ferry I did not want Bob to know. I questioned if I still wanted the job if this was how they operated.

I called Poul right away.

"Listen to this," he said, "It's wild. This guy Luis Medina met Bob months ago at a meeting and asked if he could sit with him sometime to get his advice about being an executive director. Bob agreed and offered to come up to see him at his site, in Dobbs Ferry. They picked a date, and guess which date it was, even though they set it months ago?"

"Today?" I asked.

"Yes, today," he said. "While you were there in one room interviewing, Bob was in the next room meeting with Medina. And here's what's good. When Bob heard you were there, he told him, 'I'd hate to lose Mark Redmond, but if I were in your shoes, I'd hire him in an instant.'"

"Poul, do you know the odds of this happening?" I asked.

"About three million to one?" he answered.

I was called a few days later to meet with Luis Medina for the final interview. It was pretty much a repeat of what I had told his people a week earlier. At the end, he asked me why I wanted the job.

"It's the next step up," I answered.

"It's about ten steps up," he said.

I knew what he meant. There was a very big difference between running two small residences in Brooklyn and an eighty-four-bed campus in seven houses. And I'd have to live next to the grounds. The job came with a house, and it wasn't an option: It was mandated so that I'd be available to deal with crises when they arose, any time day or night.

I turned to Luis and asked, "Why do you want me for this job?"

"Because if you're good enough for Poul Jensen and Bob Mc-Mahon, you're good enough for me," he replied.

So I tendered my resignation and let the staff at both houses know I was going. I then told the kids, starting with the small Bushwick crew. They gathered in the living room and I let them know I'd be leaving soon. One of them, a nine-year-old who was fairly new, who I had barely had a chance to speak to in his short time there, looked directly at me and said, "I hate you."

These boys had suffered so much loss and rejection by the adults in their lives, so his response didn't shock me. To at least this one boy, I was yet another person abandoning him.

The Epiphany crew took it much better. The staff and kids threw a going-away party for me on my last day, which was a blast. Someone took a group picture of me and the guys, that, almost three decades later, I still have, enlarged and hanging in my Vermont office. They also gave me a card, signed by all of the kids. Most of what they wrote was some variation of "Thanks for what you did here and good luck in your new job," with a signature beneath it.

But tucked away in the corner of the card was something one of them had written but did not sign:

Do not forget the homeless.

For a long time I tried to match the faces in the picture with what each one had written, in an effort to figure out who had written that final remark. But I finally gave up; I could not make the match. So I've regarded it as a life-long reminder by an anonymous source, prodding me to always remember what is important, and why I do the work I do.

EPIPHANY YOUTH HOSTEL, APRIL 1992

· *eight* ·

PUTTING EPIPHANY ONTO A GOOD COURSE was an incredible challenge. Doing so at St. Christopher's in Dobbs Ferry would be even more so.

Not only was it a bigger facility, with quadruple the number of youth living there, it was also coeducational. And I had never worked with young women before, not even at Covenant House. I had dinner before I started with Sister Paulette Lomonaco, who was the head of Good Shepherd Services in New York City and a well-deserved legend in our field. When I told her I was about to take over a campus, and it was coed, she asked, "Have you ever worked with girls before?"

When I said I had not, she smiled and said, "And this place is coed? You are about to find out just how difficult this work can really be."

I had no reason to doubt her. The St. Chris kids were younger than what I was used to at Epiphany, mostly ages fourteen to sixteen. Almost all were from New York City, and of course, the poorest sections. Except for two white teens – a boy and a girl – over the next five years every youth was a person of color. Most had been in multiple foster and group homes and had not fared well. St. Chris–Dobbs Ferry was often the end of the line for them. If they didn't succeed here, there really was nowhere else to go.

Despite being located in one of the most affluent counties in America, the physical campus was a dump. The school building was covered with graffiti on the exterior. The seven cottages where the kids lived were rundown and drab.

There was very little structure to the program. No rewards for those who behaved properly, no consequences for those who did not. No recreation program, so kids were bored and frequently got into trouble, simply out of a lack of anything entertaining to do.

Staff members had schedules, but they frequently scammed the system so one person would call in sick, ask another staff member to fill that shift and thereby get overtime, and they'd then split the financial surplus between them, promising to reverse roles the next time around. The supervisors, who were paid more than line staff, gave themselves the easiest shifts – daytime, when the kids were in school. As the kids were coming back to the cottages, supervisors were in their cars heading out the driveway.

My work was certainly cut out for me. I inherited an assistant director who, like me, was Caucasian, but widely despised and regarded as racist by the majority of staff, who were people of color. Luis Medina did me a favor and got him transferred to another campus the agency had, and I hired an African American man named Al Randolph, a veteran in this field and widely respected. He and I worked shoulder to-shoulder-to clean things up. It wasn't easy, and it frequently wasn't pretty, but over time we were able to get staff to stop the nonsense they were pulling or we sent them packing. We started an active recreation program. We formed boys and girls basketball teams that competed against county high schools. I obtained donated bicycles and personally took kids out several times a week. We recruited volunteer mentors for kids, and we persuaded our maintenance workers to let kids work alongside them after school each day so they could learn carpentry, plumbing, and painting. I had them get rid of the graffiti on the side of the school, and when anyone dared to tag it again, we'd paint right over it. We renovated cottage after cottage; it took a few years, but in time all of them became as home-like as possible. We started family visiting days and barbeques so parents and relatives could come and see their kids. We started therapeutic groups run by trained, licensed counselors. We started a gospel choir for kids who were interested in that. I launched a leadership group and took those kids on ropes courses and other activities that would help them to reach their potential.

It was a great thing to watch the kids change and blossom. The feedback we received from parents and relatives reflected this. We'd frequently hear, "My child is changing for the better. Whatever you are doing on that campus, it's making a difference." It wasn't all roses. For example, the following things occurred, not necessarily in this chronology, but they happened.

· ·

A boy found out his girlfriend on campus was seeing another boy, so he left and came back at night with a loaded gun to kill him. I managed to call the police and persuade them not to drive up with their siren on so he wouldn't hear them and run. He was apprehended and arrested.

· ·

My ninth day on the job, the Rodney King verdict was announced. When the kids saw on television the rioting going on in Los Angeles and other cities, they wanted to do the same on campus or in downtown Dobbs Ferry. One boy, who had tried to commit suicide two weeks earlier, managed to persuade them to instead follow the example of Dr. Martin Luther King and calmed them down.

· ·

A fourteen-year-old girl with a history of suicide attempts bolted from her cottage at eight o'clock on a freezing cold December morning, heading for the train tracks below. After receiving the urgent call about her departure, I bivouacked through the woods in order to try and find her, but couldn't. A dozen boys her age followed me down there and did, eventually, find her and bring her back. I took them all out to dinner that night to thank them.

· ·

Our third night living in the house next to campus, twelve girls in one cottage decided to break out at eleven o'clock, knowing we were at minimal staffing during the overnight shift, in order to start a riot. They succeeded. It went on for three hours and ended with one girl going to the hospital.

· ·

A young man was beaten up by one of the aides at the school, who, I quickly learned, were thugs who regularly struck students for even the most minor infractions. I filed an abuse complaint with the Department for Children and Families, which infuriated the other school aides but impressed my staff members for doing what was right.

I accompanied our boys' basketball team to a game in a high-poverty section of Yonkers. When it looked like we were going to win, the referee called the game off, and we were chased to our van by angry fans. I clutched my seven-year-old son's hand as we piled into the vehicle and managed to escape.

· ·

One of our part-time African American staff members came by to pick up his check. He was a wonderful man, much-beloved by the kids at St. Chris. I watched him drive off. Ten minutes later he stopped to get a slice at a local pizza parlor and was shot three times by an off-duty New York City policeman in a dispute over a parking spot. He died, and when the authorities could not locate a family member to identify the body, I was called to the morgue to do so.

· ·

When one young man's mother died, I decided to go to the funeral in the South Bronx and bring a few of his friends with me. When the woman's former husband absconded with the money that was supposed to go to the funeral parlor, the parlor refused to start the service as relatives made calls trying to raise the funds needed while her body lay in state. The boy was embarrassed beyond belief.

· ·

Our recreation staff took a campus trip to Rye Playland Park. I stayed behind, and that night at halftime on Monday Night Football, the local station announced, "Riot at Rye Playland tonight, story at eleven." I had a sick feeling it was our kids, and I was right. I ended the evening at the police station.

· ·

I dared to take my family on vacation for a week. One of our staff, knowing this, drove her husband up to my house and watched him break in and rob it. One of our female youth saw this, notified the police, and later identified him. I returned from vacation and the staff member could not understand why she was being fired.

· ·

If you have any desire to read the details of these events, feel free to read my first book, *The Goodness Within: Reaching Out to Troubled Teens With Love and Compassion* (Paulist Press). And as disturbing as these anecdotes may be, there was also what I call The Incredible Case of Gerald Farr.

Mr. Farr was a part-time staff member at St. Chris who functioned as a "rover." While all other staff members would show up for their eight-hour shifts and be assigned to one particular cottage, the rover was an extra person who would patrol the grounds and help out wherever needed. An African American man in his mid-thirties, he told us his full-time regular job was as a firefighter in the New York City Fire Department. In fact that is pretty much all he talked about, especially with the kids. He talked to them all the time about what it took to apply there, what the qualifications were, what the job was like, and how much he loved it.

One summer Sunday afternoon I was at home and my work phone rang. I immediately picked up and the administrator on duty said, "You'd better get over here. Your office is on fire."

Fire was always a worry at St. Chris's. We'd already had one fire about a year earlier; a group of girls in a cottage were mad at another girl, took a pair of jeans out of her closet, lit them on fire, and threw them in the woods out back. Guess what happened next?

But this call was particularly frightening because my office was in the basement of a cottage that housed twelve young women on the floors above it. I dropped the phone and ran out the door.

My office was on the other side of campus from where we lived. As I sprinted over I noticed two things that were welcome sights: the girls standing at a safe distance on the front lawn of their cottage, meaning they were safe, and Dobbs Ferry fire trucks heading down the driveway.

I ran to the back of the cottage, where the door to my office was located. To my surprise, Gerald Farr was standing there, dressed in full fire gear.

Why is our rover dressed like a firefighter at this moment? was my first thought, but when you are in middle of dealing with a fire, those kinds of questions get put in your mental parking lot to be figured out later. Without even saying a word to him, I put my key into the door lock, only to find that I didn't have to turn the key as I always did: It was already unlocked.

Why is my door unlocked, when I know the last thing I did on Friday was to lock it? was now parked next to the first question.

I pulled open the door. Black, thick smoke billowed out. Mr. Farr turned to me and said, "I'm going in. If I'm not back in two minutes, send the firemen in after me."

He got down on all fours and started crawling in. He yelled

things back to me, but I couldn't make out what he was saying or trying to communicate. By then the Dobbs Ferry firemen were suited up and approaching me, carrying hoses. I told one of them that a staff member was in there. A group of them went in and seconds later Gerald Farr exited, coughing and hacking. One of the firefighters gave him oxygen, and once he caught his breath, they asked what he had seen and he filled them in.

The next few minutes are a blur to me. Other fire departments pulled up. The grounds around the building were crawling with firefighters. Many were surrounding Mr. Farr, patting him on the back. He was the hero, no doubt about it.

When they left him alone for a second, I went over to him.

"I think it was arson Mr. Redmond," he said. "I think somebody set the fire." I couldn't believe what I was hearing. I thought for sure it had been some kind of electrical malfunction; after all, it was a very old building. Arson? My office?

There were two male staff members on duty that day upstairs in the cottage. I went over to them and asked, "There's a possibility this was arson. Did either of you happen to see anyone by the cottage at all this afternoon?"

One man looked at the other and rolled his eyes. The other one smirked.

"What?" I asked. "Did you see someone? Who?"

"Your hero over there," one said, pointing at Gerald Farr, who by then was again surrounded by firefighters congratulating him for his brave work.

"Are you kidding me?" I said. "Are you telling me you saw Mr. Farr up here earlier?"

He turned to his shift-mate and said, "Remember? I happened to look out the back window and said to you, 'What's Farr doing out there by Mr. Redmond's door?'"

"I do," said the other staff member, "and I said to you, 'I'm sure he'll be up to see us in a minute.' But he never did, he never came up here. And then a few minutes later we smelled smoke."

"Are you two trying to tell me you think it was Gerald Farr who set the fire?" I asked. "I saw that man risk his life to put it out."

"All I'm telling you is that he was the only person I saw outside your door today," the first one said. "If anyone else was up here, I didn't see them."

I went back over to Gerald Farr.

"Thank God you were here today," I said.

"Yeah I know," he replied, "and that I happened to have my firefighter gear in my car trunk."

I continued. "Now, when you were working as the rover today, did you happen to see anyone up by this cottage?"

"No, I didn't, because I never even made it up to this end of the campus today," he answered.

I thanked him again and walked away thinking, So I have two staff members identifying this guy as being outside my office door, they smell smoke shortly thereafter, and he denies he was even up here?

I walked over to the Dobbs Ferry police chief who was then on site.

"You're never going to believe this one," I told him.

I filled him in. He listened and said, "I'm going to go question Mr. Farr. In the meantime, we know an accelerant of some sort was used in there to get the fire going, and we also know how that person got into your office. They used a blue crowbar to pry open the west-facing door and exited out the north door. If we find that blue crowbar, we'll find our arsonist."

That then answered the question I had about why my door was unlocked when I first got to it. The arsonist pried open the west door, walked down the hallway and set my office on fire, then exited through the north door that was closest to it, and since he didn't have a key, would leave it unlocked.

The chief and some of his staff invited Mr. Farr over to the chapel offices on the other end of campus. About an hour later the chief came back to me and said, "He says he never claimed to be a New York City firefighter."

"I'll be right back," I said. "I'm going to go get his file, which is in another building. It has his job application in it where he wrote that he is."

I found it, and there it was, in black and white.

They questioned him for a few more hours, and as I finally headed over to my house to go to bed, by coincidence, Gerald Farr was being led out of our chapel, in handcuffs. He saw me and shouted, "I didn't do it Mr. Redmond, I didn't set your office on fire!"

"That's for them to figure out," I replied, as I pointed to the police. "As for me, I only know one thing: You're fired!"

Later on the police secured the legal right to impound his car. What did they find in the trunk?

A blue crowbar, with wood chips in it that matched the door to my office.

What an idiot, I thought. Not only is he a criminal, he's a dumb criminal. He could have tossed that crowbar into the woods or the Hudson River or a million other places, but he puts it back into his trunk.

Now why would Gerald Farr set my office on fire, and then go in dressed in full fire gear to try to put it out? (We later found out he had pilfered the gear from a volunteer fire department on Long Island somewhere; they wanted it back after they read what he had done.)

It didn't take me long to figure it out, once all of our staff were back on Monday. It turned out he was dating one of our staff. She began to have doubts that he actually was a New York City firefighter and started to spread the word among others. I believe that he set my office on fire in order to go in and help put it out to convince her and everyone else that he was actually a member of the FDNY.

Not that he admitted that. He actually had a different rationale that his lawyer offered in court: Mr. Farr was concerned about the lax security in my office. He wanted to show that someone could easily break in. He did so but then heard someone outside and panicked and lit a match in order to provide light for himself. The match then somehow lit papers on fire, which quickly spread.

A grand jury was empaneled, and I had to go testify. I sat in the waiting area across from one of the Dobbs police lieutenants, a man I knew well from several brushes that St. Chris kids had had with the authorities over the years.

I looked at him, shook my head, and said, "Why are we even here? This is ludicrous. We're talking about the cost of my time, your time, the judge's, the jurors, the court officers. The taxpayers of this state are picking all of this up. Can you believe this?"

He shook his head too. "This is our system of justice," he said. "I guess so," was all I could respond.

In the end Gerald Farr took a plea. I heard his lawyer persuaded him to do so since his defense was so weak and didn't make sense. I believe he received a sentence of six years.

Someone who worked in this field longer than I had once advised, "The kids are the easy part. It's the staff that will drive you over the edge." In truth, the vast majority of the staff I've worked with are committed, capable, talented, and kind. But then there are the Gerald Farr's of the world, and yes, they do drive you nuts.

· *nine* ·

ROSANNE AND I DIVORCED while I was at St. Christopher's – Jennie Clarkson, after ten years of marriage. We had both been unhappy for a long time and had been through a series of marriage counselors, none of whom were able to help us work things out. We agreed to shared custody of Aiden, who was then age seven. I'd stay in the house supplied to me by St. Christopher's, and she bought a place nearby.

The day we signed the divorce papers, I left the lawyer's office in Manhattan and I felt happy. It was like I had a new lease on life. I even had a girlfriend, a really nice woman I had met at work. I walked toward Grand Central Station where I'd take the train home to Dobbs Ferry, feeling lighter and free. On the way I stopped at a deli and bought a sandwich, planning to eat it on the train. But after I boarded and unwrapped my sandwich, I couldn't take more than a bite. I suddenly felt nauseous. I packed it up, figuring I had a stomach bug or something.

Once home, I made dinner for Aiden, put him to bed a few hours later, and called my parents and siblings to tell them that all the legalities were completed, and I was free to start my life over. I felt relieved.

That night I couldn't sleep. I tossed and turned the entire evening. The next morning at seven, I dragged myself out of bed, showered, and got Aiden to his school bus, but I still didn't want to eat. I trudged through the workday. That night, I went to bed completely exhausted but, again, could not go to sleep. Still no appetite the next morning, and I had to admit it was not a stomach bug bothering me but something else.

I had been seeing a therapist for about a year while working through the turmoil of whether or not to end my marriage. He had helped me a lot, including coming to the decision to divorce. I had stopped seeing him months earlier, and the last time we were together he said, "You know, a lot of people, especially men, when the actual divorce takes place, it hits them hard emotionally."

"Well that's not going to happen to me," I said. "Besides, even if it did, what would you recommend?"

"Medication. I'd recommend you go on medication."

"What?" I exclaimed. "There is no way on God's green earth I am going on medication."

But another day of not eating and sleeping and I was back in his office. When I walked in, he saw me and said, "You don't look well."

"I haven't eaten or slept in three days."

"You're depressed."

"No, I'm not. I'm happy. I'm finally out of this marriage. This was my decision. I'm happy."

"Insomnia and lack of appetite are two major indicators of clinical depression," he said. "I think you should go on medication."

"I already told you, I'm not going on medication."

When I got home that night I went for a walk. For some reason I started thinking about a book I had read in high school, Elisabeth Kubler Ross's *On Death and Dying*, in which she talked about the five stages of grieving. I remembered the first was denial. Then anger, bargaining, and the last was acceptance. But there was one more, and it had the same first initial as one of the others. What was it?

I remembered just as I returned home. It was depression.

It was my mind's way of telling me that my therapist was right. I was depressed.

One more day of not sleeping and not eating, and I was in the pharmacy.

I handed the pharmacist the prescription and he said, "This will be ready by tomorrow. Please come by then."

"No! you don't understand," I replied. *"I need those medications now!"*

The poor guy looked startled and got to work mixing chemicals. As anyone who has ever been on anti-depressants and anti-anxiety medications knows, they do not work immediately. Not even close. They take weeks, at least, and that is only if they are the right medications for your body and in the right dosage. And so began my descent into a living hell.

I lost forty pounds in only a few weeks. I remember holding up a banana and looking at it and trying to convince myself I could eat it. I went to a nutrition store and bought some awful tasting powder that, when mixed with water or milk, was supposed to put on weight. The medication I was prescribed to help me sleep would relax my stomach a bit, so that's when I would shove as much food into myself as I could, late at night, right before bedtime.

Even so, I got thinner and thinner. I later found out that the staff at St. Christopher's were certain I was addicted to crack cocaine. That was the big drug taking people down in the nineties, and if someone became super skinny, super fast, they were assumed to be on crack. The staff believed that's what was happening to me.

I dragged myself into work. It wasn't a day-to-day battle to survive: it was hour by hour. There were many times I'd look at my watch and say, "Okay, I've made it to two o'clock; if I try really hard, I think I can make it to three." My bed at home felt like it had a magnet in it, drawing me to it constantly. Not that I'd sleep even if I got there; I'd just lie there looking up at the ceiling, writhing with anxiety.

I had to tell my boss, Luis Medina, what was going on. There was no way I could hide it. He had been a trained clinical therapist, so he was sympathetic. If not for him, I likely would have lost my job, the house that came with the job, and then custody of Aiden.

When you are in a state like this, it's easy to become convinced that it's permanent, that you have finally discovered the real you. I was going for therapy twice a week, and he asked me if I felt suicidal.

"No," I replied, "but before this I could never understand why someone would take their own life. Now I understand it. If this was your permanent state of being, I can see why you'd want to get out of it by taking your life."

He later told me that scared the hell out of him.

I did read years later that many suicides are performed not by those people who have had chronic, life-long periods of depression, but by people who have never been depressed before. The sudden, seemingly endless, sharp and intense pain causes them to lose hope.

Several times I came close to checking myself into the psychiatric unit of the county hospital. The only thing that stopped me was that I knew kids from St. Christopher's who were in there. Here I was, the director of the program, and I needed hospital-level care? I might even be placed in the same unit as theirs. This would be beyond embarrassing.

I confided in my siblings, and each of them had the same reaction: "You? Depressed?" And I knew what they meant. I was usually a font of energy and optimism. To be depressed was totally contrary to my nature. They were so incredibly kind and understanding. Several times I'd drive to wherever one of them lived to try and find an escape, and they fed and took care of me. I am still very grateful to them and their spouses for the kindnesses they showed me during that dark time.

I had a spiritual director at that time, Sister Thelma Hall, whom I had been seeing periodically for the past few years. I called her up.

"I'm depressed," I told her.

"Come right over," she said.

Sister Thelma was great. Understanding. Kind. Sympathetic. She gave me *The Depression Book* by a Zen meditation teacher named Cheri Huber. It looked like a child's book, written in a juvenile font with amateurish drawings. I took it home and placed it on a shelf. I had been devouring everything I could find on depression written by neuroscientists and psychiatrists, plus well-known books by those who chronicled their own depressive states, such as William Styron. The book Thelma gave me looked silly.

But when you become desperate for relief, you look anywhere, so I picked up *The Depression Book* one night and found it immensely helpful. It contained so many wonderful insights. I have since given the book to many friends who are therapists, and all have found it to be of great benefit to their patients. I have also given it to friends who have suffered from depression, and I know they, too, appreciated it.

One of the main teachings in Huber's book was the Zen expression, "That which is accepted is healed." I found that to be very true. The more I tried to make the depression go away, the more I tried to figure it out – to reason my way through it – the deeper it seemed to stick. But when I'd finally throw my hands up and say, "I give up … this is just the way it is … I can't make this go away, so I will just try and put one foot in front of the other and live life the best I can," that's when the depression would ease up. By accepting it, it was being healed. I was being healed.

It never went away for long, though. After several weeks of living a nightmare, I'd begin to feel relief. I'd think, Thank God, this is over, but a day or two later I'd be right back in it. Night terrors. Panic attacks that felt like I was having a heart attack. Inability to eat or sleep. It felt like it took every bit of energy to walk across the room. My confidence at work, or in any other area of my life, was nil. I could barely concentrate on anything. In one phone conversation with my brother, he said to me, "Do you realize you've just told me the same thing three times in the last fifteen minutes?"

At some point it was explained to me that recovery from depression takes place in a zig-zag fashion. You feel lousy, then you feel good, then you feel lousy, then you feel good. And when you slip back down, it's extremely frustrating. I had confided with someone at work what I was going through, and one day he said to me, "Mark, last week you looked good, but now you look terrible again, what's going on?"

"I know," I replied. "I was good last week, and now I feel like crap again."

He admitted that, when he got his divorce years earlier, the same thing happened to him. "You feel bad, then you feel good, then you feel bad, then you feel good."

"How did it end?" I asked him.

"One day you feel good," he said, "and you wait for that to end, but it doesn't, and you just keep on feeling good."

"How did that feel when that happened?" I asked him.

"You feel like the luckiest man on the face of the planet," he replied.

As the months went by, I did start to finally feel a bit better. I read a book by a woman who had experienced depression, and she described it as being under water, looking up, and being able, even for a second, to break through the plane of the water and take a breath, and how incredibly wonderful that felt, even if only for a short while. It was true. I remember walking out into my front yard on a fall morning, looking up into the blue sky, and physically noticing that the depression had lifted, that I felt normal once again. Someone said to me, "After depression is over, you realize how wonderful 'normal' really is. You don't have to feel happy to be happy. Just being 'normal,' being not depressed, is wonderful." It is.

But in these first few months, the depression and anxiety would always make their return. One such time, I called my therapist on a Sunday afternoon. I felt incredibly anxious, like I was completely falling apart. He picked up the call and said, "What you are experiencing is akin to what people who live in California experience when there is an earthquake. There is the big shock, and then there are after-shocks that go through. They aren't as big or as devastating as that first quake, and all you can do when you are experiencing them is to hold onto a doorway or something and ride it out. That's what I think you are going through now."

Within an hour I felt better.

A few weeks later, I was again deeply depressed. A social worker on our staff who was leaving came up to me and said, "You look like hell again, what's up?" I told her that the depression was back, I couldn't make it go away, I was incredibly frustrated, and that I felt like this was going to be my life forever.

She grabbed me by the collar, pulled me in close, and shouted, "Listen, my father died suddenly and my mother was a complete wreck, I mean a complete wreck. And that was just something she had to go through. She couldn't make it speed up and go away. She just had to live with it, and she did, and in time she was okay, but that's you right now, get it?"

I could feel my body loosen up as she spoke and by that afternoon the depression had lifted.

I could see that I was slowly getting better, and I think it was a combination of the meds, therapy, people I could confide in, but also exercise. There is a ton of literature extolling the benefits of exercise as treatment for depression, some proclaiming it is as effective as, or more effective than medication. So as tired as I was, I forced myself to get on my bicycle and ride. I'd go for hours. In some ways, I feel like that bicycle saved me. I grew emotionally attached to it. Twenty years later people would say to me, "When are you going to get rid of that rusty old thing and buy yourself a new bike?" and I'd reply, "You don't understand. That bike saved my life. I can't get rid of it." But I finally did. I gave it to someone I knew who had just come out of prison. He saw my bike and liked it. "Here, it's for you," I told him. "It helped me, maybe it will help you too." He was thankful to receive it, and I felt like I had found the right home for it.

Meditation also helped, specifically the version known as centering prayer that I had learned about years before on retreat. I had periodically dabbled in meditation, but I had this strong instinct that it was now essential to my recovery and to my future life. I took time out every morning to do this for the first twenty minutes of the day, and it has remained an important spiritual practice for me.

My dreams helped a lot too. At one point I was leaving a therapy session and turned in desperation. "I'm doing everything you've asked," I said, "but I'm still in agony. Is there anything else I could be doing?" Without hesitation he said, "Yes. Try to remember your dreams, and when you come back tell me about them." This sounded pretty woo-woo to me, but I was up for anything that might help. I bought a small tape recorder and kept it on my bedside table so that when I would wake up in the middle of the night, I could record whatever I was dreaming. Or when I woke up in the morning, I'd immediately try and recall what I had dreamt that night and write it down.

It worked. Somehow I was able to train my mind to wake myself up when I had a dream, and if not, to remember it in the morning. I wrote them all down. They were incredibly helpful. It was like they provided clues as to what was going on deep inside and what I needed to face. I still have them, probably a dozen notebooks filled with dream memories, and I've kept them on a computer file since 2005. Some were nonsense, others, very helpful. Here's one I remember even now, twenty-five years later:

I'm in shorts and a t-shirt, running along a desert path or in the mountains, as if I am in a race, perhaps, or training for a marathon. I am exhausted. And I can't get my rhythm down. My cadence is all off. I'm having trouble sequencing my steps correctly so I am practically stumbling. Then this other runner passes by me. He looks good. Nice running outfit on. He seems strong. Prepared. He pats me on the back, encouraging me. I look up at him. It's me.

I still depend on my dreams. Whenever I have a big decision to make, I ask my mind to deliver a dream that will guide me. It hasn't failed me yet, and I've actually turned down or accepted jobs based on a dream I had.

Eventually the depression and anxiety went away – for good, or at least for a few years. In all the reading I did, depression was often described as "highly relapse-able," and I did have a few more bouts in the years ahead, but never as severe as that initial one, and I learned how to deal with it. In time it went away for good, and even though I am the first one to tell people who experience depression to consider medication, I weaned myself off of everything over time.

This whole episode changed me. I regard it as a gift. I look at my life in terms of "before the summer of 1994 and after." It broke something in me that needed to break. I was very shut down emotionally before then. My friends at Covenant House would tease me, when I was there, about not being able to express emotions, and I had no idea what they were talking about. Now I do. I would simply freeze at any kind of emotion shown to me by another. It would scare the hell out of me, and I wasn't even aware of this until now.

The depression also created a different, and deeper, level of compassion in me for those who suffer, in particular the youth with whom I work. Those kids feel like crap most of the time. Their self-worth is at the bottom. They feel like their world is falling apart. I never knew what that felt like. Now I do.

Because of what I went through, I have also been able to help others when they are going through depression. In my network of family and friends, it is known that when one of them is dealing with depression, I'm the one to call. It has been a privilege to guide several of them through it, and I never would be able to do this if not for having endured it myself.

I view depression as a spiritual experience now, and value this quote by Franciscan priest Father Richard Rohr.

The "cross," rightly understood, always reveals various kinds of resurrection. It's as if God were holding up the crucifixion as a cosmic object lesson, saying: "I know this is what you're experiencing. Don't run from it. Learn from it, as I did. Hang there for a while, as I did. It will be your teacher. Rather than losing life, you will be gaining a larger life. It is the way through." As impossible as that might feel right now, I absolutely believe that it's true.

So do I.

· *ten* ·

AFTER ALMOST FIVE YEARS of being at St. Christopher's and living on-site, I was worn down to the bare metal. We had made tremendous progress in terms of improving conditions on the campus and the level of care we were able to offer the teenagers there. But still, we had increased the number of youth from eighty-four to ninety-six and all of them suffered from some kind of trauma early in their lives. Whether physical, emotional, or sexual, it would manifest at any given moment of day or night. One or more of them could act out and spiral out of control, lashing out at staff or another youth, or make a suicidal gesture. If it happened at night or on the weekends, which was not uncommon, I'd have to spring into action, leave my house, and deal with the situation. Five years of living like that, and I was exhausted. I was having trouble getting a good night's sleep. I'd take a vacation, go away, and then start counting the days until my next one.

I had to admit it: I was burnt out.

I knew my time at St. Chris's was done, so I resigned, offering to remain in the house and in the job for another three months, which would give Luis Medina time to find my replacement. He actually offered me a different job, director of operations, for which I was grateful, but I'd have to give up the house. By that time, I was ready for a move.

So it was during this in-between time that, one freezing cold December night, I lay down in my bed and the beeper went off. I had just returned from our annual holiday party, which had been held at a nearby hotel. I was bushed. And I thought, You know what? For the first time in five years, I'm not going to answer that. Whatever the problem is down there on the campus, I will let the administrator in charge deal with it.

But when the beeper went off again, I knew there must be something serious going on, and I called down.

"What's up?" I asked.

"Five girls from Gould Cottage are out running around, and we can't get them back in."

"Are you kidding me? It's zero degrees out there, and these girls want to be outside and play games with us?"

"I know, I know," he said. "It's crazy, but we can't get them in."

"I'll be right down."

I put my clothes back on and a winter coat, left my house, and jogged the few yards to the fence that separated my place from the campus. There was a gate with a padlock I'd have to go through, and to my surprise the five girls were right outside of it, huddled together and laughing. I slowly and quietly put my key into the padlock, but it was so cold out there the lock had frozen and would not open.

Unable to open the gate that way, I knew my next option was to push hard on the gate and slip through the narrow opening it would create. I had done it many times before, but never at night and never in a rush, and I worried that, unless I did it quickly, they'd hear me and run. My plan was to surprise them and, hopefully, persuade them to just go inside.

I pushed on the gate and dashed through the gap. The girls instantly saw me, and all but two of them fled. I said, "Come on, this is ridiculous, let's go to that cottage," pointing to the nearest one, and they went with me.

When we got there, the counselor on duty was already at the door, holding it open for them, but when she saw me she screamed.

"Oh my God, your face!"

"What?" I asked.

"Your face! Go to the infirmary. Now!"

I had no idea what she was talking about; I could not feel any pain, likely due to the bitter cold and adrenaline. But I started to jog toward the infirmary, which was all the way across campus. Midway there I put my hand up to my face, looked at it, and found it covered with blood. I felt my face again and could tell that my nose was literally flapping in the wind. Apparently, when I dashed through the gap in the fence, there was a piece of metal there that sliced my nose vertically. (If you've ever seen the movie *Chinatown*, there's a gruesome scene in which Jack Nicholson has his nose cut, not by a fence, but by Roman Polanski wielding a knife. That's how I looked.)

I got to the infirmary just as two kids were exiting from it. When they saw me, they, too, yelled, "Oh my God!" I went inside and the nurse on duty was the first person not to greet me in that fashion. He simply said, "We've got to get you up to Dobbs Ferry Hospital, stat."

He drove me there and dropped me off, unable to stay due to his obligation to get back to the ninety-six youth living on campus. I walked into the emergency department, my nose dripping blood, and they put me in an exam room right away.

It was so cold that night that the roads had frozen, causing multiple car accidents. People were being brought in on gurneys who were in far worse shape than I was, but eventually a nurse came in to look at me and said, "Any cut to the face and we have to call in a reconstructive surgery specialist."

"How long till he gets here?" I asked.

"*She'll* be here in an hour," was the icy response, which I very much deserved, my sexist remark on full display.

An hour later she arrived, came in, took a look at my nose, and said, "I think I can put that back together for you pretty easily with some stitches."

By this time I had seen the cut pretty clearly via mirror, and it did extend slightly below my nose to that space above the upper lip.

"Doctor, I have a request," I said.

"What is it?" she asked.

"Well, I'm a single guy. And I have a girlfriend. And my moustache means a lot to me."

"And?" she asked.

"Doctor, can you save the moustache?"

She looked closer, took my head in her hand and pivoted it so she could see from different angles, and finally said, "Yes, I think we can save the moustache."

"Thank you!" I said with relief.

She stitched me up and I headed home, moustache intact.

A few weeks later, I had to go to the medical center where that doctor worked to have the stitches removed. I looked forward to seeing her, but someone else took them out. Then, walking down the hallway afterward, headed for the exit, I saw her.

She spotted me right away. Without even saying hello, she grabbed my head in her hand and twisted it around at various angles, peering intently at my nose.

"I did a great job!" she said. "What do you think?"

"I agree! And you saved the moustache!"

"That's right, I saved the moustache! And how are things with your girlfriend?

"Not so good. She broke up with me."

She frowned. "Really?"

"Yes, really."

She shook her head.

"Well ... that's her loss then!" she said.

Which made me feel a whole lot better.

· *eleven* ·

HAVING MY NOSE ALMOST SLICED OFF MY FACE was the final confirmation that I was doing the right thing leaving the directorship of the campus and moving off-grounds. I found an apartment in nearby Yonkers, where Aiden and I moved a few weeks later. I became operations director at St. Christopher's, which meant that I was now consumed with our IT system, making sure all vehicles were maintained, ordering supplies, getting bids for renovating our buildings, and other operational matters.

I wasn't happy in this role, so I started to reach out to executive directors of other nonprofits I knew to see what was available, but nothing was coming up. Then one night, I came home to hear a voice message on my machine from Mike Duggan, the director of a nonprofit in Stamford called the Domus Foundation.

Mike and I knew each other from Brooklyn in the early eighties. He had graduated from Holy Cross in Massachusetts a year after me, and instead of joining the Faith Community at Covenant House, signed up with the Jesuit Volunteer Corps and became a full-time volunteer in one of the poorest neighborhoods in Brooklyn. He ended up marrying one of the other volunteers, who happened to be the niece of a nun working at Covenant House. It was this nun who connected us.

I had gone over to Mike and his wife's place in Brooklyn one night for dinner while our one-year-olds played in the backyard alongside us. He and I hit it off right away. We were both from rambunctious Irish Catholic families. While I had played rugby in college, he was on the football team. We had a lot in common.

At some point in the nineties, he and his wife had left Brooklyn and moved to Connecticut, where he became executive director of Domus. While the formal title was Domus Foundation, it was not the kind of foundation that granted out money, such as the Ford Foundation. Domus's mission was to work with low-income children and teenagers who came from poverty. It had two residences for teenage boys who had been removed from home and were in the foster care system or had been arrested and were now in the juvenile justice system.

Mike's phone message was something along the lines of, "Mark, it's been a while since we've talked, but call me, I may have an opportunity for you." For some reason I didn't call him back, which is uncharacteristic of me, but a week or two later, he left a second message, "I hope you are on vacation, which is why you haven't answered me. Please give a call."

I did, and a week later at breakfast, we sat in a diner, and he told me that Domus was growing and had been selected for funding by the State of Connecticut to open up more programs for at-risk youth, and that his board of directors agreed he needed to hire an associate executive director. I was intrigued, especially when he told me that the state had recently passed legislation creating charter schools and that Domus was thinking of applying to start one the next time the Department of Education requested proposals.

I had always been deeply dissatisfied by the school on the grounds of St. Christopher's. It was a weird setup, in that I was in charge of running the campus and reported to Luis Medina. The school was an entirely separate organization, legally and in every other way, with its own board of directors, school superintendent, and management. It made no sense organizationally. I felt that, for five years, I had been trying to create a structured, therapeutic campus, yet our kids went to a school for six hours a day where chaos reigned. It seemed the people who ran it didn't care one bit whether or not their students were getting an education. Every spring they held a graduation ceremony, and yet not one student in all the years I was there graduated with a high school diploma or even a GED. The school was a total joke, and I had no authority to change it.

So the idea of starting a school where we could actually do it right – where children from poverty could actually get a decent education? Now that was something I could get behind. I told Mike I'd take the job.

I started at Domus in September of 1998. At least once a week I'd ask Mike to let me know if he heard anything about the opportunity to apply to start a charter school. Not that I didn't have plenty of other things to do; there was a plethora of tasks for me to take on. The houses where the kids lived needed to be renovated, so I started lining up contractors and getting bids. There were grant opportunities Mike threw my way, and I started working on those. No shortage of work.

Then one afternoon in late October, I ran into Mike in the driveway of one of our houses. He handed me a document that was as thick as a phone book and said, "We have a hell of a lot of work to do in the next six weeks." I looked at the cover. It said "Connecticut Department of Education" and it was the application to start a charter school.

I thumbed through it right away. Talk about intimidating. This was going to take a massive effort to get everything together by the December 18 deadline.

At that time there were already ten charter schools in Connecticut, all of them brand new. I called the principals at every single one, asking if they would offer me advice and guidance in filling out the application. Most ignored me and didn't return my call, but of those I did speak to, every one said, "No way can you fill that out in six weeks; you need at least six months. It's that complicated."

My response was always the same: "I don't have six months. I have six weeks. Will you help me?" No one gave me an outright no. Most just ignored me. There was one principal however who agreed to help; I drove to her school to see it and she gave me a copy of her successful proposal.

I then found out that under the Freedom of Information Act I had the right to enter the file room of the Department of Education in Hartford and have access to all the winning proposals from the year before. That's what I did: I sat there and rifled through those proposals, taking notes. So all those charter school principals who wouldn't help me? They did help me. They just didn't know it.

With that knowledge under my belt, I began to work with Mike and our Domus team to frame out what our school would look like. Mike told me he had been approached by teachers and administrators at Stamford Public Schools for years, asking that Domus create a school for students who were under-performing, had frequent behavior problems, and were eventually dropping out in ninth or tenth grade. This was Domus's target population – where they had the most success – and the district knew it.

Charter schools were still fairly new in America in 1998. Each state approached the concept differently, and in Connecticut's version each would be funded directly by the legislature so as not to draw dollars away from the local district. And each charter school would be run by a separate nonprofit organization, not by the district itself. In essence, public dollars would be used to fund a private entity.

Mike and I sat with four of our staff in the basement of one of the Domus group homes and hammered out what our school would be like. We agreed it would consist of middle school, grades six through eight. We proposed small class sizes, with no more than twelve per class, two classes in a grade. We'd really focus on language arts and math because that's where kids were failing the most. We'd have a longer school day. Parents would have to commit to a certain number of volunteer hours per month. And we'd mandate school uniforms to create a sense of order and discipline.

We also had to come up with a name. Domus had a name for every program it ran, for example, Passages and Avenues. Our school needed one too. Donn Reid, a longtime Domus staff member, came up with a name we all liked: Trailblazers. Trailblazers Academy. It made sense, because that's what we considered ourselves, blazing a new trail for youth to succeed in school and in life.

I worked on that proposal day and night for the next six weeks. Thanksgiving Day 1998, I was in my office at Domus writing the report. Aiden was with his mother for the holiday. I took one break, to go to a high school football game and see one of the Domus kids there, and later on, to go to a Boston Market to buy myself a take-out Thanksgiving dinner. Then I went back to writing.

As December 18 drew closer, I actually started to think that we'd pull it off, that we had a chance to submit a decent proposal on time. But the more I homed in, not only on the start-up budget, but also the mandatory five-year budget and fiscal projection, the more I realized I could not make the numbers work.

That's why, on the evening of December 17, in the basement of one of our residences with Mike, and less than twenty-four hours to submit the proposal, I turned to him and said, "As far as we've come and as hard as we've worked, I don't think we should submit this tomorrow. We just do not have the revenue we need to operate the school."

"Let me call the district superintendent," he said. "This is his last year – he's retiring – maybe he can help. Let's look up his phone number, and I'll call him now."

We grabbed what was known back then as a "phone book" (pre-Web pretty much), looked up his name, and even though it was past nine, Mike called him. He picked up, and Mike's end of the conversation went something like this: "We're trying to start this school. ... It will be for your middle school students who are falling through the cracks now and will likely drop out of high school. ... We need a commitment from the district for operating funds. ... The proposal is due tomorrow at 5 p.m."

From that point on all I could hear was the occasional uh-hunh and okay from Mike. I could only imagine what the superintendent was thinking on his end, which was probably, Are you guys nuts?

Mike finally got off the phone and said, "Okay. The district's in for a million a year every year. We're good."

In my mind, Mike had just pulled off the ultimate sales pitch of the century.

"Okay," I said, "we're back in business. I am going to go back to my computer and redo the budget. If you can find me a twenty-four-hour Kinko's somewhere, I'll head there afterward, get the copies made, and drive it up to Hartford tomorrow."

Mike found one in White Plains, New York, halfway between Domus and my house. I got there at around 2 a.m. and handed over a thick document, telling the person there I needed twenty-two spiral-bound copies by nine o'clock.

I headed home, got a few hours sleep, and returned to Kinko's. When I was handed the copies, I looked at one and saw they had messed it up. The pages were not in order and some were even missing.

I asked for the manager. He came over and I told him the job had to be redone. He apologized and said, "We're backed up right now, we'll get this to you sometime later today."

"You don't understand. I need this job done right. I need twenty-two copies, and I need it done immediately. These copies are due in Hartford by five o'clock, and I have to drive them there. Doing it sometime later today is not an option."

"Um, okay," he said.

A little over two hours later, I had the copies, checked them, thanked him, got in my car, drove to Hartford, and entered the Department of Education building – the very one where, only a few weeks earlier, I had exercised my rights as a citizen, perusing the winning charter school proposals. Now, against all the odds and in an incredible crush of time, we were submitting our own.

I left and got a massage.

Two months later, we were informed that eleven proposals had been submitted, including another one from Stamford besides ours, and that the Department of Education would be selecting only two for funding. We were asked to attend a meeting in Hartford a week later where we would be given the chance to explain our proposal, defend it, and answer questions from department officials.

Mike, another Domus employee, Julie DeGennaro, and I went that day. They put us in a room with another group of applicants while we waited our turn to be called. These people were from New Haven and introduced themselves. They were all students at Yale Law School and explained that this was something they had been working on for several years. They had already received money from Yale alumni, and I believe that either one of the graduates or the law school itself had given them a free building.

Okay, I confess that as soon as I heard, "We're from Yale Law School," I was intimidated. We're talking the same school that produced Hillary and Bill Clinton, Sonia Sotomayor, Gerald Ford, Clarence Thomas, and scores of other American legal luminaries. This is who Domus is competing against? And they've got money? And a building? And have been working on this for years?

"How about you?" one of them asked us. "How long have you been planning your school?"

I looked at the floor. So did Mike. What do we tell her? "Gee, this is something we came up with three months ago, five of us in the basement of a group home. We have no money, no building, no nothing, except an idea?"

I can't remember who answered her, me or Mike, or exactly what we said, but it was very likely something like, "So, how do you think the Red Sox will do this season?"

I sat there thinking, We are just completely out of our league here, I mean completely.

Two months later, in April 1999, Mike received a call from the mayor of Stamford, Dan Malloy, that, of the two charter schools selected for funding that year, ours was one. We later found out that the other was the group from Yale.

That night all of us from Domus rushed to a bar in downtown Stamford to celebrate. We were ecstatic. The whole thing seemed incredible. We had gone from nothing but an aspiration to the very possibility of an actual school in only a few months.

At the end of the night, though, I pulled Mike aside and said, "Listen, this is awesome, and I'm glad we're celebrating now, but it's April, and this school has to open on September 1. That gives us a little over four months to pull this whole thing together. We're going to need help – a lot of help. I think we should bring on Garland Walton full-time."

Mike agreed. Garland had been a high-level member of Mayor

Malloy's office who had recently left. She was super smart, organized, and available.

She was also in the bar with us at that moment. Mike walked right over to her and offered her a job. She said yes. I breathed a sigh of relief.

That relief would be short-lived. I got up the next morning and thought about the challenge ahead of us. We didn't have a building. A principal. Books. Computers. Phones. A curriculum.

Teachers. We needed six certified and licensed teachers. By April, the vast majority of teachers were already committed to their schools for the following fall. How would we find teachers?

And students. We needed students. We needed to persuade forty-eight parents that their children should leave the schools they were in and give a completely new and untested one a chance.

We dove in. We plowed ahead. We knew that if we took a minute to think about the enormity of it all, we'd be crushed. It was kind of like writing the proposal a few months earlier. Everyone told me it was an impossible task, but I didn't listen to them, and I am glad I didn't.

We decided that priority one was finding a principal. We recruited several volunteers from the Domus board of directors and others from the education field for a hiring committee. We ran ads, résumés came in, we narrowed it down to three or four finalists, who came in for interviews. We narrowed it down to two finalists. Both were teachers with good experience who interviewed well. It was a close call, but we decided to offer the position to one of them, and we sent our regrets to the other.

The person we selected had impressed us with his positive spirit and energy. I joked that he was a walking *Seven Habits of Highly Successful People*, because every sentence he uttered was peppered with the words perseverance, determination, or resilience. We all agreed that this kind of attitude was what we needed to get the school off the ground, and frankly, it was the spirit Mike had inculcated at Domus – that whatever obstacles lay before us, we'd manage to get through them.

Then he started. Suddenly Mr. Positivity became Mr. Negativity.

"How do I know this school is actually going to open? What guarantees are you giving me? Why haven't you people made more progress than this? Why haven't you hired teachers? Where are the books?"

Our answer was, "This is why we hired you," but I had this sinking feeling that we had made a big mistake hiring this guy, and that he was going to bail on us.

Which is exactly what he did, by the end of week one. Not only that, he went to the local paper, the *Stamford Advocate*, and told the reporter that we didn't know what we were doing at Domus and that the school would never open.

"Our worst fears are coming true," a local activist was quoted in the article.

Thankfully, Mayor Malloy had our backs and told them, "Starting a school like this is a Herculean task," and that he still had faith in us.

We called the person who had been the runner-up and offered him the job. He declined. He had already found another one.

I was really worried. We had no leader, the weeks were passing, and September 1 was getting closer. With less than four months to go until opening, Mike reached out to a Stamford teacher he knew, Carol Bjork. The students had recently voted her the teacher they liked and trusted the most. He persuaded her to leave her position and become our principal. I was elated. When I met her it was obvious why the students admired her so much. She seemed like an exceptional person who really cared about students and would work her fingers to the bone to get the school up and running.

Carol got to work recruiting teachers and somehow brought on the six we needed. Mayor Malloy offered us the entire wing of an under-utilized school building in the city; we took it. The Domus board president gifted us one hundred thousand dollars so we could start buying the things we needed, like books, computers, school uniforms, and everything else.

One of the main tasks Garland and I were focused on was recruiting students. She put together an impressive brochure describing Trailblazers Academy, offering it as an alternative to mainstream schools. We ran ads. We put up posters. We were given addresses of rising fifth and sixth graders in the Stamford school system. We contacted them all. All through that summer we held public meetings at which parents and students could learn more and ask questions.

We were flooded with applications. There were so many parents who knew that, if their children stayed in the mainstream schools, they would not likely receive a decent education and would probably drop out once in high school. Demand was so great, we had to hold a lottery to select our first forty-eight students.

I was tasked with calling those families that had been selected. To this day, it is one of my happiest memories – to deliver that message and then hear the shrieks of delight and thanks from parents when I gave them the news.

By that August we had the teachers hired, a building, and students, but there was still an enormous amount of work to be done in only a few weeks' time. There were moments, though, when incredible things happened. As we were trying to figure out how to order a phone system, Sacred Heart University called us, serendipitously offering the system they were replacing. The same thing happened when we were ready to order school desks and chairs; another school called us at that moment offering us some of theirs. I began to think, God must want this school to open; that's the only explanation.

Still, I woke up every morning with a searing headache and a knot in the pit of my stomach. I was terrified that those forty-eight students were going to show up on September 1, and we were not going to be nearly ready to welcome and educate them. Despite all the forward momentum, there were definitely moments when I felt like quitting. I received not one, but two job offers at this time and thought about taking them just to relieve the incredible stress I was feeling. I knew I was harming my physical and mental health by continuing as I was.

But I stayed, and looking back, if there was any one reason why, it was because of what the ten- and eleven-year-old children applying to Trailblazers had written in their applications. Every parent had to fill out an application, but so did each child. Besides the standard questions of name, address, and last school attended, we asked two more. Their answers to both were precious. Here are some examples:

PLEASE DESCRIBE A TIME WHEN
YOU HELPED SOMEONE OR SOMEONE HELPED YOU.

I gave a homeless man money.

When my mom got a new toilet I put it in for her.

*Someone once helped me with my math because
I was stuck on a problem, then I got it!*

I like to do good deeds.

Served food to the homeless.

Help out old people with groceries.

*A girl was doing bad in math so I tutored her and
she got an A in her grade.*

I go to the grocery store for the seniors.

*I volunteer in the library. I help people to find books
and I help the kids in the summer reading club.*

When I saw an old lady get hit by a car I called the ambulances.

*My Grandma and I help each other at home,
I also do community service at the soup kitchen.*

I helped people when they were hurt. I helped animals.

WHAT DO YOU WANT TO TELL US ABOUT YOURSELF?

*I'm intelligent, outgoing, I love to go to church
and the community center.*

I'm kind but I stand up for myself.

*I get along with people.
I'm kind, love animals, help people when they are sad.*

I don't think I'm smart. I feel I try but I don't get anywhere.

I am a bright person and I get along with people quite well.

*I want to be in a school where people know how to act.
I really like to learn new things that I didn't know before,
but sometimes they turn out to be too hard for me.*

*I like hanging out with friends because they make me feel good.
My favorite color is purple.*

I am a smart student who loves learning new things each day.

I'm very nice, kind to others, respect others that respect me.

I like to learn how to be the best I can be.

If I like what I'm doing I will try my best.

*That I like basketball and I like reading and I have a bad temper
because if something bothers me I easily get mad.*

*I am nice but pretty shy. Good in school.
Never gets in trouble in school at all.*

I want to lose weight and build self esteem.

I like to try my hardest.

I'm a nice person always willing to help.

I want to do better in education. I'm an usher.
I like following my mom and I love the Lord.

Sometimes I'm good. I don't read very well and that bothers me.
I love Jesus.

I'm a very sensitive person.

I am a very shy but nice boy. I want to learn and
do best in school. I am in special education and I really need
help expressing myself.

I love kids. I love to go to church.

I am nice, smart and helpful.

I'm a nice person to be around.

I'm a good person, sometimes I get mad, I get out of hand.

I'm helpful, talented, smart.

I came from Egypt a year ago.
In Egypt I went to a private school and I want
to have a good education so I can go to college.

I like to meet people. I'm a hard worker and eager to learn.

I have good learning qualities.

I want to tell you that I am a fast learner and
I like to learn new things every day.

I'm a teacher's pet and I like to play.

I'm an intelligent, bright, willing to learn young boy.
I would like to offer my skill to Trailblazers.

I'm a nice outgoing kid.

I'm very friendly.

Then there was this reply, written by an eleven-year-old boy:

PLEASE DESCRIBE A TIME WHEN YOU HELPED
SOMEONE OR SOMEONE HELPED YOU.
I don't remember.

WHAT DO YOU WANT TO TELL US ABOUT YOURSELF?
That I am not dumb.

· ·

At the moments I felt most stressed out and ready to just bail on the whole thing, I'd look at that one application and what he had written and knew I had to somehow hang in there. That there was a boy in the city of Stamford who wanted to prove to the world that he had a mind, and that he was actually smart, and that this school was his best, if not only chance to do so – that's what made me stay.

An official with the Department of Education could see the crushing strain all of us were under. He called me and offered us the chance to postpone opening by a year. I was relieved and thought we should take it. He then called Mike and made it an official offer. Mike told me he thought he'd say yes, but he called me the next day and said he had turned him down, that we would be able to open on time and ready.

I was furious, but it turned out to be a good lesson for me for the years ahead when I'd head up my own organization, because the following year the State of Connecticut declined to fund any new charter schools due to budget difficulties. We would've been shut out. Mike had been right, and I learned that when an opportunity is presented to you, take advantage of it because it very well may not be there again at the promised time.

On September 1, 1999, forty-eight students showed up at Trailblazers Academy, all wearing khaki pants or skirts, and shirts with the Trailblazers emblem. They were greeted by Mike Duggan, the Domus staff, all the Trailblazers staff, and me, standing outside and clapping and cheering for them as they walked in. We had books, computers, desks, chairs, a curriculum and everything else a functioning school required. Somehow, some way, we had pulled it off.

Ninety-two percent of the students qualified for free or reduced-price lunch; the city-wide average was 30 percent, so we got exactly who we wanted at Trailblazers: children of poverty.

I didn't go for a massage this time. Instead, I promptly jumped on a plane and flew to a monastery in the Arizona desert that I had read about. I was exhausted. I prayed, meditated, and hiked in total silence for ten days. The monks there fed and took care of me, and I slowly came back to myself.

That first year at Trailblazers was difficult at times. We still lacked so many things, especially the physical space we needed. At one point I gathered the teachers and aides in a room and showed them a scene from the movie Apollo 13. It was the one in which the three astronauts are trapped in the capsule, and the mechanism that purges carbon dioxide is not functioning, so they will die if it continues to build up. The engineers at the ground crew in Houston are huddled in a room and given the identical contents that exist in the capsule, with the instruction to build something that will extract the CO_2 using only with what they have in front of them. They, of course, succeed, verbally tell the crew in space how to do it, and it works.

"This is us," I told them. "I know we need a better building, we need better IT, we need about a hundred other things, but we have what we have, just like those engineers did, and we have to figure out how to make it work." And they did. They figured things out.

Trailblazers made it through year one; five of the six teachers left at the end of it, but we found new ones. We added an eighth grade and improved in year two. I then left Domus, but followed the school and always stayed close with Mike; we still meet for coffee once a year. Trailblazers continued to grow, even expanding to a high school. Other districts with failing schools asked Domus to help out, and Mike and his team began educating youth who were in the juvenile justice system.

I would love to say that Trailblazers Academy is still up and running, but after twenty years, the funding became problematic and it closed. I was saddened by that, but I still take great satisfaction in knowing that thousands of children who came from poverty had the opportunity to receive a quality education, many of whom did not drop out and later went on to college.

And because of what we did, that one young man, who by now must be in his thirties, had the chance to prove to the world, "I am not dumb."

TRAILBLAZERS ACADEMY STUDENTS

· *twelve* ·

AFTER MY POST-DIVORCE DEPRESSION, I started thinking about dating. Everyone I knew advised me, "Now don't go and get serious with anyone." A friend at work who had been divorced told me that everyone had given her the same advice, "But I, and everyone else I know, ignored that and does just the opposite: we dive right into a hot and heavy romance right from the start."

Which is exactly what I did. It was with a woman who also worked at St. Christopher's. She was a lovely person, but after a few months, I ended it. There was a part of me that knew my friends were right. One of them sat me down and told me, "I have a feeling you have to go through a number of romantic adventures before you marry again." Others expressed similar sentiments.

I called one of my younger brothers, who was still single. "I'm out of practice," I said. "How does this dating stuff work these days?"

"Dating sucks," was his response.

But a male coworker told me, "Dating is going to be easy for you. In fact, I predict you'll have met the perfect person for you and be married within three years, five at the max."

As it turned out, dating was easy at first; everybody had someone they wanted me to meet. I was set up on probably twenty blind dates. I look back now and chuckle. I'd be going out to restaurants and picking up the tab. A friend who was still single called me and said, "Redmond, are you kidding? You'll go broke that way. This is why God invented Starbucks. Coffee dates, strictly!"

And when I went on a blind date and wasn't interested, which was every single time, and because this was prior to email or texting, I'd send a hand-written note to the person explaining that I really did enjoy their company but I wasn't interested in going out again. One woman wrote back, "Wow, I never received as nice a rejection as that! Most of the time I just don't hear from the guy again and I take it for granted he's not interested. Thank you!" This was obviously before the term *ghosted* was invented.

Having exhausted all the blind dates available to me, I was faced with Now what do I do? This was pre-Match.com and Tinder. Then a woman at work, who had heard I was now single, asked if I biked. I told her yes.

"My husband and I belong to this local bicycling club," she said, "and we always see so many young, single women on the rides, and we wonder where are the young single men?"

I immediately joined that club.

Over the next five years I became a pretty good cyclist, even to the point of taking part in fifty-mile rides all around the metropolitan area.

But I did not meet one single woman to date on those rides.

The years went by and I did manage to go out with several women, but the relationships always ended. Either I broke up with them, or vice versa. Then one afternoon I was driving on the Cross County Parkway, headed to my apartment in Yonkers, when a thought popped into my head. It wasn't a voice I heard or anything like that. It was a spontaneous thought that was seemingly implanted in my mind:

You will fall in love again. You will get married.

And it's not a total stranger. It's someone you already know.

Someone I know? I went home and thumbed through my address book, wondering if there was someone in there I had overlooked and should be thinking about. No one though.

A few years later I had a phone call from that same "dating sucks" brother. He had just completed the Boston-to-New York Northeast AIDS Ride, in which he and three thousand other people cycled for three days to raise money for AIDS research.

"You'll never guess who I ran into during one of our breaks," he told me.

"Who?"

"My old high school junior prom date, from twenty years ago.

She's a reporter for a Connecticut television station. There I was among three thousand people in a Bridgeport park, and somehow we spotted each other. She was covering the ride for that night's broadcast."

I immediately flashed back to my brother in his tuxedo two decades earlier, driving off in our father's Cadillac to go pick up his prom date. I even remembered her name.

"Marybeth Christie?" I asked. "She must be in her mid-thirties by now. She's probably married? Children?"

"No," he replied. "She's still single."

I had just started the job with Domus and said to him, "I'm working in Connecticut now, and so is she? You know, I'd like to meet her."

"Why don't you just call her?" he asked.

"No way," I immediately replied. "She'll think I'm some kind of nut. 'Hi, you went to the prom with my brother twenty years ago, do you want to go out?'"

"Suit yourself," he said.

Six months went by, and I was working feverishly with Mike Duggan and the Domus team trying to start Trailblazers Academy. There was a school board hearing one night, and I was there to support Mike. The media was there in force, and I spotted a female television reporter.

I went up to her and asked, "By any chance do you know a reporter named Marybeth Christie?"

"Sure," she answered. "We work at the same station. She has the desk next to mine."

I pulled out my business card, wrote on the back of it, "Hi, you went to the prom with my brother twenty years ago," and asked this woman to give it to her. She agreed, and I left thinking, "This is easy, she'll call me and we'll meet."

Wrong, wrong, wrong. And dumb. I didn't hear from her.

Another six months went by, and one day I picked up a magazine I had been reading all my life, *Maryknoll*. It's a Catholic magazine containing stories about missionaries who are working in some of the most war-torn and poorest areas of the world. The nuns had us read it when I was in grade school, and as an adult I subscribed and read it faithfully each month. It inspired me. And in this particular issue, whose name did I see as an author for one such article? Marybeth Christie. She'd written about a nun helping indigenous people in Guatemala who live in a garbage dump, and about a priest working with gang members in Nicaragua.

"Hmmm," I thought. "That's interesting," surmising that she must have left the television news industry.

Shortly after that, I was invited to the house of a male friend for a Sunday dinner, right after Thanksgiving. He was married with two children, and after the meal, when his wife and kids had departed the room, he leaned over and asked, "So Redmond, what's the latest with the ladies?" Most of my married guy friends had this image of me as a middle-aged Carrie Bradshaw, that I was living this *Sex and the City* lifestyle they could only fantasize about. I could not help but feel they were trying to live vicariously through me. The truth is that I was mostly bored and lonely.

"I was dating someone but it ended ," I said.

"What are you going to do now?"

"I don't know, but there is this one woman whose name keeps popping up over and over again. It's kind of strange. I'd like to meet her. The problem is I don't know how. Maybe, after the holidays are over and the new year begins, I'll try to think of some way."

"Listen," he said, "I was unemployed and everyone told me I'd never find a job during the holidays, but I found a job during the holidays. If I could find employment during this time of the year, you can find romance."

Believe it or not, I was influenced by that, so when I arrived home that night, I remembered that one of my best friends was a Maryknoll priest who was also a medical doctor. He had done missionary work with AIDS patients in Tanzania in the 1980s but was now back in America, and perhaps he knew this Marybeth Christie. I emailed him and asked if he did. "Yes," he emailed back, to which I replied, "Can you get me her email address?"

He agreed to ask her.

A few days later he gave me her address, and I immediately sent a message that began, "Hi, you don't know me, but you went to the prom with my brother twenty years ago."

She emailed back, then I emailed her back, and on it went. This was before the days when you could check your email on your phone, or even from your work computer. You had to go home and check your personal computer, which I hurriedly did every night after work.

After about a month of this back-and-forth emailing, I received a message from her stating something along the lines of, "I am starting to feel like Meg Ryan's character in *You've Got Mail*. Do you really exist, and if so, can we please meet?"

"Yes!" I replied. "But I have a teenage son. I don't know if you know that." I had met women before for whom this was a relationship deal-breaker.

"I know you do," she answered (she had been an investigative reporter after all). "That's fine."

We agreed to meet on a Thursday night in December in front of a restaurant in downtown Stamford. We had never spoken on the phone, and I had never even seen her picture, so I stood there not knowing for whom I was looking. As each woman walked by I wondered, "Is that her?"

Then I saw a woman walking down the street, wearing white pants, a pink sweater and a yellow jacket. She came up to me and asked, "Mark?"

"Marybeth?"

We turned to go into the restaurant, but it was closed for an office holiday party, so I suggested we walk up the street to another place I knew. We went to cross the street, and I don't remember doing this, but months later, Marybeth told me that there was a car coming, and that as it approached, I tucked my right hand under her left elbow, and that when I did this, she felt a distinct physical sensation, and a thought popped into her head (just as it had in mine, years earlier on the Cross County Parkway), which was:

"This is it. This is the person I am going to spend the rest of my life with. This is the person I am going to marry."

Which is exactly what happened.

WEDDING DAY, MAY 26, 2001

· *thirteen* ·

I HAD BEEN THE ASSOCIATE EXECUTIVE DIRECTOR at Domus for five years and believed I was ready to be an executive director somewhere. Tacked up on my office wall was a quote by psychologist Abraham Maslow.

A musician must make music, an artist must paint, a poet must write, if he is to be ultimately at peace with himself. What a man can be, he must be.

I believed I had the experience, ability, temperament, and intelligence to take on this level of responsibility. I also knew Mike Duggan wasn't going anywhere from Domus anytime soon; he was younger than I was, and his retirement was a few decades away. By mid 2002, Marybeth and I were newly married, she was pregnant with Liam, and we were both open to moving elsewhere in the country.

So one day, I sat on a bench overlooking the Hudson River and called someone I knew who was the director of the New England Network for Children. This was an umbrella group for all the nonprofit organizations in those six states working with and helping children and teenagers who were in foster care, homeless, runaways, or suffering from addiction and mental health illnesses.

"Are there any executive director openings in New England?" I asked her. "Maine? New Hampshire? Any state up there?"

"There's a rumor this organization called Spectrum, in Burlington, Vermont, will be looking for a new executive director," she replied. "I'll let you know if it's true."

I was thrilled by the very possibility and went home to tell Marybeth the news. I had been to Burlington once, for a weekend, seventeen years earlier. It was a really nice city, with a beautiful downtown, restaurants, theaters, several universities. And I loved the very idea of Vermont – rural, a simpler way of life, progressive politics, and a lot less expensive cost of living than the suburbs of New York City.

Liam was born on October 7, 2002, and a few weeks later I received an email that contained the job description for the executive director of Spectrum Youth and Family Services, with instructions on how to apply. I went to the Spectrum website to learn exactly what the organization did and who it helped. I forwarded the information to someone who knew me and the work I had been doing for several years.

"This job is perfect for you," she said. "Everything they do there you have done at some point in your career."

I emailed a cover letter and résumé. I heard back from a board member, Mary Lee, who said she was in charge of the search committee and would schedule a phone interview with other board members and Spectrum staff. It was held a few days later. I ensconced myself in our bedroom while Marybeth tended to our newborn son. Every question they threw at me I felt I answered well. Liam started howling near the close of the interview, and someone on the other end asked, "Is that a baby?"

I laughed and replied, "Yes, we had a baby boy a few weeks ago. I'll tell him to keep it down."

At the end, Mary Lee asked me, "Are you serious about taking this job?" I knew what she was getting at. This was a big move for Marybeth and me – both of us leaving jobs we had, leaving the New York metropolitan area where we had spent much of our lives, a new baby, and my son Aiden was a junior in high school. If I were the one doing the interviewing and asking the questions, I'd be wondering, Should we take this candidate seriously? Is he really willing to do all this if we make an offer?

"Yes," I replied, "I am serious about this."

I received an email from Mary shortly afterward telling me I was moving on to the next phone interview round. I also found out that I was one of thirty-six candidates, some of whom were current and former Spectrum staff members. My hopes sank a bit when I heard that. If I were a board member looking for a new executive director, I'd likely want one who already knew the organization as well as the Vermont political and fundraising landscape. I considered myself to be a longshot.

I did well enough on that next phone interview to be invited to Burlington for the next round. I flew up on the Sunday after Thanksgiving and was surprised to look out my window when we were over Vermont and see snow. When we landed, I found a cab and told the driver 177 Pearl Street. He dropped me off in front of a building with "Spectrum Youth and Family Services" stenciled on the front window. Inside, I was directed upstairs and finally met Mary Lee in person. She introduced me to the other board members and Spectrum staff who were on the interview team.

There was nothing they asked that surprised me or I could not handle. I talked about my twenty-one years of experience working with homeless and at-risk teens and young adults, the things I achieved, and the mistakes I made, from which I learned so much.

Mary drove me to the airport the next morning and on the way there said, "We're down to three candidates, and you're one of them."

This was getting serious.

I was invited for the next round a week later, which would take place from Sunday morning through Monday afternoon. This time we drove up, Marybeth's seeing Burlington for the first time ever, and of course the same for Liam, who by now was two months old. It was December and already bitterly cold. Marybeth fell in love with Burlington at first sight. She walked around downtown, with Liam in a Baby Bjorn, doing Christmas shopping while I went on interviews.

I met all of the Spectrum program leaders during my rounds. I kept seeing this one man coming in and out of buildings, and I wondered when someone would introduce me to him so he could explain which part of Spectrum he ran. Then I figured it out: He was my competition. (The third candidate had dropped out.)

At one point I was led to a large conference room, and the

entire sixty-person Spectrum staff was present, including the current executive director, Will Rowe. Mary introduced me and it then became an "Ask the candidate whatever you would like" session. Most of the questions were pretty standard: "Why do you want this job?" and "What experience do you have?" Then a female employee with a baby in her lap said, "We heard your wife just had a baby. How are you going to do this job with a newborn at home?"

My first reaction was to think, "You can't ask that. That's illegal." But I could not say that, and answered something along the lines of, "Yes, this will be a challenge. This is my second child, so I know how much work a baby entails, but I believe my wife and I can handle this."

By late Monday afternoon I was pretty interviewed-out, but I had one final one to go, with the full Spectrum board. I thought it went well, and at the end, one of them asked me, "What's the difference between being a manager and a leader."

I don't know if it was because I was tired or just letting my guard down, but I replied, "Near the end of my tenure at St. Christopher's in Dobbs Ferry, I had an African American staff member shot and killed by a Caucasian off-duty New York City policeman in a dispute over a parking space. The local police called to the scene could not find a family member, so I was called to the morgue to identify the body. The next day our mostly black staff and mostly black and Hispanic kids living there were distraught beyond belief. I went to every rally and march and even spoke at some of them. I was often the only white person there. I have to confess to you that I had had tense relations with the staff for most of my five years there. But after this, one of them turned to me and said, 'The staff here really love you now.' I asked her why, and she replied, 'Because you are out here with us when it matters.'

"That's leadership," I told the board. "I was always a good manager, but then I became a leader."

I thought for sure I'd be offered the job after this interview, but Mary pulled me aside and said, "We now want references from your present executive director, board president, and someone you supervise."

I had already given them three references from my days at my two prior workplaces, so I was taken aback by this latest request. And I hadn't even told Mike Duggan that I was interviewing for this. He had no idea I was even up in Vermont.

I called one of my brothers who worked in the business world and explained my dilemma.

"How badly do you want the job?" he asked.

"Badly," I replied.

"Then give them the names of those references," he said. "This is what businesses are doing now so they don't get burned. They are checking out candidates from every possible angle, up, down and sideways."

So that's what I did: I told Mike and he was extremely gracious. He knew of Spectrum and told me he'd give a good reference, and I know the Domus board president did, as well as one of my direct reports.

One more big consideration was Aiden. He was in the second semester of eleventh grade in high school. Ever since his mother and I divorced when he was in second grade, we had shared custody of him. He stayed with me every other week. If he didn't want me to go, I wasn't going.

I told him the situation and he responded immediately, "You go, Dad, because I am practically done with high school anyway. I can come up and visit you and spend the summer, and then a year later I'll be in college." Ironically, he and I had been talking months earlier about his applying to St. Michael's College, which is only minutes from Burlington, so this fit in with our plans. (He ended up getting into St. Michael's but decided to go to Providence College instead.)

Now all I had to do was wait to hear from the Spectrum board president. I was 90 percent sure I'd say yes if offered the job, but I did have some hesitation. In that final interview, the board was open with me about the challenges facing the organization. They alluded to financial difficulties. The staff was fractured into two opposing camps. A few months earlier, two Spectrum young men had participated in the murder of a drug dealer in an apartment Spectrum rented; and a young woman who had been living in a Spectrum residence ended up in a heroin-and-prostitution ring in New York City and killed.

In that week of waiting to hear back, I had two dreams. In the first, I am on some Caribbean island with a beautiful beach. It's early morning and people are going out to position their lounge chairs and umbrellas in order to claim a spot; but it fills up quickly. If you don't get there before everyone else, you won't be on the gorgeous beach and will miss out.

That dream told me that this opportunity to move to Vermont and lead an organization was time-limited. If I didn't jump on it and take it early, I'd miss out.

The second dream was even clearer. In it I am dressed in a suit jacket and tie, driving north, up into New England. I arrive at some kind of ballroom, I go in and the place is packed. People are seated at round tables, all dressed in semi-formal attire. Up at the front is the mayor of Stamford, Dan Malloy. He calls me up and introduces me to the crowd: "This is Mark Redmond. He is moving up here to take on a very difficult job. He doesn't know anyone, and he will need a lot of help. Who here is willing to help him?"

One by one the hands start to shoot up. "I will," says one person. "I will help him," shouts another, and it continues from there, with virtually the entire room full of hundreds of people, raising their hands and offering to help me.

The dream ended, and when I woke up, I knew what it was telling me, because, honestly, my greatest hesitation about taking the Spectrum job was that I didn't know anyone in Vermont other than the few people I had met on the board of directors and some staff. And that is a very big part of a nonprofit executive director's job – connecting with people who can donate funds, make major gifts, help on legislative matters, and connect you to the right people who can make things happen for the organization. I knew practically no one. I was starting from scratch.

But this dream told me not to worry about that, that people would come from all walks of life and corners of Vermont to help me. (Spoiler alert: They did.)

I turned to Marybeth and said to her, "If I get offered that job, I think we should take it and move to Vermont."

A few days later the board president called and offered me the job. I said yes.

· *fourteen* ·

WE WERE SCHEDULED TO LEAVE our apartment on Tuesday, February 18, 2003, but a blizzard hit the East Coast, and the moving truck Spectrum had paid for could not make it down to Yonkers due to dangerous road conditions. That gave us one more day to pack ourselves, which we needed, because we had only returned from a week-long family ski trip in Colorado the day before. The next day, the completely-filled truck pulled away from the curb, and Marybeth and I drove separate cars, with Liam in a car seat in hers. Only four months old, he cried, I think, for the entire six-hour trip – to the point where we pulled over and switched vehicles so we could share in the suffering.

We arrived well past midnight in Burlington and moved into a rented house that Mary Lee had found for us to live in for the next few months. When I woke up the next morning, I turned on *Good Morning America* to hear that, "The coldest place in America today is Burlington, Vermont, at minus thirty-three degrees." It felt like it.

A few days later, at Spectrum, I walked in, introduced myself, and was directed upstairs where I saw my predecessor Will Rowe. He promptly pushed himself away from his desk, smiled, and said, "It's all yours!" Will had been the director of Spectrum for eleven years. It was only a seven-person organization when he arrived, and it now had over sixty employees. He had done a great job building it up. He was also a kind and gracious man. We had a three-week transition period, and he could not have been more helpful. I have heard all kinds of horror stories from executive directors about battles with their predecessors, and nothing could be further from the truth in my experience with Will. He has since passed away, and I owe him a debt of gratitude for helping me so much in my introduction to Spectrum.

After those first few weeks, the problems started coming at me, fast. Money was one. A big one. When I had flown up for that first in-person interview months earlier, I had dinner with the board treasurer. "Our fiscal year just ended," he told me, "and we lost $167,000, but don't worry, by the time you get here, all these cuts will have been made, and we'll be in good shape financially."

When I told Marybeth this her reaction was, "Don't believe that. You'll have to do it."

She was right.

When I took a close look at the financials, I saw that Spectrum was bleeding money. Not only that, there were no savings, no cash reserves, no investments, no endowment. The agency had been paying its bills only because of a one hundred thousand dollar line of credit with a local bank, and that was fully extended. We could not even do direct deposit for employees' paychecks. People had to come in and pick up their checks, and we hoped they were late in doing so. The letter carrier would come in, and we'd practically mug the poor person, hoping to find checks in there so we could quickly deposit them and pay some bills.

I had no choice but to make cuts, to close some programs and lay people off. That's not what I intended or hoped to do when I took the job, but the very existence of Spectrum was at stake. If I didn't make these difficult decisions, then the entire place was going under. One by one I had to call people in and give them the bad news that they were losing their jobs.

One employee we had not laid off said to me, "If one more person here is let go, morale is going to sink."

"Really?" I replied. "You know when morale is really going to sink? When you go to cash your paycheck, and the teller says, 'Sorry, but there's no money in Spectrum's account to pay you.' And trust me, we are right there."

But I knew she was right. Morale was plummeting. I knew it would. I tried to keep the best face on it all, to give people some hope, but even I, at night, would toss and turn, tormented by wondering if I had made a terrible mistake coming here. Marybeth and I had both left jobs. We had an infant son. We were looking to buy a house. And Spectrum was barely afloat. At one point I said to our board president, a Certified Public Accountant, "I don't know if we're going to make it," to which he replied, "At least we're still in the game." That became my mantra for the next few months: "At least we're still in the game."

Over the next few months our strategy worked. At least on paper, we could see our financial situation start to improve; on an accounting basis, we were making progress and getting closer to solvency. But we were still way low on the actual cash we had to pay people and bills. I went to the Vermont Community Loan Fund to see if we could get second mortgages on our buildings. They came through for us, which gave us breathing room for a while; but very quickly we were faced with not being able to make payroll again.

I called our banker and asked if I could come over. He agreed. We already owed the Chittenden Bank one hundred thousand dollars for a line of credit that was overdue by a year. "Can you give us another hundred thousand?" I asked him, almost certain he'd throw me out of the room.

"We have been monitoring your fiscal situation at Spectrum," he said, "and can see you are making difficult cuts but they are paying off. So yes, we will give you another line of credit in that amount."

I almost leapt up and embraced the guy. Instead, I thanked him and headed over to the nearby Immaculate Conception Cathedral, got down on my knees, and thanked God for the generosity of the Chittenden Bank. In subsequent years, I have told whoever is our finance director, "We will always bank there (now called People's United Bank), even if someone else offers us a seemingly better deal; they had our backs when we needed it the most."

We never missed a payroll, and in time we paid off the second line of credit, then the first line, then the second mortgages, then the first mortgages, and we even found ourselves in a position to start an endowment.

But those were just the money problems at Spectrum. The real problems were programmatic.

Spectrum was a paradox. It didn't take me long to see that there were some truly excellent things going on to help kids and families. A team of licensed mental health and addiction counselors who seemed highly professional were doing some outstanding work. We had other staff working on addiction prevention in schools all throughout the county. We had staff involved in juvenile justice work, helping teenagers who had committed a crime to make amends for what they had done while continuing in school. A team of staff helped unemployed youth find jobs. This was all really impressive work.

Yet at the same time, in the same organization, was some unbelievably low performance and slipshod standards. I don't think I was in the job two weeks when a reporter showed up at our door wanting to interview me about the rape of a teenage girl that had occurred in a Spectrum apartment.

"The what?" I asked him.

He told me he had just been in court where a charge had been leveled against a young man associated with Spectrum who had sex with an under-age female while a Spectrum staff member was in the apartment.

I called the Spectrum worker assigned to this young man, and she said, "Oh, yeah, I meant to tell you about this. I was in court today about it."

I was aghast.

A few days later I received a call from one of our supervisors. "A father with whom we've been working just killed his former wife, and it turns out he has been having an affair with his Spectrum worker."

Unreal.

Spectrum had a house in Burlington for eight teenage boys who were in the foster care system. I went to see it during my first week there. It reminded me of my first visit to Epiphany in Brooklyn. Dirty. Graffiti. Holes in the wall. I asked the woman in charge, someone with a master's degree in social work, why it was in such horrendous condition.

"These kids come from poverty. They are probably going to

spend their lives in poverty. This is what they are used to," she said.

She was gone from Spectrum very quickly. A few weeks later, one of the staff members from that house stopped by my office on a Monday morning, and I asked him how the weekend had been.

"Oh a few problems, but nothing major," he replied.

"Like what?" I asked.

"Well we had this one boy who had gone out and a few hours later he ran onto our porch with the police chasing him. They maced him, and we're still not exactly sure what he did to get in hot water with them, but we'll find out. And then this other boy had some kind of sexual encounter with a man across the street We're not sure if it was consensual or not, but he ended up attacking the neighbor with a two-by-four. We're looking into that. And then the police showed up at the house on Saturday night with their drug-sniffing dogs, and our worker on duty, when he saw that, insisted on taking his backpack out of the house and putting it into the trunk of his car."

My jaw dropped.

"I need you and all of your staff here in my office tomorrow at 9 a.m.," I told him.

They dutifully showed up the next day, and I went over all the calamities that had occurred the prior weekend. They sat there impassively, then one of them blithely stated, "Well, yeah, and in the weekend before that we had X, Y and Z happen," and another of them said, "Right, and the week before that, remember when that boy did A, B and C?"

I quickly realized that the staff had become completely inured to the atrocities happening in that house. The dysfunction there had become normalized for them. They simply took it for granted that every day would contain another outrageous act that no longer seemed very outrageous to them.

Spectrum had another house for girls in the foster care system with an equal number of problems, and a house for boys who were convicted of sex offenses. I read a confidential report on the latter that had been written by the State Department for Children and Families (DCF); it was shocking, and I immediately shut the place down.

With all this going on in the background, I scheduled an appointment to go meet the chief of the Burlington Police Department, because, as I learned a long time ago, in this line of work, it's always smart to be on good terms with the top cop. I went in and introduced myself. She sat there, looked up at me, and almost spat out the words, "Spectrum? Boy do you have a long way to go to get the reputation of your agency back."

"Nice to meet you as well," I replied.

When I had interviewed months earlier, the board had told me that not only were relations with the police bad, but the dozens of small businesses on Church Street, Burlington's main commercial walkway, detested Spectrum as well. During my time with Will Rowe, the former executive director, I asked, "Which business owner hates us the most?"

"That's easy," he said. "Yves Bradley, the guy who owns The Body Shop. He can't stand Spectrum and even caused us to lose some grant funding."

Following the advice from *The Godfather*, which was, "I keep my friends close and my enemies closer," I wrote a letter to Mr. Bradley introducing myself and asked to meet with him to hear his concerns. He contacted me, and in a meeting at his store, I heard him out. A lot of what he said made sense. There were some young people doing pretty outrageous things in downtown Burlington, even to the point of committing crimes, and Spectrum staff were making excuses for them, even shielding them from any consequences.

I assured him that things would change at Spectrum in this regard, and they did. Not every staff member agreed with me on this. They no longer work at Spectrum.

As for Yves Bradley, the store owner who hated Spectrum so much? He is now one of our biggest proponents. He donates money, gives us hockey tickets when he has spares, found us a new building to move into when we were looking to expand, organized clothing drives for Spectrum, and even put a Giving Tree in the window of The Body Shop one Christmas. He is truly one of our greatest champions.

· fifteen ·

WHEN I WAS APPLYING for the Spectrum executive director position and had that first interview with board members and staff, one of the things people kept repeating was, "We have to get these kids ready to be on their own by age eighteen," or "That eighteenth birthday comes really fast." After the third or fourth reference to this, I interrupted the interview and said, "I have to ask, what is this about age eighteen? Why is it so special, why the sense of urgency?" A social worker replied, "In Vermont, foster care ends at age eighteen. If you are living with foster parents or in a group home, you have to move out on your eighteenth birthday."

I was shocked. For one thing, I considered Vermont to be forward thinking in so many ways, practically a Progressive's paradise. (Bernie Sanders, after all, right?)

"Listen, I hope you hire me for this job," I said, "but even if you don't, that needs to change. In Connecticut, kids in foster care can remain up until age twenty-three if they wish, and when I was in New York, it was twenty-one. My own son is seventeen, and he is an honor student at a Jesuit high school. If I tell him on his eighteenth birthday, 'Happy Birthday, now you have to leave my house, find your own place to live, feed yourself, buy health insurance, and everything else,' I doubt he'd be able to do it. But we're talking about kids who do not have thriving and healthy families to go back to, who do not have marketable job skills, and who maybe have a high school diploma, and probably not even that. You're asking them to make it on their own at eighteen? It's not going to happen. The vast majority are going to end up homeless or, more likely, eventually do something wrong and end up in prison."

They obviously did hire me for the job, and while I was swamped the first few months, trying to learn about Spectrum and deal with dozens of different problems and crises, I didn't let go of this issue and continued to ask advocates and other nonprofit foster care providers what they thought of this policy. They all basically agreed with me, but they were so used to it – it had gone on for so long, – that it didn't even register with them as a serious problem that had to be dealt with and the policy changed. One nonprofit leader said to me, "Yeah, you are right, but even if you started working on that today, it would take a good five years to get it through the legislature and into law."

I knew what he was saying, but I didn't let it deter me. I did my research and found out that Vermont was the only state in New England to discharge youth from foster care at age eighteen. The other five helped kids up until twenty-one, twenty-two, or twenty-three.

I also discovered that, in a recent study of the Vermont Department of Corrections, 36 percent of all Vermont prisoners had previously been in foster care. This was incredibly damning evidence of a failed policy. The state was cutting foster kids off at eighteen, primarily as a way to save money, but then these same kids were popping back up in the prison system, costing the state forty-five thousand dollars per year for a male and upwards of fifty-five thousand for a female. Add to that the incalculable human cost of a life ruined, and the threat to public safety.

So after only seven months on the job at Spectrum, I wrote an editorial and emailed it to the *Burlington Free Press*. I didn't know anyone there, I just wrote it and sent it off to "Dear Editors," having no idea if they'd run it or not.

They did, a few days later, giving it the title "Foster Care Cut-Off Age Rule Must Change." "For a state that is forward-thinking in so many ways," I wrote, "Vermont is shockingly out of step with the rest of the country when it comes to its treatment of youth who are in the foster care system." The reaction was immediate. On the nonprofit side, and from foster parents, I received dozens of emails and messages thanking me for bringing the issue to light, agreeing with what I had written and why the policy needed to change. The Vermont DCF, however, which was responsible for foster care in the state, did not take kindly to it. One of their division directors wrote a rebuttal editorial, opening with, "Mark Redmond makes a number of statements in his commentary that are inaccurate."

DCF was a major funder of Spectrum, so I knew I was taking a risk by writing what I did, but I felt it was too important an issue to ignore; it was affecting so many foster kids negatively, not only at Spectrum but for many of the fourteen hundred foster kids in the state. I wrote it believing that, by shedding light on the issue, legislators would react and do something about it.

None of them did. Nothing happened. I kept waiting for the governor or a few legislators to take action, or even one of them, but my op-ed caused only a momentary stir, and that was it. Foster kids continued to be discharged at age eighteen, many of them later ending up homeless or in prison, just as they always had.

Two years went by. Frustrated at the lack of progress, I decided to meet with a woman who worked as a lobbyist in the legislature for another nonprofit. I showed her the op-ed and then explained that not one single thing had happened to advance this issue during the forty-eight months since it had appeared. She advised me to do two things. "One," she said, "is that you have got to go around to every advocacy group in the state that has anything to do with this population and convince them that this issue has to move to the top of their agenda. Two, go meet with the Speaker of the House and seek her advice as to which legislators you should approach to get their support for it."

I moved ahead on both fronts. I went around and gave the same speech at meetings of every advocacy group that had anything to do with abused and neglected children, teens in foster care, at-risk youth, or transition age youth. I explained the facts: how these kids were getting cut off by the state at eighteen, how they were nowhere near ready to live on their own, and what percent were ending up in corrections. "I am asking that you make this your number one issue this year," was my request, and all of them obliged.

As for the Speaker of the House, only in a state as small and un-bureaucratic as Vermont can you call the Speaker of the House at her house, which is exactly what I did. Gaye Symington was her name. She took my call, and we arranged to meet in her office. After I showed her the op-ed, she asked clarifying questions and then pulled out a sheet listing all state legislators by party, town, and committee. "Go see this one," she said. "He will be interested in this issue. And that one: She is on a key committee that might be able to take this on." She continued like this, naming about a half-dozen legislators I should go see.

So I did that, traveling all around the state to meet with each one, explaining to them why the age cut-off had to change and how it was negatively affecting so many foster kids. Not all of them were sympathetic, but most were. And when the legislature opened in January 2006, I found myself invited to testify at the House Human Services Committee on the issue.

The legislature in Vermont is in session for only a few months, and in 2006 I was hopeful they would pass a bill officially changing the age of discharge up to the twenty-second birthday. All the advocates helping me on this were optimistic that it was going to happen. Then at the last minute, a bill was passed ordering DCF to instead study the issue for another year.

I was ready to pull my hair out. "Study the issue?" I said to one advocate. "What is there to study? The evidence is overwhelming that kids are being hurt by the present policy. We all know what the right thing is to do on this. Why delay it to study the issue?" One legislator told me, "When we don't want to do anything on an issue in the legislature, we pass a bill to study it instead." I told one advocate this and he replied, "That is often true, but don't give up hope or stop your efforts, because it's not always the case. You may succeed in the end."

I didn't give up. I kept repeating my stump speech until one day I got lucky. (Or as I said to a group of college students while telling them this story, "You make your own luck in life.") I was in a large group meeting, talking about the need to change the law, and how in its present form it was hurting kids. In the meeting was the governor's new Secretary of Human Services, Mike Smith. Mike had been a Republican legislator at one point, worked in the insurance industry and became a leader there, and was now one of the most powerful members of the governor's cabinet. That was all I knew about him, but after listening to me speak, he revealed that, when he was young, he had been in quite a bit of trouble himself. "I could very well have gone the route that your kids do," he said, "and ended up homeless or in prison; but I joined the Navy Seals, and that put me on a different path." The oft-quoted "All politics is personal" was certainly true in this case. We now had someone in the governor's office who was sympathetic to our cause.

And so it was that, in January 2007, in his traditional opening remarks to all house and senate members on his plans for the upcoming session, three-term Republican Governor Jim Douglas announced his intention to change the foster care discharge age, and that he would introduce a bill calling for such. I wasn't there for the speech, but others were, or heard it broadcast live on Vermont Public Radio, and my phone was ringing off the hook. "Do you know what Governor Douglas just said? It's going to happen this year!"

I spent the next few months testifying again about the issue, and of course, it was not as simple a matter as just passing a law. There were many details I wanted to see covered in the legislation, but in the end, the house and senate passed a bill that allowed foster youth to receive supports from the state up until the twenty-second birthday. Steve Dale, the Commissioner of DCF, had also played an important role in the legislation, and when he told me the governor intended to sign the bill, I said, "He should sign it at Spectrum, because no one did more than we did to make this happen."

And so he did. On June 6, 2007, at the Spectrum Drop-In Center, Governor Douglas signed into law Act 74, "An Act Relating to Foster Care Services and Supports." The room was filled with cameras and reporters, advocates, other providers, legislators, Spectrum staff and board members, and several teenagers in foster care. The governor signed the bill and gave the pen to one of them, a young woman. It was a triumphant moment, and I could not help but think back to that conversation I'd had with an advocate early on, in which he advised that it would take "a good five years" to make this change. We did it in four, I thought to myself.

A reporter called me and asked, "How did you get Mike Smith, a conservative, Republican, military veteran to support this as he did?"

"It's a good lesson," I replied, "because you never know someone's backstory. We all see a person and put them in a certain box based on their gender or political party or past job. But it's so often not the case, and to me the lesson is that if you really believe in something, a cause or issue, put it out there in front of everyone, because you can never predict who is going to surprise you and help."

It's been years since that bill was passed, and the legislation accomplished exactly what we intended. I go around Vermont and meet with nonprofit leaders, and they talk about foster youth staying in their group residence or foster home past age eighteen, leaving when they are ready at twenty, twenty-one, or twenty-two. Even at Spectrum, in our residences, the eighteenth birthday is just another birthday to celebrate, not to kick someone out. They stay until they decide they are really ready to move on to the next step.

This whole experience was, to me, very gratifying, and to this day I have a large photo in my office of the governor signing that bill. It was a true example of how a democratic system can work, how a systemic injustice can be corrected, and how you can use persuasion and passion to move the legislative system to do what is right for people. Hundreds, if not thousands, of young people in Vermont have been helped by what we all did together.

GOVERNOR JIM DOUGLAS, JUNE 6, 2007

· *sixteen* ·

ALMOST FROM THE DAY Marybeth and I landed in Vermont, we started looking for a house to buy. We had been renting an apartment in Yonkers, then renting the house in Burlington, but we were looking forward to finally owning our own place. The market was super hot in and around Burlington in early 2003, and if you didn't arrive with check in hand, chances were you'd lose out. Marybeth, toting Liam, would join a realtor, driving around and trudging through places for sale while I was at work.

She found us a nice house in Essex, only about twenty-five minutes from Burlington, so it'd be easy for me to drive in each day. The house was in a fairly new neighborhood and in good condition, with plenty of rooms and space and even a yard, which, back in Yonkers, was only a dream. It'd be a nice house in which to raise Liam.

We settled on a closing date and about a week before, on a Saturday morning, Marybeth suggested we drive there and take a walk through the neighborhood. We did, and walking down the block, we met a woman in her yard and introduced ourselves.

"You'll love it here," she said. "The schools are good. It's safe. People are really nice and look out for one another."

And then she asked us a question: "Will you be looking for a church to join?"

I thought that was a bit unusual, but then I wondered if this is just what Vermonters do when meeting someone for the first time, ask about a church. After all, we had been living in Yonkers, and that is not what they did there, but perhaps it was customary here. (I have since learned that Vermont is the least religious, least church-going state in the country. As one person told me, "If you lived in Alabama, every person there would ask you what church you are joining. You somehow managed to find the one person in Vermont who'd ask you that.")

"We're both Catholic," I responded as Marybeth nodded. "We'll probably look for a Catholic church nearby once we've moved in."

"Well if you are looking for a contemporary Christian church," the woman continued, "please let me know. I'd love to tell you about mine."

We did move into our new house a short time later and met another husband and wife across the street, and I told her about the neighbor who was promoting her church.

"I know which church that is," she said. "We call it the Hollywood church."

"Hollywood church?" I asked.

"Yes," she said, "because every service is this big-screen, multimedia extravaganza. Lights, loud music, really something."

I met a different neighbor shortly after that, and told him about the woman promoting her church to us.

"Yeah, my wife and I went there once," he said. "It was messed up. We're not going back there."

Hearing that, I was convinced I need not join that church. It reminded me of the megachurches you read about, which too often promote a pie-in-the-sky, feel-good spirituality bereft of any emphasis on social justice and reaching out to help the poor. Whatever problems the Catholic Church may have, which are many, it does not give short shrift to Jesus's teachings about feeding the hungry, sheltering the homeless, and challenging the underpinnings of a society and economy that create such suffering. To me it is the church of Dorothy Day, Oscar Romero, the martyred El Salvador missionaries, Mother Theresa, and others whom I so admire. As Pope Francis says, it is or at least should be, "The church of the poor and for the poor."

A few months later, the volunteer coordinator at Spectrum sent out an all-staff email: "Who is available this coming Sunday, 10 a.m., to go to a church to pick up some items their fifth grade youth group wants to donate to us?" Of course it was this particular church, so my first reaction was to think, "I don't want to go. I don't have a good feeling about this place. Let somebody else here do it. Surely one of the other sixty employees here will step up and volunteer to go."

At the end of the week I asked our volunteer coordinator if anyone had volunteered.

"No one," she replied.

Argh. I said I'd do it. After all, I lived closer than anyone else, and I was the director.

I showed up that Sunday morning and found my way to an upstairs room, where about twenty fourth and fifth graders were waiting for me. They sat cross-legged on the floor. Four or five adults were with them. I was introduced to the children and did my standard five-minute presentation on what Spectrum is, who the young people are that we help, and why they are on the streets and without families. Then one of the adults carried up a laundry basket full of things like deodorant, towels, toothpaste, and soap, and placed it before me, announcing that these were things the kids had collected. I thanked them, promising to deliver them to the kids at Spectrum.

I glanced at my watch and thought, "Nice, only ten minutes, now I can go," and I actually started for the door, when the adult male at the front of the room motioned for me to stay.

"Mr. Redmond," he announced to the class, "before you go, one of our children has something special for you. Emily, can you please come up and show Mr. Redmond what you brought?"

I stopped and watched this little girl, maybe age nine or ten, dragging a big black duffel bag up to the front of the room. She brought it right up to me, laid it at my feet, looked up, and said, "My brother died this year, and my family wants to donate this to you to give to a boy at Spectrum."

I unzipped the bag and it had a lot of the same things that were in the laundry basket; but then I noticed a white leather-bound Bible, so I pulled it out. There was a card placed inside of it. "To a Young Man at Spectrum" was handwritten on the envelope.

The card was pre-printed, and on the front was written,

To a young
Man at Spectrum

"Always remember…" and on the inside, "God is watching over you." A picture of the girl's brother was taped to the other inside page. I was startled when I saw it; because this girl was only in fourth grade, I was expecting to see a boy around that age. But it was a young man, similar in age to those we work with at Spectrum. In the picture he was smiling, happy, handsome. Someone had written the dates of his birth and death; he was twenty-one when he died, and it was only a few months earlier. They had also written, "God bless you, from the family of Brad."

I leaned over to the adult next to me and whispered, "How did her brother die?"

"Heroin overdose," he whispered back.

Those two words ripped right through me. It was one of those times in life when someone says something that completely changes the way you look at a situation. It was like a moment of spiritual awakening, when you suddenly see things very differently, very clearly. And the first thing I saw was my own blindness; my own foolishness; my own prejudice. And I saw that, while this church may not be the kind that I would want to join, or the kind of worship I prefer, there are a lot of good people here, some of whom, like this little girl and her family, are in tremendous pain. And if this church is where they find hope and peace and healing, what right do I have to judge that?

I have none.

I knelt down to face Emily and told her, "You have my word that I am going to give this to the right young man at Spectrum." I then reached over and hugged her, thanking her for the gift she and her family had given.

That week we had a two-day strategic planning retreat with all Spectrum staff. It had not gone well. There were still staff at Spectrum who were not at all happy that I had been selected as executive director over an internal candidate they favored, and they made that clear. Other staff were not pleased with all the changes I was making. It had been a tense two days, and I, for one, was glad it was drawing to a close. I had brought the duffel bag and card with me and decided to end the meeting by telling the story and seeing if anyone there knew a youth who could use the contents.

I started to tell the story, but holding that card, it almost felt like I could feel the pain of that family. It was as if the card itself transmitted the agony of those parents and that little girl, and I broke down. The tears just streamed out of me. I tried to read what was in the card, but it was almost impossible. I struggled to get out the words and ended by saying, "This is why it is so important that we do the work we do here. For some reason we missed this young man, or he never found his way to us, but there are so many others out there like him, and it's a reminder of why Spectrum exists and why we do the work we do."

I could barely look up at the staff. I was so embarrassed, but when I did, I saw that some were crying too. I realized in a way that it was good that it had happened. They now saw me as a person, not an executive making controversial decisions.

One of our workers told me that he had counseled a young man who had been homeless, lived at Spectrum for a few years, and was now accepted at Vermont Technical College. "He could really use the things in that bag," the counselor told me, and I replied, "Great, give it to him, but I am going to get the address of the girl and her family and I want him to send a thank you card." And this worker later assured me that the card was sent.

I thought that was the end of this story, but four years later I received this letter from Brad's mother, along with a check for $250.

Dear Mark,

Today is my late son's birthday; he would have been 26 years old, but for a tragic accidental overdose of heroin. He liked to go out to dinner, the little Indian restaurant on North Winooski Avenue, Nectar's, Perry's, or Shanty on the Shore's "all you can eat shrimp." This birthday I felt in my spirit that I'd like to fund the boys in your group home going out to dinner, I hope that the enclosed check will cover it. I'd like those boys to know that they are so precious and valuable. Their lives have great significance and they are recognized for choosing to be involved with the program and working toward a good future for themselves. The thought of a group of guys going out, having a good meal together, laughing and enjoying themselves will do me good. I wish we could be doing that with my son, but I'm blessed to be able to do this small thing in loving memory of him.

God bless you in your work with the youth of our area. Wishing you and yours a blessed Easter.

I tried to reach out and meet this mother several times, to the point of making an impromptu visit to her house, but we never connected. Then ten years later, I was in New York City on a Friday afternoon, getting ready for my niece's wedding the next day, when I received this email from one of the staff in our Drop-In Center.

A woman who would like to remain anonymous except for her first name came by to see us today. She does not want a thank you, or any public recognition. She was out looking for hungry teens to give sandwiches to, and came across Drop-In. She said she used to see teens all over Church Street just hanging out, but was left wondering today where all the teens were. When she came to Drop-In she realized that the people she was trying to help were already here. She came at a great time with lots of dancing, healthy lunch eating, and positive energy among the kids. She was positively overwhelmed by the atmosphere, and services here. She came to my office, and cried as she told me about her son who used to come to Burlington for negative purposes, and would have been 35 now if he had not overdosed on heroin years ago. She knows our organization, and used to send Mark donations to take the kids out to dinner sometimes. Continuing to interact with Spectrum was too painful for her because of memories of

> *her son, so she stopped donating and reaching out some years ago. Today she felt that God sent her here, so she gave us a cash donation of $160, and asked that it be used for food for the Drop-In program. Thank you!*

I was in some store on Fifth Avenue with Marybeth and Liam, shopping, when I received this. It gave me the chills. I had to sit down. This was a fourteen-year story, and I now understood why it had been so difficult for me to reach this mother. She was just in too much pain. But now might be the time, so I found a way to reach her.

We met over coffee. I asked her about her son and what he had been like. I asked about her daughter, Emily, who by then was in her twenties. I let her know how grateful I was for what she had done back in 2003 and for what she had done most recently. I told her that her story had given hope and healing to many people.

And this church – the one I thought so poorly of and maligned, at least in my own mind – has been incredibly generous to Spectrum over the intervening years. I can contact them at any time and ask them for donated coats, boots, sweaters, blankets, whatever our kids need, especially in the winter, and they always come through.

And I did something I never thought I'd do: I went to one of their services. Marybeth and Liam and I were invited to a Christmas show they put on, and we went. And yes, it was kind of Hollywood. They had singers and drummers and dancers and fake snow falling from the ceiling. They really put on a show. It was like Broadway comes to Vermont for one night, but I also found it meaningful, sincere, and spiritual. And at the end of the night, the members of that church packed my car with wrapped Christmas presents, to take back to the kids at Spectrum.

· *seventeen* ·

I KNEW FROM THE DAY I STARTED at Spectrum that fundraising was going to be a big part of my job. I had watched what Mike Duggan had done at Domus. In essence he left the running of the day-to-day operations to me and one other person while he developed relationships with potential supporters. And it worked: The amount of money donated to Domus skyrocketed. I needed to do the same kind of thing at Spectrum.

When I arrived, Spectrum was 97 percent reliant on federal and state dollars for its budget. Two percent came from the local United Way, and Spectrum raised forty-nine thousand in other donations for the remaining 1 percent. I knew that had to grow, especially in light of government cutbacks that were sure to come. Speaking with someone who had worked in the Clinton administration, I described for him our revenue sources, and he said, "If I were you, I'd act as if every one of those federal and state dollars will be disappearing over time." I believed him, and the first time Spectrum lost one of the big federal grants we had relied upon for so many years, I went nuts, calling representatives from our Congressional delegation in outrage. It did no good.

I knew I needed to make contacts with people in Vermont who could make things happen for us – who could help raise funds – but I was new in town; I barely knew anyone. Then one day, as I was walking into a Burlington restaurant, Halvorson's, for lunch, I thought I recognized someone I saw leaving – someone I had worked with briefly twenty-four years earlier at the Metropolitan Life Insurance Company on Madison Avenue. I walked back onto the street and yelled, "Hey Jeff! Jeff Norris!"

He wheeled around and said, "Who are you? How do you know my name?"

I laughed and said, "We worked together at Met Life in 1979."

He remembered me and we shook hands, exchanged phone numbers, and agreed to meet soon.

We met about two weeks later at the same restaurant. Jeff had left his job at Met Life only a year earlier and moved up from Connecticut with his wife and two children. He was living only about two miles from me in Essex. I told him what I had been up to in the intervening decades, how I had ended up in Vermont, and the challenges I was facing at Spectrum.

He told me he was the chief operating officer for an investment firm in Burlington, which had just hired Rob Miller, who had previously been commissioner of the Vermont Department of Economic Development. Jeff offered to set up a lunch so I could meet him.

A few weeks later, sitting with Jeff and Rob Miller, I asked Rob, "Who are the people in this city and county and state I really need to know?" He was great and provided me with a list of people and said I could use his name when trying to reach them.

I still have that handwritten list somewhere, but even in my mind, I know who they are. I systematically worked through the entire thing, calling or emailing or writing each of them with this message: "Hello, I am the new director of Spectrum. Rob Miller has referred me to you as someone I really need to know. Can I stop by?"

It worked. I'd go see these people at their work sites or at a coffee shop, or if I could persuade them to come in and see Spectrum, even better. I'd end each meeting with two requests: Is there anyone else you think I should know? and Can I put you on our mailing list?

As the mailing list grew, so did the amount of money we raised via donations. But we were still in a precarious financial position. I was about to lay off the person in charge of our mentoring program, which I hated to do. We had thirty-six volunteer mentors at the time, each of them assigned to one youth who needed an adult who would be a responsible, caring presence. It was one of the best things going on at Spectrum, and I despised the idea of ending it. Then Jeff called me out of the blue and said, "Our firm wants to donate sixty thousand dollars to a worthy nonprofit. How about yours?"

We kept mentoring going. Sixteen years later it still is, and hundreds of kids, most from households of poverty, have been greatly helped.

Someone then advised me to meet Sister Irene Duchesneau, a nun from a religious order based in Montreal who had been assigned to the Fanny Allen Hospital in Colchester for decades. I don't think she was five feet tall, but she was a total powerhouse of energy and spirit. It turned out her order had a foundation, and she invited me do a presentation in front of its board. They must have liked what they heard because they gave us a big grant, the first of many to come from them.

Sister D also told me she had heard from someone she knew who was a major philanthropist in Burlington, and when she told him they were giving money to Spectrum, his reaction was, "Why are you giving to that place? They have a terrible reputation." When I heard that, I asked for his name and phone number. I called Pat Robins out of the blue, asked if he could come in and see what we are doing at Spectrum, and he obliged. After a one hour visit, he not only started contributing in significant sums, he contacted the president of a company he had helped to found and insisted that this man come in to meet me. He did, and the company gave us one of the largest donations we had ever received.

It kept going like that. Marybeth's father was a trustee of Providence College, and at an event there, he met the bishop of Vermont, Kenneth Angell. He told Bishop Angell about me and the work I was doing at Spectrum, so I arranged to go meet him at the chancery. I knew of the bishop and his tragic story – that his younger brother, David, a writer and producer of the Emmy Award–winning television shows *Cheers* and *Frasier*, had died along with his wife in the first plane to hit the towers on 9/11. Bishop Angell listened to me talk about the work we were doing at Spectrum, and as I was getting ready to go, he said, "There is a foundation based in L.A. in my late brother and his wife's name. I am happy to write a letter recommending they give a grant to

Spectrum." This was not what I was expecting – not why I had gone to meet him – but of course, I obliged and said I would very much appreciate that.

The David and Lynn Angell Foundation gave us fifty thousand dollars with the stipulation that it was a one-time, one-year gift.

It continued for ten more.

I was at Spectrum for about a year and a half when, one day, I read in the *Burlington Free Press* that someone had made an anonymous $50 million donation to nearby Middlebury College, which was followed by another anonymous donation of $10 million. We were just pulling ourselves out of debt at Spectrum at that time, paying off the second mortgages and lines of credit that were keeping us going, but most of the buildings we owned were in pretty rough shape, including the ones where the kids lived. They needed a lot of renovation as well as replacement furniture, which required a lot of money that we did not have.

The multimillion-dollar donations to Middlebury irked me. I had just been there to tour the college; my son Aiden was a senior in high school, and that was one of the colleges he was considering. It was a truly beautiful place – a quintessential New England liberal arts college with a gorgeous library and art museum and state-of-the-art dormitories; a hockey rink the Bruins would have been happy to play in; a golf course on the campus; its own ski slope a few miles away; and the cafeteria was as nice as any restaurant I had seen in Vermont. After the tour, I started calling Middlebury College "The Land of Oz." Presenters at the parent-student orientation practically boasted that they had the highest tuition rate of any college in the country. Later on I learned that the endowment was over $700 million. Today it's over a billion.

And this institution needed a $50 million donation? Followed by $10 million? I didn't think so.

Here we were at Spectrum, struggling to help, basically, the same age group as Middlebury, but our kids were almost exclusively from backgrounds of extreme poverty. If one of them managed to earn a high school diploma or GED, we were thrilled, absolutely thrilled. But we knew the chances were very slim that our success stories were going to later be in a position to donate back to us. It wasn't going to happen. Schools like Middlebury have a self-generating flow of donors. Most of their students come from affluent backgrounds, and when they graduate, they are likely to become great successes in fields like medicine, law, engineering, business, and technology, and thus able and willing to donate back to their alma mater.

We don't have that, or anything close to that, at Spectrum; so when I read about these large donations to Middlebury, I could not help but ask myself, If someone was in a position to donate that much money, why give it to a place that is obviously already so wealthy and with such encouraging financial prospects? Why not donate that money to a place like Spectrum or Covenant House or Partners in Health that could really use it, and the donation would have a dramatic impact on the lives of impoverished people?

I thought about trying to get a reporter at the *Burlington Free Press* to write a column expressing this; I was friends with one of the weekly columnists there, Chris Bohjalian, who also happened to be a best-selling novelist. I considered asking him, but my wife's reaction was, "Why don't you write it yourself, as an op-ed?"

So that's what I did. I wrote it, emailed it to the editors at the *Free Press,* and the next thing I knew, it appeared on September 24, 2004, under the title they had given it, "Who Will Donate to the Disadvantaged?"

My editorial had an immediate reaction. The *Burlington Free Press* was really the paper of record in Vermont at that time. Almost everyone read it. I walked down Church Street, the main pedestrian thoroughfare, that day, and I must have been stopped twenty times by people I knew, telling me how much they liked the column. I felt like a rock star. Then an email came through on my computer screen from Rich Tarrant, one of the wealthiest people in Vermont. I had never met him, but I had always wanted to; he had graduated from St. Michael's College in the 1960s, was drafted by the Boston Celtics, and then went on to cofound a very successful software company based in Vermont. He was a wealthy man. Every nonprofit leader in the state wanted to meet him, and now he was asking to meet me based on what I had written in the paper. I did meet Rich about a week later, which was followed by a twenty-five thousand dollar gift to Spectrum, the first of many to come from him and his foundation. A few weeks later I was invited to a Vermont radio station to be interviewed about my column. Another wealthy and generous Vermonter, Bobby Miller, happened to be listening, and he mailed in a donation for ten thousand dollars.

My wife said, "You hit a nerve," and she was right. I began to think that this column might have potential to get to an audience larger than Vermont. So one rainy Friday afternoon I had a spare hour at work and walked over to the Borders book store on Church Street and made my way to the magazine section, specifically the business magazines. I pulled a bunch of them off of the rack: *Fortune, Business Week, Crain's, Forbes, Fast Company, Money, Inc.* I perused them all and noticed that, in *Forbes*, there was a regular op-ed page entitled "On My Mind" written by a guest columnist. I put all the magazines back except for *Forbes*, which I purchased, and walked back to my office where I pulled up Forbes.com on my computer. I clicked Contact Us, pasted my op-ed into the Message section with an intro that stated, "Please consider this for your 'On My Mind' column." I hit Send and went home for the weekend.

The following Monday an editor from *Forbes* called to tell me that they were going to run the column in their next issue, and he was sending a photographer up to take my picture the next day.

Wow.

For the next few days, the *Forbes* editor helped me to improve the piece, adding information about the multimillion-dollar donations that regularly go to other universities similar to Middlebury, such as Princeton and Harvard. They also asked that I insert a paragraph about the scholarship money Middlebury does give out to its accepted students who otherwise might not be able to attend. As I thought that was fair to mention, I agreed. But the main point was essentially the same, and they ran it on November 15, 2004, with the title "Defining Charity Upward:

Why do wealthy people give to well-endowed universities serving successful kids, instead of to nonprofits that help the truly needy?"

I had thought the reaction in Burlington was big, but this was bigger. Way bigger. Donations to Spectrum came in from all over the country: five thousand dollars from a husband and wife in Texas; double that amount from someone in Colorado. Lots of smaller donations from all over the country. I even received one from Paris Hilton's grandfather, Baron Hilton. I wondered if my article resonated with him because, at the time, his granddaughter was making headlines for all the wrong reasons

And I received some moving notes with the donations. This was from a businessman in Florida (who has continued to support us in even larger amounts).

Dear Mark,
Enclosed is a check for $4,000 to help in your efforts.
We little guys have to stick together.

And this letter, which came with a check:

Dear Mr. Redmond,
I was touched by your article in Forbes regarding the rich
giving to the rich. I never attended college myself and
therefore do not have a school I regularly contribute to,
however I do have two grown sons in college that I support.

The reason your article touched me is because I am orig-
inally from the Northeast, born in Massachusetts and
raised the first ten years of my life all over New England.
I am a product of the foster care system through the '60s.
The experiences of my youth, as with everyone, have had
an effect on my entire life, most notably never feeling like
you fit in, never fully trusting other people, or that you
were loved enough. Not feeling loved enough, in my case,
equated to being chosen, never choosing. Often times the
person choosing me was not a good fit. Yet I did not feel I

was good enough or worthy of the people I admired. I do understand how some of "your" kids feel.

I did develop a strong desire for independence and to be self-sufficient. Given this, I worked very hard and today have a successful career. I cannot endow Spectrum Youth and Family Services with spectacular amounts of money, but I would like to make this my lead charity and will offer to you whatever I have available.

The amazing thing is that almost all of these donors have continued to support us in the decade and more since. When I was about to start at Spectrum, my father-in-law said to me, "I don't like it when I donate to a nonprofit and the only time I hear from them again is when they are asking for more money." I took that to heart and stayed in contact with all these generous people from around the country, sending them notes and articles about Spectrum, but only once or twice a year actually asking for a donation. I think that is why they have stayed faithful to us. A few years later, a new staff member at Spectrum asked me, "Why are these people who have nothing to do with Vermont, who don't live here, donating to us?" "Because they care," I responded. "They care about the homeless and the poor."

Then I did something else. My wife's grandfather Emmett McNamara, who was ninety-five at the time, insisted I send the article to Warren Buffett. My initial response was, "Forget it, Granddad, Warren Buffett probably has six layers of assistants to keep him from people like me," but I sent it anyway, with a letter stating, "I work with homeless and runaway teenagers in Burlington, Vermont. *Forbes* magazine published the attached opinion piece that I wrote. Hope you enjoy it." To my shock, Mr. Buffett sent my letter back to me, with this message written in ink:

Mark – I agree with you. I am for all types of philanthropy, but I think it makes most sense where there is a high societal

need and a small or non-existent natural funding
constituency. Our priorities are not in your area, but
we try to follow the above formula.

Warren Buffett

As surprised as I was that he had written back, I had to admit I was disappointed he had not enclosed a donation. But his hand-written message would come in handy, very handy, three years later when I made another connection to the Buffett family. It was again Marybeth's grandfather who provided the impetus. He had visited Spectrum that fall and was impressed by what he saw. The day after Christmas 2007, he flew up from Florida to see us on Long Island, where Marybeth and I were visiting relatives. We went to a restaurant for lunch, and during the meal he said to me, "You are married to one of my granddaughters, and another one was dating Warren Buffett's sister's grandson, and she has gotten to know Doris Buffett pretty well. You should ask my granddaughter to put you in touch with Mrs. Buffett to see if she will donate to Spectrum."

It sounded like an outlandish idea, but so did writing to Warren Buffett in the first place, so I called my wife's cousin to see what this was all about. "Yes," she said, "I know Doris Buffett, and she is a very nice woman. She has her own foundation, but don't email her – don't even type out a letter – just take your organization's letterhead and handwrite a letter to her telling her who you are, mention my name in it, tell her what Spectrum does, who you help, and what you need money for." I was still pretty dubious about the whole thing, but nothing ventured, nothing gained, so that's exactly what I did, with one additional attachment to the letter: a copy of her brother's note to me from three years before with a "p.s.: Doris, I am pen pals with your brother."

I was pleasantly surprised when I received a phone call a few weeks later from Mitty Beal, identifying herself as the person in charge of Doris Buffett's Sunshine Lady Foundation. She told me that Doris had received my letter, was impressed and intrigued, and that I should submit a formal proposal in six months. I was thrilled, and I told my wife's cousin, and of course, her grand-father, who could not be happier.

Then the stock market crash of 2008 occurred, sending the economy into a tailspin and the start of a worldwide recession. I called Mitty and said, "I have a feeling you will not be making gifts to any new organizations now," and she replied, "I am sorry, but we won't be. We lost a good percentage of our foundation's value in the crash, and in fact we are wondering how we can meet the commitments we have already made to our long-time recip-ients." I told her I understood, and just as I was about to hang up the phone, it occurred to me to ask, "Is it okay if I keep you informed about Spectrum and what is happening with us going forward?" "Sure, that would be fine," she replied.

So for the next several years, every article that came out about Spectrum – every bit about us on the radio or television, every interview I did – I'd send to this woman. I never asked for a dime. I just kept her informed. And one day about three years later I took a look at the stock market and thought, You know, this thing has largely come back from 2008, and I bet the Sunshine Lady Foundation is in good shape again. So I called her and came right out and asked, "Would you be open to receiving a proposal from Spectrum now?" She replied, "We have been following you and Spectrum for the last few years, and we'd love to receive a proposal."

I knew without hesitation what I wanted to ask for. I had known for a while that it was time to re-create the transitional residence we had on Maple Street. Homeless kids started out in the shelter, and those who were able to find and keep a job, at-tend school or a training program, and save money, moved over there. At Maple Street, the kids would get their own keys to the front door and keys to their own rooms, pay nominal rent, and learn independent living skills. For my first few years at Spectrum, there was always at least one opening in the Maple Street house for a shelter youth who was ready to make the move over; but we became a victim of our own success. Although in the early years, we had a number of kids bailing out of the residence in the first few months – or even more likely, our staff was asking them to leave because they were not following the program – over time we found kids really succeeding there and staying longer, which is exactly what we wanted. But the downside was that the house frequently became full, with no openings for a youth in the shelter who was doing everything we asked and ready to make the move over. For the first time we had to start a waiting list at Maple Street, which then created a backup in the shelter, which led to our having to turn kids away at the door. Bad all around.

We realized that we needed to start another transitional living residence. The problem, of course, was finding the dollars to build one, and just as challenging, operate it on an ongoing basis. The present residence was funded through a combination of federal and state dollars, none of which was likely to be secured for an additional residence. It seemed daunting, but no one could deny the need.

So that's what I asked Mrs. Buffett's assistant for – money to start another transitional residence.

I put it in a proposal, and a few weeks later she called me and said, "We will give you two hundred thousand as a matching gift. If you can raise that much yourself, we will give you that amount."

"Thanks, I'll take it," was my response.

We sent out a press release, and when the newspapers, radio, and television got hold of it, there was a big reaction. The Buffett family had never given money to a Vermont nonprofit, so this was huge news in our little state. Reporters were calling me constantly, asking if they could speak to Mrs. Buffett, to which I would reply, "Listen, *I've* never spoken to Mrs. Buffett before." But her assistant did give me Doris's cellphone number, and for the first time in all these years I had a conversation with her. She could not have been nicer, expressing great admiration for what she had learned about Spectrum. She told me the last time she had been to Vermont was in 1948, for a summer camp. She also agreed to speak to reporters, and that I could give them her number. She also gave me some valuable fundraising advice: "When you have a matching gift like this Mark, never tell people how much you've raised, because if you play your cards right you can triple or quadruple it."

Spoken like a true Buffett, I thought to myself. I also knew she was right.

It wasn't hard to raise the matching two hundred thousand dollars. One family alone, who had already been so generous to Spectrum for multiple years, wrote us a check for the full amount. The student body at nearby St. Michael's College voted to pool their funds and give us ten thousand dollars. A local builder, who had for years donated a thousand dollars annually, wrote us a check for twenty-five thousand. I was advised to contact another businessman, who was reputed to be at his desk at five every morning; I woke myself up at that early hour, called him, he answered, I asked if I could come over right away to see him, he said yes, and when I got there he told me he'd donate five thousand dollars.

Another time, our board president called me on my cell on a Friday night. When I answered, he said, "I was just in a restaurant in downtown Burlington, and while there I ran into State Senator Tim Ashe. I told him what we want to do regarding a new residence, he said he thinks he might be able to get you some state money for this, and that you should call him." Senator Ashe had, at one time, been on the Spectrum board himself, so I knew him and called him the following Monday morning. Within a week, he had me presenting at the Senate Institutions Committee on which he served. They gave us $144,000.

By this time we certainly had enough money to build/buy/renovate a residence and furnish it. The challenge now was the operating costs. I knew that it cost about $250,000 per year to run a residence like this, with staffing costs as the primary expense. My board was reluctant to go ahead and approve expending funds to start a new residence, not knowing if we'd have the dollars to actually operate it year after year. I approached the new commissioner of the Department for Children and Families, Dave Yacovone, to see if he had room in his budget to fund it. He was sympathetic, because he well knew the predicament facing homeless young people and the need we were facing, but he told me he just did not have the dollars available for this. "You've got to go to the legislature to see if they will fund it," he advised.

This was not going to be an easy task, because it was common knowledge that the legislature had to come up with $71 million in *cuts* that year, and here I was asking for new money for a new project, and it could not be one-time money; it had to be permanent money in the base budget. Because of my work on Act 74 a few years earlier, I did have good contacts in the legislature. I started with Mark Larson, whom I used to supervise when he worked at Spectrum and was now one of the key members in the House. His advice was, "Start with this person, and then go to this person, and then to this one."

So that's what I did: tracked legislators down and met them in coffee shops on weekend mornings, or in the cafeteria of the legislature, or wherever else they wanted to meet. I'd start off each conversation the same way, "I know you have to cut $71 million this year, and I know you may laugh me out of the room when I ask you this, but I need $250,000 in new money, in the base budget, in order to create this new residence for homeless teens that is so desperately needed." I kept waiting for the Are you out of your mind? response, but no one said that. Each one was respectful, heard me out, and advised me whom I should see next. And I just kept going and going and meeting and explaining and pleading, one after the other, and one day a lobbyist called me and said, "I was just at the Senate Appropriations Committee, and in the midst of discussions about cutting, cutting, cutting, they are also talking about giving Spectrum the money it needs to start this new residence. In fact, Commissioner Yacovone was in there urging them to do so. How did you do that?" I chuckled in response.

So against all the odds, we succeeded, and the legislature appropriated about 75 percent of the operating funds we had requested, which was fine with me. I told our board we'd raise the rest each year, and they agreed. And we moved ahead. We ended up deciding to use one of our own buildings, moving staff out of a section of the second floor. That meant we were hunting for another nearby building for them to work from, which we miraculously did in record time. Renovations commenced, amidst all kinds of drama regarding zoning, permitting, building codes, historic preservation regulations, and on and on.

We did it, and on May 30, 2012, we had a ribbon-cutting ceremony to open a new eight-bed residence for formerly homeless youth. It was a great moment, and many of the people who had been key players in moving it forward were there to celebrate. Two who I wished could be there, however, were not. Marybeth's grandfather, age 102 at this point, was too frail to make the trip, and Doris Buffett had prior plans; but I sent them both plenty of pictures and news articles. A lot of people made this project happen, but those two people were key.

SPECTRUM PEARL STREET RESIDENCE

Five years later, we had a different need.

When the coldest months hit, all of our beds were filled, especially in the shelter, so we'd turn kids away when they needed us the most. If it was below a certain temperature, each of them could apply to the state for a voucher to stay in a motel, but to say that was not ideal would be an understatement. These motels were not healthy, safe places for anyone, especially a teenager. They were filled with drugs and other illegal activity.

I told the Spectrum board about the situation and asked for their support to start a Warming Shelter somewhere in Burlington that would be open from November through March. "I have no idea how we will pay for this or where it will be," I told them, "but I know it's needed." They gave me the green light.

I approached probably every synagogue and church in the city looking for a basement, a hall, anything. None worked out, usually for good reasons, such as the fact that they were running a daycare or school in their space. I approached Bishop Angell's successor, Louis Matano, and received a lecture about why the liability risk of a shelter in a church property prohibited this, and, "Even if you do find a Protestant church or synagogue willing to do this, they are not taking on the true moral issues of the day, which are abortion and end of life."

A year later, he was replaced by Bishop Christopher Coyne, who was in favor of the idea right from the start. "We have two parishes downtown," he said, "and a newly installed pastor. Go see him, and if he's game to do this, so am I."

I went to see Father Lance Harlow, who offered us two spaces. We ended up selecting the church hall in the Cathedral of St. Joseph's, a co-cathedral. There was plenty of room for ten cots, which were supplied by the Community Health Centers of Burlington, and the University of Vermont Medical Center offered to launder the sheets every day. We went around hat in hand to our regular donors asking for extra gifts to get this operational before the weather turned frigid. People were great. They really came through for us, and we were able to house ten youth there that entire winter.

Our Development Director asked some of the youth what they felt about being at the Warming Shelter. These were their responses:

. .

*"I'm thankful for the Warming Shelter because if
I wasn't there I would be sleeping outside in the freezing cold.
Before I was there I didn't even have a sleeping bag,
cause someone found it and threw it away when I left my camp.
And I love the staff. They are fantastic, awesome and cool."*

. .

*"If I wasn't at the Warming Shelter I would probably still be
sleeping in the Macy's parking garage. It's really been a blessing.
The Burlington community has been really awesome too.
People are always dropping off food at nights so we always have
something to eat if we're hungry."*

. .

*"I'm really grateful for the Warming Shelter cause it's a safe
place to stay when I have nowhere else to go. I really feel the
staff care about us. And I appreciate that it's warm. And the
beds! They're actually really comfortable."*

. .

*"If I wasn't at the Warming Shelter I would probably
be sleeping in laundrymats like I did last winter,
cause it's too cold to sleep outside. I really enjoy
it there and always feel safe. The environment is
welcoming and the staff are nice."*

. .

"I'm grateful for the Warming Shelter because I would still be sleeping outside if I wasn't there. It's great and I'm really thankful for all the support."

· ·

After that first winter, we were left wondering how to keep the Warming Shelter going.

So ... back I went to Doris Buffett and the Sunshine Lady Foundation.

All I can say is thank you, thank you, thank you.

· *eighteen* ·

ANOTHER PART OF FUNDRAISING for a nonprofit organization consists of events. In my first few years at Spectrum, we tried several, including a dance marathon, an "adult prom," and bike rides, none of which made much money, and all of which consumed a great deal of staff and volunteer time. When I hear someone say, "We're doing this event to raise awareness," I always respond, "I can write an article and get awareness. Awareness doesn't pay the bills. If we do an event, it has to raise money, or we don't do it at all."

After enduring all these busts, one day in 2012 I spotted something intriguing on Facebook. Covenant House had an event called the Executive Sleep Out, in which they had Manhattan business executives sleeping outside in the cold, each of them appealing to family and friends in order to raise funds.

I hit the Share tab on Facebook, sent it to our development team at Spectrum, and asked, "What do you think? Is this something we could do in Burlington?"

"Sounds good," they replied. "Let's give it a shot. We'll do it in the spring."

"Uhm, no," I replied. "This is not camping. We'll do it in March. March sounds colder than April. I don't care if we do it on the last day in March, but we'll do it in that month." The average night-time temperature on March 30 in Burlington hovers just below freezing.

"Okay," they replied. "People can bring tents."

"Uhm, no," I said again. "The homeless kids I know don't have nice North Face tents to sleep in. We'll give people a cardboard box and a black tarp to put under their sleeping bags. No one will get hypothermia. No one will die. They will be cold and uncomfortable, which is the idea, and they will get up the next day and be so grateful they have a nice warm bed to sleep in the next night." I did agree however to a large overhead canopy when my staff argued, "Even a homeless person would not sleep out in the pouring rain or snow, which may very well happen." So I gave in on the canopy, although I insisted, "No sides to it. If there is a wind whipping in off of Lake Champlain, I want people to feel it."

We needed a place to sleep outside, and it took only one call to the wonderful people at the Unitarian church across the street from our Drop-In Center; they agreed we could sleep out on their lawn, which was in a nice, visible spot right at the top of Church Street. Leonardo's Pizza down the block from us agreed to donate the dinner, and August First Bakery and Café, a few blocks away, agreed to provide breakfast and coffee for the morning.

The hard part, of course, would be convincing business and community leaders to sleep outside, in the cold, in March. We thought that, with any luck, we could persuade twenty people to do it. I started with Spectrum board members, many of whom were heads of various businesses, banks and law firms. Almost all of them agreed to do it. (I particularly enjoyed egging on Mike Smith, who was president of Verizon in Vermont by that time. "Come on Mike, you were a Navy Seal; this thing will be easy for you." He agreed to do it, driving all the way back from a meeting in Portland, Maine, for it.)

Then I started in on the members of the Vermont Business Roundtable, which I had only recently joined. I attended their annual meeting in January of 2012 and had emailed a few of them beforehand, asking them to be the inaugural members of the Spectrum Sleep Out. One of the first people I ran into at the meeting was Mike Seaver, president of People's United Bank in Vermont. He looked at me and said, "You want me to do what? Sleep out under the stars? In March?" (He signed up.)

One by one, I started to get people to say yes, and then I'd email another potential candidate, stating, "So-and-so, who is president of this company, is doing it, therefore you have to do it." And it worked. Person after person agreed to this outlandish idea, agreeing to do their best to set a personal fundraising goal of two thousand dollars.

By the day of the Sleep Out we had forty-four people registered, more than doubling our initial expectation. Together they raised over ninety thousand dollars, more than quadruple the amount we had ever raised at an event before, with expenses of only about 2 percent.

I, of course, was out there with them. It started out like a pep rally, with all of us gathered in the Drop-In Center eating pizza, laughing and joking. I gave a short speech, telling them how grateful I was that they were doing this, and how the kids in our shelter knew what they were doing, and how impressed they were that anyone would take on something like this. We then went around the room so they could individually introduce themselves.

"Hi, I'm Brian, I'm a partner at the Dinse Knapp McAndrew law firm."

"I'm the president of People's Bank."

"I'm the founder of a software company in town."

We were near the end, when a woman said to the crowd, "My name is Tawnya Safer, and I'm sorry, I think I've made a mistake. I'm a housewife – a mom – and I work as a staff assistant. I'm not the head of a company or a partner at a law firm. I don't think I belong here."

The man standing behind her, Dan Feeney, the owner of a very successful Burlington company, gently put his hands on her shoulders and said, "That's not true. That's not true at all. You've raised money to help homeless kids? You're going to sleep outside in the cold and the snow tonight? Then you're a leader. You're a leader just as much as any other person here tonight is, and you have every right to be here."

We've done the Spectrum Sleep Out nine consecutive years, and there are only two people who have done it each and every time: myself and Tawnya Safer.

At ten o'clock we headed over to the church lawn. It was snowing (I again gave thanks for the wisdom of my staffers who advocated for the canopy), and the temperature was in the mid-twenties – in other words, perfect. Some people jumped right into their sleeping bags; others, including myself, chatted out on the lawn for a while, but eventually we all settled in. Two Spectrum staff members sat in chairs nearby, taking turns staying awake and watching over everyone for safety. The police had also been alerted that we were doing this and were a quick phone call away if, for some reason, we needed them.

Even though I had worked with homeless teens for decades, I had never actually tried something like this before, and it was eye-opening. Once all the laughing and camaraderie was over, actually trying to sleep outside like that, in the freezing cold, is almost impossible. And the cold is the least of it. Burlington is a small city, but there are still all the lights and the continual noise. From the occasional ambulance to a police car to a truck making a late-night business delivery to the church bells – the noise never seemed to die down.

And then there was this sense of vulnerability, especially when the local bars closed and people were noisily walking by, and even yelling over to us things like, "What are you people doing out there?" or "What's this all about?" At least for me, that's when my mind started racing, What do I do if one of them comes over and harasses us? I know we have staff who are awake and watching over us, but what if they can't handle it? What if we have to call the police? How long will it take till they get here? On it went, until I realized that no sleep can happen while you are worrying this much.

I don't think I slept an hour. The Sleep Out changed me that night. It gave me a new awareness and understanding of just how incredibly difficult being homeless is. I mean, we had it easy. We had people protecting us. We had an overhead canopy. We were well-fed. We knew this was just one night. What would it be like to be a kid who had to sleep outside and didn't have all those things? And then had to get up in the morning and try to go to work or to school? Exhausted from lack of sleep and aching from lying on the cold ground for hours, I could only imagine how truly terrible it must be.

The Sleep Out changed many people that night. Some of those who participated wrote the following reflections:

Friends and family,

Succeed by Helping Others Succeed … it is a simple phrase yet a powerful group of words when strung together.

Two months ago, Mark Redmond from Spectrum Youth and Family Services reached out to me to see if I was interested in helping him raise awareness on the ever-growing problem of teenage homelessness here in Burlington and throughout Vermont. "Dan, I need your help, and are you willing to sleep overnight on a tarp and cardboard box on the lawn of the Unitarian Church to raise much-needed awareness and funds for Spectrum?" was all Mark asked.

All I asked of you – my friends and family – was to help me help Mark succeed at his project and you came through with flying colors.

I want to thank you from the bottom of my heart. I will not forget that you individually helped deliver success to a worthwhile organization.

For the record, I slept a total of 90 minutes with 40+ other friends of Spectrum between 11 p.m. and 5:15 this morning. I was chilled to the bone with snow falling part of the night and a steady wind. At the end of the night, I packed my sleeping bag, walked down Church Street, hopped in a cab to my home, and jumped into my warm bed. That is not happening for many tonight. Succeed by Helping Others Succeed … what a simple phrase. Thanks again.

DAN FEENEY

. .

Last evening and into this morning, I was part of a life-changing experience. I left the Spectrum Sleep Out not only as a supporter of Spectrum, but as a changed person.

I was frozen. Literally. I could barely open my eyes. They were frozen shut from wearing my contacts and having my eyes water during the early morning hours when the crisp blowing wind would meet my face. I was exhausted. I was in a daze. The roar of the emergency vehicles, which streamed through the city streets, and the sound of early morning party goers, left me with this nagging feeling, we have to do more. Yes, even more.

At approximately 4 a.m. I heard a loud rattling sound. It startled me at first. I didn't recognize it. I tried to locate where the sound was coming from by lifting my oversized wool hat just a tad above my eyes. Everything echoes differently on the empty streets of Burlington at 4 a.m. It was a person, pushing a cart. It was one of us, I thought, a homeless person. Then my eyes filled up with tears and I thought, no this is just me for one night, and I still have a home. That person pushing the cart does this every day, probably around 4 a.m. searching for food, or bottles or articles of clothing someone left behind during the every-day activities and happenings of downtown Burlington.

I thought a bit about my childhood as I was lying there overnight on the lawn at the end of Church Street. I re-called how Mark spoke during the opening of the evening, and how I couldn't stop nodding my head. We all have a story in life. Each and every one of us. Some choose this path and some choose that. Some intertwine and some couldn't be further from the other. We are born into this world all the same, but our journeys are all so different.

Thank you for allowing me to be a part of this amazing event. Spectrum Youth & Family Services is an amazing outreach, which offers not just food, a warm bed for the night, and free healthcare, but it offers something even more than that, something that everyone needs, and that is HOPE. Our community is in good hands with Spectrum. Spectrum Youth & Family Services is the HOPE that our community needs. Spectrum is the real deal.

I hope we are able to raise even more money over the next couple of weeks so more lives can be changed and offered a new beginning. I hope I can be a part of this great organization in some form or another in the near future. It felt like I was surrounded by family and friends. Helping people is like being "home." The Sleep Out event is over for 2012 but the impact will forever live on in my heart.

TAWNYA SAFER

. .

Mark – I want to thank you and your team for the inspiring Sleep Out. It was a very humbling experience at many levels. I somewhat expected that I would be a bit cold, but even with several layers of clothes, hat, and a decent sleeping bag, I was absolutely freezing at different times and was literally shivering for much of the night. The nighttime noise was the most unexpected for me. Laying on the ground with my head in the sleeping bag, I couldn't see what was going on. I had an incredible heightened awareness of the smallest to the largest sound, of which there were many. Despite sleeping with 43 others, and having your two staff "keeping watch" I felt vulnerable and not all that safe. I kept imagining what it might be like for a 15-year-old to be all alone with those sounds and cold night after night. At any point, I knew that I had

*an option and that in just a few hours, I would have hot
coffee, food, my car, a shower, the day off, the weekend
playing with my family, etc. Easy for me. Not easy for that
15-year-old.*

*Life twists in ways that we often cannot understand.
Homelessness could touch anyone.*

*Spectrum ... you raised awareness in a very real way.
Take good care,*

MARY LEE

· ·

*I have to tell you I was expecting the Sleep Out to be a
simple camp-out. It was anything but simple. It was a
gigantic eye-opener for me. You and your staff should be
very proud of what you do. You all have inspired me in
many ways. The stories and your talk were a slap of reality
that I know nothing about and flat out ignore. I want to
change that.*

*Just want to say thank you for inviting me.
I was very proud to be part of the event and will continue
to do so in the future. Keep up the great work!!!*

ANDY BOWEN

· ·

*I would not change this whole experience for the world.
I think everyone needs to experience this. I just can't believe
so many kids go through this every day and night. I had
people around me. I was safe. I was able to have food
and drink right away that morning. I had a bathroom.*

*I had warmth. I had people who cared that I was there.
I HAVE a home.
I could not be happier to be a Board member of Spectrum.
I was nervous. But I did it – and what I endured was zero –
nothing compared to the lives our homeless youth in Vermont.
I am glad Mark asked me. I am glad I said yes. My hope is
we can continue to raise awareness and continue to get the
facilities in place for these kids. We have only scratched the
surface – we have many more miles to go.*

MICHELLE LITTLE

. .

*Participating in this event was one of the best decisions
I have made this year – really. Initially, it was "Oh
yeah, I'm up for that," when in reality I was thinking
"Mark Redmond is nuts, he will never get anyone else to
participate – I'm safe, it's so far in the future – it will never
happen."*

*Note to self, NEVER underestimate the will and the drive
of Mr. Relentless (dressed in easy-going clothing), he is from
New York after all, and he believes and lives the mission
of his organization. Lo and behold, Mr. Relentless and his
team had met and surpassed the goal of 20 participants,
and I was woefully behind in fundraising and borrowing
an appropriate sleeping bag. (Note to Self: NEVER
underestimate the will and drive of a team led by Mr.
Relentless – likes attract, be very afraid of the special way
they walk, talk, and especially the "determination gleam"
in their eyes.)*

*Day of event dawns, money is raised, sleeping bag borrowed
– and myriad excuses start floating through my mind: "The
doctor did just tell you the broken bone in your foot is*

*healed – but take it easy. It's going to snow, it is snowing.
Doesn't the kitty look like it isn't feeling well? Etc., etc., etc."*

*I did not weenie out. I did what I do in most stressful
occasions, I shopped and baked. Twelve or fifteen dozen
chocolate chip cookies, and bought lots of Easter candy, "for
the campers." I got to the event early, helped at registration,
and did the other thing I do in stressful situations, I opened
up my heart to Hope. And oh wasn't there Hope in the
room. It was there when I arrived in the smiles the Relentless
Ones were wearing. Hope got bigger with the arrival of each
camper, and it leaked out the front door of the building and
surrounded the block as we walked across the street to open
our sleeping bags and hearts. We learned more that night
about the Hope that Spectrum holds out to their clients. The
Hope that if you choose the more difficult path, the next
day – the next morning, the next conversation, the next job
interview – will be better, and help fill up that personal Hope
Bucket. That personal Hope Bucket that helps you place one
foot in front of the other in forward, positive movement.*

*So to my fellow campers, thank you so much for sharing
your Hope, and to the Relentless Ones, I will forever be in
your debt. After all, what are we without Hope?*

PAM MACKENZIE

. .

And I received this Facebook message from a woman who heard
about the Sleep Out. She wrote that she had been a homeless teen
in the 1970s and stayed at Spectrum at that time.

*I hope that you get a ton of support through this Sleep
Out. As one who has been there, the fact that people are
willing to show support to these homeless teens gives them*

Hope. Someone cares! About them! When you are home-less you do not think that anybody ever even thinks about you, not for one second.

· ·

The Sleep Out was so successful that we continued with it the next year. This time we were able to recruit eighty-eight people, and they raised $155,000 for us. We were thrilled, and it was the same type of experience: freezing cold, the lights, the noise, the vulnerability, and about an hour of sleep, at least for me.

We kept doing the Sleep Out, year after year, with the number of people participating growing as well as the dollars raised.

SPECTRUM SLEEP OUT, MARCH 2019

Each year there was something unexpected. One year a dumpster right behind the Spectrum shelter caught fire in the middle of the night, so the noise of the fire trucks arriving woke everyone up. (I was accused of setting the fire, which I vehemently deny!) Another year a horizontal snowstorm came barreling off of Lake Champlain and completely covered all of us lying on the ground. People looked like snowmen coming in for coffee that morning. One year the ground beneath us was a complete sheet of ice, so it felt like trying to sleep in a refrigerator. Another time it was an enormous mud bowl out there.

Another year I kept hearing this loud, bellowing male voice all night long, and I could not fall asleep. Finally, at around three, I got up to see who it was. It turned out it was a homeless inebriated man on the church lawn, pestering our staff who were tasked with staying up and keeping watch. I went over to the person in charge, our development director Sarah Woodard, and asked, "How did this happen, and what are we going to do about this?"

She looked at me and said, "Well you can call the police, and when they arrive they will approach him, and he will probably scream and cause a big scene, and everyone will wake up, and they will all probably wonder why the director of Spectrum is calling the police on a homeless man."

She had a point.

I walked over to him and said, "If you don't work here, you need to keep quiet." And he actually did. The best part? A few hours later, when everyone got up and went into the church basement for breakfast, there he was with us, feasting on an egg and cheese sandwich with a coffee. Sarah, the good person she is, had invited him in for breakfast.

The next day I apologized to a friend who was doing the Sleep Out for the first time. "I'm sorry that guy was there making noise all night and probably keeping you awake."

"Don't apologize," he said. "That added to the experience because I'm sure if you are actually homeless, that kind of thing happens to you all the time when you are trying to go to sleep. I now have a better understanding of what it's like."

Another interesting twist to the Sleep Out occurred in the second year. About a week before the event, someone I did not know at the time, Julia Andrews, emailed me. She explained that she and her family lived in Westford, which is about thirty-five minutes outside of Burlington. Her daughter Celia was age nine and had heard about the Sleep Out and wanted to do it in her backyard the same night as ours. "Would that be okay?" Julia asked, to which I replied, "Sure, feel free." Shortly afterward Julia emailed me the link to Celia's GoFundMe.com page.

A few days later, my son Liam, age ten at the time, asked me if he could do the Sleep Out with me and everyone else on the lawn of the Unitarian church, and I told him no, that we had a rule that anyone out there had to be age sixteen and over. "But look what this girl in Westford is doing," I told him. I pulled up her GoFundMe.com page and said, "Why don't you sleep in our backyard like this girl is doing?"

"Should I go around the neighborhood with an envelope and ask people to donate?" he asked.

"No," I replied, "you should start your own GoFundMe page like she did and email it to every grandparent, aunt, uncle, and older cousin you have."

Three days later he slept outside, on our back patio, with Marybeth dutifully keeping watch over him from the adjacent living room.

Celia raised over $1,200 and Liam raised $650.

Thus was born the Spectrum Student Sleep Out. It takes place on, or shortly after, the adult one, with hundreds of middle school, high school, and even college students sleeping in parents' back-yards, football fields, Little League fields, church lawns, town squares, and college quads. The Student Sleep Out usually raises tens of thousands of dollars for us.

I try to visit most of them to say a few words and thank these kids. At one of them a parent said to me, "You started a movement."

"No I didn't," I replied. "The nine-year-old girl from Westford did."

And it's true. Celia Andrews wanted to help homeless kids and had the compassion and initiative to ask her mother if she could do it. We nominated her for the Association of Fundraising Professionals in Northern New England Demont Scholarship Award for Outstanding Youth in Philanthropy. It was a five thousand dollar college scholarship.

Celia won it. She deserved it.

CELIA ANDREWS

· *nineteen* ·

BURLINGTON IS THE BIRTHPLACE OF BEN & JERRY'S ice cream, and in fact, Jerry Greenfield himself is a faithful and generous donor to Spectrum. Once a year, Ben & Jerry's has a Free Cone Day at its store downtown, and the line extends down the block.

That gave the owner of a local burrito place, Boloco, an idea: Free Burrito Day, with the caveat that if people do choose to give something for their burrito, the funds would go to Spectrum.

I was grateful that Boloco offered to do this and volunteered to help in whatever capacity desired. Local celebrities, including the mayor of Burlington and the University of Vermont hockey coach, stood behind the counter rolling burritos, while my job was to stand there holding a large bowl that had "Please donate to Spectrum" taped to it.

It started at 11 a.m., and immediately a long line formed. There were college students, businesspeople, and families. Most received their burritos and put one or two dollars in the bowl, some contributed larger amounts, while others put in nothing.

At one point I saw three men in line whom I recognized as being from Burlington's homeless population. They were dressed practically in rags, were unwashed and unshaved. They seemed to me to be possibly inebriated to some degree, although not acting out in any way.

The Boloco manager had previously given me several Get Another Free Burrito cards to hand out to whoever I wished. This seemed like the perfect opportunity, so when the first homeless man came through and was handed his burrito, I offered him one of the cards. When I did so, he responded with a smile I will never forget. Beatific is the only word that comes to mind. He didn't say anything, but he looked absolutely delighted.

Then he did something I did not expect. He reached into his pocket and pulled out two pennies and motioned to place them into the bowl I was holding. My first reaction was almost to pull back and say, "That's okay. You don't have to do that. This isn't meant for you."

But I didn't. I resisted that impulse. I recognized that this individual, as homeless and poor as he appeared, had as much right to give back as anyone else, and to deny him that would be to deny him his dignity.

He put the two pennies in the bowl. I smiled and thanked him. As he walked away, I couldn't help but think of the Gospel story in which a poor widow at the temple came and donated two small coins, and Jesus responded, "This poor widow put in more than all the others; for they all put in out of their surplus, but she, out of her poverty, put in all she owned, all she had to live on."

A few months later, I persuaded one of the wealthiest people in Vermont to come and visit Spectrum, to see our shelter, Drop-In Center, and everything else we offer to homeless and at-risk youth. I had heard that he had recently made a six-figure gift to another nonprofit, so I planned to ask him to do the same for us. After touring him through, I asked if he would donate.

"What's the range of giving?" he asked.

I thought for a moment and responded, "This year one family made a quarter-million-dollar gift to us. And a homeless man gave us two cents. That's the range."

He looked at me quizzically, eyebrows raised, but didn't say anything.

I then added: "And both gifts mean exactly the same to me."

· *twenty* ·

EVERY THREE YEARS AT SPECTRUM, we engage in strategic planning. We bring in a consultant who works with our board and leadership staff to identify which initiatives we will focus on in the coming years.

The first few times, we ended up with pages and pages of directives, outcomes, indicators, and on and on. This is a common mistake for both for-profit and nonprofit organizations. By the time we did it in 2015, we realized that if we came up with just three or four initiatives, at most, to focus on, that was fine. I also insisted we adhere to something I had once read in a management book: Write your strategic plan in pencil. That is great advice, because even in the course of three years, so much can change, including opportunities to possibly pursue that would never have occurred to any of us while concocting the strategic plan months or years earlier.

So in 2015, we first took an honest look at what we thought we were doing well at Spectrum and what could be improved. It's very easy to go into these sessions patting yourselves on the back, saying, "Gee we're doing amazing work here, let's just keep doing it." True leadership means saying, "We're doing some things well, but how can we do them better, and what are we missing?"

Taking that approach, it became clear to us that one such area was that of employment for our youth. Spectrum, for more than twenty years, has had the JOBS program, which stands for Jump On Board for Success. It's a collaboration with another local non-profit, and the focus is to help youth with emotional disabilities to find employment. Since almost all the youth at Spectrum qualify for "emotional disability," the JOBS staff helped kids in our shelter, Drop-In Center, counseling, mentoring, and just about everything else we have. The JOBS staff have relationships and connections with dozens of area employers, such as food stores, movie theaters, construction firms, and restaurants.

In 2015 we were still receiving some federal funding for JOBS and, therefore, had to report outcomes to them. One of the main ones was: What percentage of your youth found a job and kept a job for ninety days? There are ten JOBS programs throughout Vermont, and Spectrum was consistently at the top with a 41 percent rate of youth making it to day ninety in a job. I had been at statewide meetings where it was stated, "Every JOBS program should be like Spectrum's."

That might have been nice to hear, but I, for one, didn't think ninety days was any great sign of success in a job. When I reached day ninety at Spectrum, my reaction was not, "Great, I've done it!" I was just warming up. All of us are, in any job. And even though Spectrum's was the highest in the state at 41 percent, I didn't think that was any great achievement.

During strategic planning sessions, we asked our JOBS staff why so few youth make it to ninety days. "It's all the soft skills," they replied. "They don't know how to show up on time. They don't know how to call in sick. They don't know how to work for a supervisor or be part of a team. They didn't grow up in families where these things were modeled for them, so they either quit or get fired within a few weeks."

Then we turned the question around and asked, "So for those youth who are succeeding in a job, what's in the secret sauce there?"

"An employer who understands who these kids are and knows how to work with them," was the answer. "But most bosses are not trained in youth work. They have no idea how to work with kids like these. They are trying to run their restaurants, their stores, their businesses."

It all made sense and led us to start thinking, What if we are the boss? What if Spectrum starts a business and puts adults in there who are trained in youth work, in how to handle kids like these? Will that improve the number who not only make it past ninety days, but improve their performance in the workforce beyond us?

Now, we are not the first ones in America to come upon this solution. I'd been following the work of Father Greg Boyle in Los Angeles for years, and even read his two books, *Tattoos on the Heart* and *Barking to the Choir*. Father Boyle started Homeboy Industries, whose motto is "Nothing stops a bullet like a job." Homeboy Industries has helped thousands of young men and women caught up in gangs by employing them in enterprises it owns, such as a bakery, cafe, a salsa line, and a silkscreening factory.

I thought about taking a trip to L.A. to see Homeboy first-hand, but then I learned of a national conference taking place in Denver in which scores of social enterprises run by nonprofits would be featured. It was expensive, though, and I didn't want it to just be me, I wanted at least two of my key staff to be with me and a few board members.

It was at this time that I received a call from Laura Latka, who had been our development director at Spectrum but was now the philanthropic advisor for one of the wealthiest families in Vermont, the Hoehls. That meant she helped them figure out how and to whom they should give their charitable donations. She called me mid-week and asked, "What are you doing this Friday at 4 p.m.?"

"I'm free," I replied.

"Mrs. Hoehl would like to meet you."

"I'd love that since I've never met her. I will be there."

Ever since Laura left Spectrum, we had been receiving about twenty-five thousand dollars a year from the Hoehl Foundation. I figured she was advocating for us, which was great, because we had not been receiving much if anything prior to that.

Mrs. Hoehl was living in an assisted living residence a few miles from Burlington. I went at the appointed time and was surprised to see in the parking lot the development director for another nonprofit, COTS (Committee on Temporary Shelter). I wondered what she was doing there, because I thought this was my opportunity to finally meet Mrs. Hoehl.

I went inside and was instructed to head down the hall and go into a conference room on the right. I opened the door and entered and was stupefied to find it packed with people. All I could think of was the TV show *Intervention* in which an individual who is addicted to drugs or alcohol enters a room like that thinking he or she is about to meet one person, and *Bam!* there's a whole crew hoping to persuade them to go to rehab.

I immediately noticed a reporter I knew from the *Burlington Free Press*, and a photographer. I shook hands with directors I knew from four other nonprofits, all of which worked directly with the homeless, like COTS, or with children and families in poverty. I took my seat on a couch, wondering what was going on.

A few minutes later, Laura came in with Mrs. Hoehl, who was in a wheelchair. I didn't know what medical condition she had, but she looked weak. I went over and introduced myself.

After a few introductory remarks thanking us for coming, Laura made an announcement.

"Each of your organizations is receiving a 1 million-dollar gift from Mrs. Hoehl today."

Stunning. That's the only word for it – we were stunned. Each of us jumped up to take our turn thanking Mrs. Hoehl. When it was mine, I whispered to her, "You stole my development director away a few years ago, and now I'm glad you did."

She laughed.

I called our board president on the way home to give him the news.

"Good for you," he said. "Now you can take the rest of the day off."

I called Marybeth, and after we immediately launched into what items I should pick up for dinner on the way home, she asked what was new at work.

"Oh yeah," I said, "we just got a million-dollar donation."

The next morning as I stood in line for coffee at a Starbucks, there on the rack was the *Burlington Free Press* with a big, front-page picture of myself and the director of COTS, big shocked grins on our faces. The man behind me looked at it and said, "Hey, that looks like you on there. Is it?"

"It sure is," I replied.

"What did you do? Why are you on there?" he asked.

"I just got a million dollars!" I replied.

I emailed two of my staff and three board members, "We now have more than enough money to go to Denver to learn about social enterprises. Book your flights."

It was a fascinating three days. There were dozens of nonprofit organizations throughout the country that had started a business. We listened to a woman who had started a bee colony in the middle of the most poverty-stricken section of Detroit and was making honey and related products like candles, and employing people from that community. We learned about an organization in Texas employing low-income immigrants to make bean soup that was packaged and sold. We went on field trips too, and I visited a bike shop that employed high school dropouts and taught them how to do repairs.

But the highlight for me was visiting a warehouse to see a nonprofit organization called Spring Back Colorado, which hired men coming out of prison or rehab who were taking old mattresses and recycling them. "Breaking down mattresses, building up lives" was its motto, and it had trucks that would go to hotels, college dormitories, hospitals, and individual homes, charging forty dollars to pick up an old mattress. (This was helped by a law in Denver prohibiting dumping of mattresses in the landfill.) They'd haul these mattresses back to the warehouse, where'd they be heated up to kill bedbugs. They would then cut the mattress open, remove the metal parts, and store them in one corner, where they would later be sold for scrap. The stuffing was pulled out and put in another corner, also to be resold. The wood was turned into wood pellets for stoves. There was one kind of foam that could not be recycled in any way, so they were covering those with fabric and selling them to the public as "Green Pup Dog Beds".

I loved the whole idea: It was helping the environment by keeping these things out of the landfill; providing employment for an at-risk population; and according to the former real estate executive running the enterprise, making enough money to be self-sufficient.

(Months later we'd visit a similar mattress recycling enterprise run by a nonprofit in Lowell, Massachusetts. I asked how many mattresses they need to recycle to break even. I was told forty thousand. That would be like the entire city of Burlington giving us their mattresses and box springs every year. So much for that idea. Plus, the staff who accompanied me were freaked out by the bedbugs.)

We came back from Denver psyched about starting our own social enterprise. One of the board members who had gone with us, Owen Milne, volunteered to form a working group to push things forward. It was comprised of myself and other Spectrum staff, Owen and the other board members who had gone to Denver, and a half dozen entrepreneurs in Burlington who had successfully started businesses. Our first move was to think broadly about all the businesses we might want to start, and list those. We ended up with twenty-six, including the beekeeping one, a coffee shop, thrift store, a chess set–making factory, silk screening, and a car detailing business.

We were not sure how to proceed from there, but Owen came up with the idea of engaging a group called Leadership Champlain based out of the Chamber of Commerce. This was a group of about a dozen emerging leaders from area banks, law firms, and corporations, and it was known that, each year, they had to take on one project. Owen asked if they'd help us develop the criteria by which we would select the business, and then to score each one so we'd come up with a finalist.

They jumped right into it. I estimate they saved us at least six months' time. They met with us as a group to try to derive what we thought the criteria should be, and came up with specifics: A business that Spectrum youth will want to do; start-up costs; financial risk to Spectrum if it fails; demand for the business in this area of the state. They then weighted each criterion, which was something I certainly never would have come up with, but it made sense, because not every one was of equal importance.

They then created a matrix in which they took each of the twenty-six business ideas and measured it according to the weighted criteria. Car detailing ended up on top.

Once that was determined, we were tasked with running focus groups with the kids at Spectrum, describing what car detailing entailed and asking if they thought this was something they'd be interested in doing. They indicated yes. I realized I needed to learn more about car detailing in terms of start-up costs and ongoing operating costs. It felt awkward to go to local detailers and ask them, "You mind if I come over and pick your brain about your business because we want to compete against you?" So I Googled "car detailing outside Burlington" and found one about forty minutes away called Mad-a-Dash-Car (get it?). A woman owned and ran it and was happy for me to come by so I could learn as much as possible. She filled me in on everything: what it would cost to start the business (not much), what soap and other liquids to buy, what equipment was needed, what she charged per vehicle, when to upcharge (dog hair was extra), and many other details. It was all very valuable information.

We now knew some key things: The Spectrum kids would want to do this work; start-up costs were minimal, especially if we rented a space rather than buy a building; people were waiting weeks to get their cars detailed now, so there would be a demand for our service, especially in a state like Vermont where winters were harsh and roads were muddy; if the business failed, it would not tank the rest of Spectrum.

I was ready-set-go by this point, but one of our board members, Mike Lane, slowed me down. He was one of the founders of Dealer.com, one of the most successful businesses ever created in Vermont.

"You can open up now," he said, "but it will probably fail. You need a business plan."

Hearing that frustrated me; I was done with the planning and the meetings, and I wanted to get some kind of business up and running and employing kids. But I also knew Mike was probably right. No: He was *definitely* right.

I had no idea how to write a business plan, and Owen and I started to look for someone who could. We made some calls and a number of people recommended Leigh Samuels, who at one point had been a strategic marketing consultant for Green Mountain Coffee Roasters. Owen and I met with her, described what we were hoping to accomplish, and offered to pay her to write our business plan.

"I'll do it on one condition," she replied.

"What's that?" Owen asked.

"That I will not be paid. I will do this only if I am not paid."

"We can live with that," I said.

Leigh brought on Nancy Westbrook, a financial services consultant; they had both served on the board of a local nonprofit called the Clothes Exchange. And Nancy had the same condition: She would only do it pro bono.

When those two started writing the business plan, it was clear we needed more information about the detailing business than what I had gained from my trip to Mad-a-Dash-Car. I hesitated to do this, but I contacted John DuBrul, the owner of The Automaster car dealership and one of our donors because he had a top-of-the-line detailing shop and could give me good advice.

"John," I said, "I know we're going to be competing with you, but I could really use your expertise about car detailing."

"I don't view you as competition," he countered. "I view you as training my future workforce. You teach these kids how to show up on time, how to speak to a boss, how to work with one another, and how to detail cars, and I will then hire them on and pay them a living wage."

That said a lot about him, and he ended up giving us total access to any information we needed to write the business plan.

With the business plan written, it was time to go to the full board of directors for their approval to move ahead and start our social enterprise. It included a big ask: We wanted to use, over the next three years, approximately a third of the gift Mrs. Hoehl had given to us to start and sustain this business.

The board members did not just rubber stamp this; they asked good questions. They pushed back, wanting to know if there was some other way to help our youth develop the soft skills in the workplace that they lacked, other than by establishing our own business. They asked what the per-youth cost was in our JOBS program versus that for this new one. What did we think the outcomes would be in terms of the success rate in our business? They went back and forth, and at one point I started to think they were going to reject our proposal.

Before I go further, I should say something about the Spectrum board. It's an interesting mix. One member was previously the speaker of Vermont's House of Representatives. The president of the largest construction company in the state is a member, as are the chief operating officer of Vermont Teddy Bear and the founder of a software startup. Also on our board is a man who, ten years ago, was living in a refugee camp in Africa and is now a graduate of the University of Vermont. Another member was a homeless teenager, eight years ago, couch surfing through high school, smoking pot every day, when he found his way to Spectrum; he is now a registered nurse, married with two children. There is also a young woman who, five years earlier, had been homeless, lived in Spectrum's shelter, managed to teach herself coding, and became webmaster for a local company.

It was she who spoke up in the midst of this worthwhile debate and said, "I wish this business had been in existence when I was living at Spectrum."

That ended the discussion. A vote was called, and it passed unanimously.

There was still a ton of work to do in order to get our social enterprise up and running. One of our board members, a partner at a law firm, drafted incorporation documents to create what is in Vermont known as an L3C company, which is a for-profit entity that exists under the domain of a nonprofit organization and can still accept charitable donations. We had to find a site, and that became complicated, not only because of zoning and permitting, but also getting permission for the discharge of the water that would be used. Hiring the director of the business would not be easy, nor the youth worker we wanted to be on staff.

None of that, however, even came close to the complexity and challenge of finding the right name and logo for the business.

Seriously.

We went around and around and around with all kinds of names and accompanying logos and could not settle on one. We knew we wanted a car in the logo, but some people thought the car we selected looked "too mean" (think Stephen King's *Christine*), while others thought a different logo made the car look comical (think Herbie in *The Love Bug*). Finally one of our board members, who worked for a local branding and design firm, offered to have his creative experts meet with us free of charge to come up with the best name and logo.

We decided to include in this meeting a few of the youth we thought might be interested in working at the detail business. The creative team asked all of us a number of questions about Spectrum's mission, how this business would fit into it, why we

THE DETAIL WORKS CREW AND ME

were doing it. And at one point one of the Spectrum youth there, a young woman, said, "The kids at Spectrum are really excited about this business opening up."

I looked at her and said, "I believe you, but why is that?"

"Because we've never had anybody believe in us, and this is finally our chance to do something where the adults believe in us."

That blew me away. We have a mission statement on a wall in our main building at Spectrum – I even helped write it – but I cannot tell you without looking at it what it says. But what that young woman said in that meeting at the branding firm? I will remember that for the rest of my life. It is the very core of what Spectrum is and stands for.

We ended up calling the business Detail Works with A Spectrum Enterprise underneath it, and the creative team came up with a logo featuring a car that wasn't too scary and wasn't too funny. We found the right building, and we figured out where the water would go. We hired the two staff, and we bought shirts with the logo on it, and we opened up, and during that first year, we made every possible mistake you could make when starting a new business, which I am told is pretty typical of every new business. But we didn't quit, and we learned from our mistakes, and after three years in existence, instead of a 41 percent rate of our youth making it to ninety days of employment, we are at 86 percent. Following our graduates as they move on to jobs after Detail Works, we know they are succeeding at an even higher rate there.

To me it's been a tremendous success, not only from the outcome statistics, but also by listening to the youth and getting their feedback. I stop by there every few months, ask the staff to leave, give the kids pizza, and tell them, "Okay, I am the boss at Spectrum. I want to know what it's like to work here. What do you like? What do you hate? What needs to change?" Without fail, the feedback is along the lines of the following:

"I love it here."
"The staff treat us with respect."

. .

"You can make a mistake here, and it's not like other places where they just fire you on the spot. Here, the staff encourage you and teach you how to do better."

. .

"I got a promotion here, and I've never gotten a promotion anywhere, at any time, in my entire life."

. .

To go there and hear this from kids who have not had many successes in school or elsewhere in life is just a tremendous lift.

Mrs. Hoehl passed away during the first year of Detail Works and never had the chance to come by and see what she had helped to make happen. Laura Latka was there for the ribbon cutting, and I made sure in my remarks to give her and Mrs. Hoehl credit. Without them, I highly doubt this social enterprise would have been created and have young people feel, for maybe the first time in their lives, that there are adults in the world who believe in them.

· *twenty-one* ·

WE WERE LIVING IN VERMONT for only about a year and a half when I received an email from the Vermont Refugee Resettlement Program (VRRP), which had been sent to me and scores of others. They were recruiting people to serve as host families for those who were about to come to the United States, having fled the civil war in Somalia, and were now living and waiting at a refugee camp in Kenya.

I forwarded it to Marybeth and asked what she thought. "Let's do it," she said.

Vermont has a long history of accepting refugees from war-torn countries, including those from Vietnam, Cambodia, Bosnia, and Nepal. Families coming from Somalia were the latest wave. We emailed VRRP that we would like to learn more, and a week later one of their staff members came by our house to meet with us. She saw that we had plenty of room, and she explained that it was a one-week commitment, and permanent housing would be found for the family after they were with us for seven days.

I asked if each family leaving Africa knew to which state they would be relocated. She smiled and said, "They just know they are coming to America."

We signed up and were told that the Arbows, a family comprising a mother, father, and five small children, would arrive at Burlington International Airport on Saturday, August 28, and that we should be there to meet them.

We went to the airport that morning and watched as a mother departed from a plane with five children in tow, ages one, three, five, seven, and nine. The one-year-old was folded into a pouch on his mother's back, while the other four trailed behind her. All five had kerchiefs around their necks imprinted with the initials

USCRI (United States Committee for Refugees and Immigrants). We wondered where the father was; we would later learn that he had decided not to get on the plane back in Kenya, choosing to remain there with his other family.

Interpreters at the airport welcomed them and introduced them to us. It was a really moving moment, watching a mother and her children escaping war and deprivation to start a new life here. I noticed Marybeth crying. We introduced ourselves, welcoming them as best we could.

It was then a matter of gathering enough cars and car seats to get everyone over to our house a few miles away. It took a while, but eventually we traveled caravan style to our place.

We arrived and the interpreters helped us as we toured through our house to show them bathrooms, showers, the washing machine, oven, and everything else. We had a pretty large backyard with a swing set, and the kids immediately gravitated toward that. A few hours later we fed them dinner. We were not sure what they liked. We had gone to Costco a few days before and stocked up on all kinds of things, especially the chicken and rice the VRRP staff had recommended. It turned out those were immediate hits; and mangoes – the kids loved mangoes. We also discovered they liked orange juice, into which they poured spoonfuls of sugar.

As night fell they all looked exhausted. We had a partially furnished basement that had been used by the previous owners as a bedroom, so we had set up six mattresses with sheets, blankets, and pillows for them to use. We led them down and helped set them up. In a little while, Marybeth and I waved goodnight and headed upstairs, leaving them to their privacy.

About two hours later, I stood at the top of the stairs to listen for any activity and could hear none, so I went quietly downstairs to make sure everyone was okay. I was so surprised and touched by what I saw. All the mattresses were empty except for one. The mother, Zaharra, was still on hers but now surrounded by all five children nestled up to her. I guessed that this is likely how they slept each night in the tent in the refugee camp.

I went back upstairs and told Marybeth, and we sat down to

watch some television. I then heard some noise and looked up to see the oldest son, seven-year-old Abdulkadir, who had come upstairs and walked into our living room. He saw me, cuddled up on my lap, and fell asleep. It was so moving to me, that we had met only hours ago and he already felt this level of familiarity and trust. He stayed there for about half an hour, then awoke and went back downstairs. I then looked at my lap.

He had peed on me.

I have reminded Abdul of this many times in the ensuing years.

Before the Arbows arrived, Marybeth had said to me, "Now, you are planning on taking some time off from Spectrum this week, correct?"

"Um, yes, I guess," I replied, and it was a good thing that I did take time off. It was a lot of work – way more than I expected. VRRP was great, supplying a staff member almost every day to take Zaharra to different places, mostly to fill out forms and register for things, including her children, for school. Marybeth was also taking her to appointments. It didn't make sense for Zaharra to take five children with her to all these meetings, so we were tasked with watching the children along with our own one-year-old Liam, feeding everyone, keeping them occupied. We took day trips with them to museums, the beach, mini-golfing; it was pretty exhausting.

On the last day they were with us, VRRP came to transport them to their apartment in Burlington. We weren't exactly sure what our role was expected to be once the Arbows left our house. VRRP left it pretty vague, and technically we could have said, "We did our one week volunteer thing, that's that," but I think right from the moment the van pulled out of our driveway we knew we weren't just going to let this family fend for themselves. One priority that came to mind immediately was food. They may have been supplied with food stamps, but how were they going to get to the store? That became our role. Once a week Marybeth and I would pull up in our two cars, click in all the car seats, get Zaharra and all the children in there and head for the grocery store. Once there, one of my principal roles was to go to the meat section and steer them away from any pork products since they are Muslim. I'd usually go with the oldest daughter, Madina, who would point to various packages and I'd say, "Mooo," for beef, "Oink, oink, oink," for pork, and make some kind of clucking noise and flap my arms for chicken. It worked. They stayed away from the pork.

This went on for a couple of months, until one day, a Somali woman who had emigrated to the United States a year or so before the Arbows, spotted us at the store and worked it out so that other Somalis would shop with them instead of us. I didn't argue.

Marybeth sent the word around to all our relatives and friends that donations of clothing, toys, games, money, whatever, would be greatly appreciated. Many people responded in kind, so we were frequently taking donations over to them.

Since the Arbows had arrived in August, we kept trying to explain to the kids the concept of winter, specifically snow, but I don't think it quite sank in until the white stuff actually materialized from the sky. They managed, however, like everyone else does in Vermont. One early spring day, I arrived at their apartment, and the kids motioned excitedly for me to go outside. It was apparent they wanted to show me something fascinating. They led me to the sidewalk and pointed to a crack in the concrete where a few green blades of grass were sprouting up. They were starting to learn English by now and a few of them could say, "Look, look!" This was what they were so thrilled about. Grass. Spring was coming.

When they had left our house months earlier, Marybeth turned to me as the vans pulled away, and said, "This is going to be really hard for that mother. Think about it. A single mother with five small children, a new culture, a totally new language." Marybeth knew that Spectrum ran a mentoring program in which we matched adult volunteers with children and teenagers who could benefit from a stable, caring adult in their lives. The volunteers committed to meeting with their mentees once per week for at least one year.

"You should get mentors through Spectrum for all of those

children," she said.

"I totally agree. Why don't we start with you?"

So Marybeth became Madina's mentor. Then we persuaded one of our male neighbors to mentor Abdulkadir. Marybeth was teaching journalism at nearby St. Michael's College at the time and asked one of her fellow professors to mentor Johara, and that professor asked one of her friends to mentor Muna; and when one-year-old Sharmarke got a little older, we recruited someone from our church to mentor him.

I know that those mentors played an indispensable role in that family. I think every mentor did the full year, with most going several years beyond that. And when a mentor had to move on for some reason, we were able to recruit another one to pick up. In fact, when Sharmarke's mentor had to end, I told him, "Don't worry, we'll find someone else for you," to which he replied, "How about you?"

He had me. I knew it was my time to step up.

"Sure," I said.

Marybeth did so much for Madina over the years that it deserves a book of its own. Seriously. She did lots of recreational things, like taking her to the movies, Six Flags, or out shopping. She became involved in her education. We went to Madina's middle school graduation, and it was so gratifying to hear teacher after teacher tell us, "Madina has what it takes to go to college."

Madina went to Burlington High School after that. She became very involved in diversity, equity, and inclusion activities, making sure the district was providing adequate education and services to students of color. She had an after-school job. Zaharra remarried and had two more children, so Madina had many responsibilities at home. We kept in close contact with Madina during this time, especially Marybeth. In her senior year of high school, I emailed her and asked if she was going to apply to colleges, and if so, what she planned to study.

"I do want to go to college," she replied, "and I want to major in something where I am going to help people."

The first thought I had was, Here's a young woman living in

poverty, and if anyone deserves a chance to cash in big on Wall Street or something like that, she does. But she wants to go to college so she can help others. Amazing.

She applied to several colleges and called to tell us that she had been accepted into a private university in New Hampshire and was all set to go.

"Don't sign anything," we told her, "until we look at the acceptance paperwork and what they are offering you for financial aid."

She agreed to do that, and when she came over for dinner a few days later, we could see that this university wanted her to take on debt of around eighty thousand dollars, and of all the freshmen enrolling there, only about half actually graduated within four years. We begged her to reconsider.

"Please," we said, "that is a ton of debt for you to take on, and if you don't graduate, it does not go away, it will follow you for the rest of your life." She had also decided to become a teacher, and paying off that much debt on a teacher's salary would be onerous and take forever.

"Why don't you go to the Community College of Vermont for two years?" we asked her. "You can even come back here and live with us if you want. It'll be practically free, and a much less expensive way to earn your basic college credits, and then you can go wherever you want for the last two years to get your bachelor's degree."

"But I want the full college experience," she said. I knew exactly what she meant: living away from home; meeting new people from different backgrounds; all the fun that comes with campus life. I wanted all that when I was her age and was fortunate enough to get it, as was Marybeth.

"Will you please think about it?" we asked. She did and let us know a few days later that she was turning down that college's offer and would instead go to community college. We asked again if she wanted to live with us, but she declined.

Madina did very well while at the Community College of Vermont, working a part-time job at the same time. After two years there, she applied to a half dozen colleges, was accepted by all, and returned to our house for dinner so we could review them. The financial aid offers were generous this time.

In the end she decided she wanted to attend the nearby University of Vermont. "You should live on campus," we encouraged her. "It'll be fun for you and a good experience."

"No, I'll stay at home," she said, and when we asked why, she replied, "I remember how you warned me about taking on debt two years ago. I don't need to live on campus. It's not worth it."

This time it was us trying to persuade her the other way, to take on debt in order to live at the university, but she had made up her mind.

Even without living on campus, there was still some debt involved with her going to UVM, so I called a friend who happened to be head of the university foundation.

"I can't believe you don't have scholarships there for New American students," I told him.

"We certainly do," he replied. "Give me her name."

He phoned me the next day. "She did not check the box for New American on her application. She checks that, she's going for free."

I turned to Marybeth and asked, "Why do you think Madina didn't check that box?"

Marybeth's response still gets me choked up. "She didn't check it because she doesn't see herself as a New American. She sees herself as an American."

We called Madina and advised her to go back to her application and check the box. She did so and received a full scholarship to UVM, one of the premiere public universities in the country.

A Transfer Student Day at the university was scheduled in August. Zaharra was working that day and could not attend, so we took a break from our vacation week and went with Madina, going to all the talks and seminars. We sat with Madina and her advisor and helped her pick out her courses, and at the end, we took a picture of her in the main quad, arms raised and a huge smile on her face.

UNIVERSITY OF VERMONT GRADUATION

For the next two years Madina studied hard, and as she always had, held down a job. She even landed a position for a while in the Civil Rights Division in the Federal building in Burlington. We'd get together with her every few months. She got engaged to a Somali man during her last year of college, and Marybeth threw a wedding shower for her. She, Liam, and I attended the wedding in the Islamic Center along with Zaharra and all of Madina's siblings. Marybeth provided the food for the reception that night. When Madina later became pregnant, Marybeth threw the baby shower for her and her friends.

Madina graduated on time, and we were all there for the commencement ceremony. It was an emotional moment, thinking back to a nine-year-old girl stepping off an airplane fourteen years earlier, not knowing a word of English, with her four younger siblings behind her and a mother who had to be completely bewildered by this new land and all the challenges before her. But Madina did it, and while it wasn't solely because of Marybeth, Marybeth had a great deal to do with it. A great deal.

A few days after the graduation, Madina gave birth to a girl.

She named her Zaharra.

After her mother.

· twenty-two ·

FOR ME, ONE OF THE BEST THINGS about Spectrum is its size. It's compact and manageable. We have about sixty full-time employees, which, for Vermont, may be big, but compared to the nonprofits in New York City and Connecticut where I had worked, it's small. When I was at St. Christopher's in Dobbs Ferry, the executive director there, Luis Medina, once said to me, "You should always work at a smallish-size place. It fits your personality." I bristled at that when he said it – "What: You don't think I can handle something big?" – but I think he was correct. I've had offers to leave Spectrum and take over organizations a lot bigger, but for various reasons, I've turned them down. Part of it is that I love where I am, and part of it is that leading an organization this size does allow me some time to spend with the kids themselves. It's very easy, when you're an executive director, to have your time consumed by meetings about budgets, strategic planning, supervision, and committees. We do have all that at Spectrum. They are necessary and instrumental to fulfilling our mission. But it's nice to take a break once in a while and spend time to get to know the youth we are serving, as well as to know our staff members better.

When I arrived at Spectrum, I made a commitment to myself that I would cook and serve a meal once a month. I occasionally do it at one of our residences, mostly in our Drop-In Center, sometimes lunch, but usually dinner; and I try and make something special, something more than tacos or burgers. There's an apricot chicken dish recipe, which I got from Fit Pregnancy magazine when Marybeth was expecting Liam, that they absolutely love. Coconut curry chicken is another hit as are pesto pasta with sausage and shrimp with linguini Alfredo. All big hits with the kids at Spectrum.

I make the meal, help serve it, and then sit down at one of the tables and eat with them. That's where I get to know them and connect with them. It's fun, and it reminds me of what all those meetings, committees, and conferences are for and why we spend our time at them.

So here are a couple of real-life vignettes, stories of different kids I've gotten to know at Spectrum since I started here in 2003. I rarely know how they came to Spectrum or what led them to seek help from us; they almost never volunteer this, and I don't ask. Almost all have a case manager or therapist at Spectrum who does know this, but by law, they are prohibited from telling me. I've changed the names below to protect their privacy, and any whom I could contact to ask for permission to tell their story, I have, and they agreed.

RANDY

Randy arrived at Spectrum at age seventeen, assigned by the Vermont Department for Children and Families to live in one of our houses. He did very well, and after about a year, earned his high school diploma, which is a big deal. Not all of the kids we work with make it that far.

When Randy turned eighteen, he transitioned to another residence we have that affords more independent living, and I sat with him shortly after he moved there. I found out he liked cars, and in fact, had a part-time job at an auto parts store in town. So I said to him, "Randy, you earned your diploma. Congratulations. That is really great. I don't know if you want to go to college or not, but maybe you would consider going to an auto tech school and learn to be a mechanic. You can do really well in that field, and you can make a nice living for yourself."

"Yes," he said, "I'm actually thinking of doing that. There's an auto mechanic school in Wyoming I'm thinking of applying to."

"Wyoming?" I said. "Why Wyoming? Do you have family there? Do you know anyone there?"

"No, I don't. I just heard that there's a good auto mechanic school in Wyoming so I am thinking of applying."

"Don't do that," I said. "We can find a good auto school for you right here in Vermont. I mean, if you go to Wyoming, you'll be all on your own."

Randy looked at me and said, "But Mark, I've been on my own my whole life anyway."

He didn't say it with any flair or any drama. He just stated it as a matter of fact, just as you or I might say, "I have brown hair," or "My eyes are blue."

I almost started to argue back with him. I almost said, "You're not on your own. You have me. You have the staff and counselors here. You have us." But I didn't. I stopped myself. Something in me felt, if this is Randy's reality, if this is how he sees himself, that he's on his own now and he's been on his own for his whole life, I don't have any right to try and talk him out of that. So I didn't.

Randy left us a few months later. He just kind of took off, which happens sometimes, even though we don't want it to. And when it does, I usually presume the worst. It often means they eventually end up in the adult homeless system or even the prison system. But about four years later, I was at a bowling alley with Liam, who I think was eight at the time, and there, about a dozen lanes over, I spotted Randy. Apparently he hadn't gone to Wyoming, or if he did, he was back. He was bowling with a bunch of young people his age, and he was laughing and obviously having a very good time. I was going to go over and say hello, but I didn't. I've found these things can be embarrassing for young people when they are with their friends; no one wants to admit they were once living in a group home or a residence for homeless teenagers.

So I just let it go, and I watched him from afar for the next hour or so, satisfied that it looked like he had done all right: He landed on his feet, he has friends, he's not alone, and he looks happy.

And that's what matters.

JACKSON

Early in my tenure at Spectrum a nineteen-year-old young man named Jackson showed up at our Drop-In Center for a hot meal.

When we found out he was living in a car, we invited him to live in our shelter. After a few months, he did well enough to move over to our transitional living residence, where he'd have his own room and be able to stay for a few years if he needed to.

A few months later, one of our board members hosted a house party that some of our staff attended, and one of them brought Jackson along to say a few words. I listened to him speak about his life and about how grateful he was for the help he was receiving from us. I've worked with thousands of homeless young people over the last four decades, and Jackson stood out because of the kindness and sincerity that radiated from him.

He always had a job while he was with us, but what Jackson wanted more than anything else was to join the Marines. I didn't encourage him, nor did I discourage him. The military can be a good character-building experience for some people who have had a difficult life up until that point, but it can also be overwhelming for others.

Jackson applied, was accepted, and shipped out to boot camp in Parris Island, South Carolina.

Jackson wrote me, and it sounded like he was doing fine. I asked my father-in-law and other family members and friends who were Marines to write to him, to encourage him, and they did that. He persevered, and when it was time for him to graduate from boot camp I knew that none of his family would be there, so I asked his Spectrum case manager, Ray Beaver, to fly down and be with him at the ceremony.

Jackson phoned me the day of his graduation. He sounded thrilled. "We are so proud of you," I told him. "Congratulations!"

Unfortunately, things spiraled downward from there. Jackson transitioned on to the next phase of military training, and to this day I don't know what happened, but within a few weeks he was in trouble and then discharged. I called and called to get some sense of what was going on, but I couldn't reach him and had no luck getting any information from the Marines.

Soon the staff in our Drop-In Center let me know that Jackson was back in Burlington and occasionally coming around for a meal. I told them, "Please have him contact me as soon as you see him again. Tell him he can come back and live with us if he wants to." But I didn't hear from him.

About a month later I was on my computer at home on a Saturday night and pulled up the online version of the *Burlington Free Press* just to see what was going on that day. I saw a headline about a suicide. A young man had led police on a high-speed chase and then killed himself with a gun.

It was Jackson.

It is very strange how the human brain sometimes works. I sat there and saw that name and my first thought was, "Sounds familiar. How do I know that name?" I look back now and realize that my mind did not want to admit what was so apparent: that Jackson was dead and had taken his life.

But I snapped out of it and quickly realized who it was. I immediately tried to reach Ray Beaver at home, but he was out. He called me back hours later. I had to break the news to him. He was as shocked and heartbroken as I was.

There was a wake held for Jackson at a funeral home in the town in southern Vermont where he had grown up. Ray and I and several others from Spectrum went to it, including the board member who had met Jackson at his house party. Someone had taped up pictures of Jackson as a child. It was just so sad. His body lay in the casket, dressed in his Marine uniform.

There was an obituary in the paper, with the standard line to the effect of, "He leaves behind the loving family of ..." A few days later I got a call from a woman who had been a neighbor to Jackson and his family when he was growing up.

"That obituary was a lie," she told me. "There was no loving family for Jackson. If he had a loving family at all, it was you people at Spectrum."

She then told me about how her son and Jackson had been close childhood friends, but for some reason, their friendship had come to a sudden halt. She didn't know why, but right before he entered the Marines, Jackson came down to see her son, all these years later. Jackson told her son that, when they were little, he had once stolen some Pokemon cards from him, and he now wanted to apologize for doing that.

She told me that she was very moved by Jackson's act, that it spoke about the kind of person he was and his integrity. I said that I felt the same way.

I kept a picture of Jackson in his military uniform from his time at Quantico taped to my office wall for years. There's still a picture of him in our office hallway at Spectrum, having dinner with a bunch of the other kids in the house, a big smile on his face. Ray's gone from Spectrum, and maybe one other person who presently works at Spectrum remembers Jackson. Everyone else who works here walks by that photo every day, not knowing the story behind that one young man's smile.

But I know who he is. I remember him. He was a special person who, like many of the kids at Spectrum, had apparently endured great suffering early in life.

We loved him, and I think he knew that we loved him. I take comfort in that. Jackson did not have much happiness in his short life, but at least for a brief period he was surrounded by people who cared about him. We loved Jackson, but for some reason, we couldn't save him.

DROP-IN CENTER OPEN HOUSE FOR LEGISLATORS

One December evening we held an open house at Spectrum to which invited legislators could come and learn more about the work we do with homeless and at-risk youth and families. We met in our Drop-In Center. About five members of the Vermont house and senate showed up. A dozen of our kids were there along with some of our staff and board members.

We started with a presentation about what Spectrum does and who we help, then opened it up for questions. A legislator asked the youth there, "How many of you have ever actually been homeless yourself, even if only for one night?"

All raised their hands.

"Where do you sleep when you are homeless?" he asked.

The answers varied: "in a parking garage ... on a park bench

... in laundromats ... behind restaurants."

He then asked, "Do any of you know someone who is out there tonight, right now?"

It was only about ten degrees above zero on this particular night. Approximately half of the kids raised a hand.

A different legislator asked, "If you could turn the clock back five or ten years, what would you do differently so that you would not be in the position you are in right now?"

The young man standing next to her answered first. "Ten years ago I was age nine and living with my family in northeastern Vermont. My parents were alcoholics, but not the kind who would each have a martini and go quietly to bed. My parents would each drink a fifth of vodka every night and then beat the hell out of each other and beat the hell out of us. So there wasn't much I could do to change things."

Then the young woman next to him spoke. "Ten years ago I was eight. My mother was a crack addict. My father was a heroin addict. He died in prison from an overdose. Eventually I became an addict. I ended up going to rehab, and I knew that if I returned to my home neighborhood, with my family and all my drug-using friends there, I'd go right back to using. But I heard about Spectrum, and I am glad I did, because now I am staying clean. I have a job, and I'm moving ahead with my life; but, yeah, same thing: There wasn't much I could do at age eight to change things."

Another young man spoke. "My parents divorced when I was little. My mother moved out of Vermont, and so I lived with my father. At fifteen I told him I was gay, and he kicked me out of the house, and I've been homeless ever since."

Stories like this went on for about the next twenty minutes. You could just see the look on the legislators' faces, a look of shock and dismay.

Finally, one young woman sitting on the couch, who had yet to say anything, spoke up. "I know when you look at us," she said, "you are probably thinking, 'Oh, these are kids who are running away just for the sake of running away, or rebelling for the sake of rebelling.' But the truth is that every kid who comes through these doors has a different story to tell, and most of those stories are quite tragic."

I was so glad she said that. You could hear a pin drop. The legislators looked almost stunned. They had heard first-hand the reality of teenage homelessness, and their beliefs about how and why people end up homeless were blown away. For a few moments, no one spoke.

The silence was broken by the legislator who had asked the original question of the kids there: "All I know is that I am going to a Dialogue Night at a local high school later tonight, and I am not going to hear stories like this."

NAT

I had an 8 a.m. finance committee meeting one morning at Spectrum, and I knew it was the birthday of one of the board members who'd be attending. I stopped at a bakery on the way in, figuring I'd buy a croissant or something and take it to the meeting with a candle in it for her. As I walked from my car to the bakery, I spotted Nat, a young man well-known to Spectrum, waiting on line for a bus to arrive. Nat had been in just about every single program Spectrum has over the years, and I would frequently see him in our Drop-In Center enjoying a meal or talking to staff. He had also once been at a barbeque in the backyard of one of our houses, when I cooked steak for everyone. From that point on, every time I saw him, he'd ask, "When are you grilling steak again Mark? Boy did I love that steak." I would also frequently see him hanging out on Church Street; he is one of those young men who, to pedestrians, might look intimidating due to his physical size and appearance, but to me, he is a big, sweet, teddy bear kind of a kid.

Before I entered the bakery I walked over to him and said, "Good morning Nat, how are you?"

"Good," he answered, "but last night I went to Drop-In to say goodbye to everyone there."

"Why is that?" I asked him, "Are you moving away?"

"No." he replied, "Today is my birthday; I turn twenty-four, so I'm too old to go in there anymore."

I felt so bad when I heard that, but I got it. At some point we had to set a cut-off age for the kids at Spectrum or we'd end up in a mission-creep situation, which isn't good for anyone. Twenty-four was really the max.

"I'll be right back," I told him. I went into the bakery and while buying the croissant for my board member it occurred to me, "It's Nat's birthday too, why don't I buy him one as well? I may not have the candle to put in it, but what the heck." So I did that.

I exited the bakery and expected to find Nat just where I left him. But he wasn't there. I sort of panicked, wondering where he had disappeared to, and then I noticed that a bus had pulled up and was now parked there, although it looked like it was ready to pull out and go. I guessed that Nat might be on it, so I ran over and pressed my face up against the darkened windows, hoping to see if he was in there. By about the third window, I was able to pick out Nat's bulky silhouette, so I banged on the glass to get his attention. He saw me and got out of his seat, motioning to the driver not to pull away yet and to open the side door.

The driver opened the door, and Nat came to where I was standing, with a quizzical look on his face.

"What's the matter?" he asked.

I handed him the croissant. "Happy birthday, Nat," I said, "and even though you are too old to be in Spectrum any longer, you will always be there in our heart."

"Thanks Mark," he said, "And I know that."

MARIAH

We took in a young woman at Spectrum who had been living in a Southern state before she came to Vermont and ended up homeless. She started at our eight-bed shelter and did well enough after only a few weeks to transition over to our independent living residence, where she stayed for about a year and a half. We then helped her move into her own apartment in Burlington. She worked a full-time job downtown, where I would periodically run into her. One time I asked her if she regretted moving to Vermont, because she ended up becoming homeless.

"No," she replied, "I don't regret it at all, because if I hadn't moved to Vermont, I never would have met the wonderful people at Spectrum."

Wow. That stopped me in my tracks. It really showed how much of an impact our people had made on her, that in her mind it was actually worth it to become homeless, if the result was that she would meet and connect with our staff members.

A few months later she sent me this Facebook message:

Hey Mark. I never really thanked you guys properly so I am sending you a message to tell you how thankful I am of Spectrum. A few years ago I didn't have anywhere to go, and you guys took me in. I knew I didn't want to be homeless anymore. I mean, I have been homeless for about 75 percent of my life, and I was really ready for a change. I didn't know exactly where to start, but you guys were there to help me every step of the way. Even when times were hard and I felt like giving up, you guys were there encouraging me and letting me know that I could do it. I started off on the streets, then to the shelter, next to the residence, and well, now I couldn't ask for more. I have an amazing job at which I recently got a raise and a nice apartment downtown. Next it is going back to school for animation so I can go work for Disney. All of Spectrum helped me get to where I am today, and I am thankful for that.

Every kid that walks through that door is wanting to make some sort of change or they wouldn't have walked in. Even though they may not say it, they are thankful for you guys too because at some point they needed your help and Spectrum provided it.

A few months later I ran into her again, and she told me she had changed her plans and decided to enlist in the United States Navy. I was surprised by her decision, but this was what she wanted to do with her life, and I told her I would support her in whatever choice she made. Right before she left town I received this message from her:

> *Hey Mark, I didn't get a chance to stop by and say bye before I go off and become a sailor, but I wanted to say thank you, and all of Spectrum, for everything you guys do. There need to be more places like this across America and it is sad there isn't. Spectrum has been behind me 100 percent in everything I wanted to do and become the last four years of my life*
>
> *I just want to say how much I appreciate everything. Four years ago I was a different person. I wasn't as confident in myself as I am today and that is because Spectrum believed in me and I saw that, and then I started believing in myself. I have grown so much with the help of you guys.*

Then I received this Facebook message from her after she finished Navy boot camp:

> *Hey Mark, everything is good. After three months of waiting to do my classes for my job I am finally in class, and if everything goes as planned I should graduate from here June 6th and be on my way back up that way for a week or so before I go on to my next duty station. I'm enjoying myself. The Navy has shown me a great time so far. I'm so excited to be part of this. Now I can go and tell all those people that never believed in me that I am somebody and I get to travel the world and do things that they will never get to see or do in their life. And thanks to you guys. You have helped me so much and helped me get this far and I am so thankful for everything you guys have done for me and I appreciate you guys keeping in touch with me. If you didn't know, my family disowned me a long time ago and now I consider Spectrum my family. When I come back to*

*Burlington for a week or so I would like to volunteer with
you guys. Maybe help cook a meal at Drop-In or visit the
Maple Street house and talk to the individuals there one
evening and let them know how much they can gain if they
stick with the program and put forth the effort.*

And one more:

*Hey Mark, hope all is well up there. I am doing great
down here. I just wanted to say hi and let you know I am
doing well. I started college at the beginning of August
and so far so good. Working on a degree in art. I follow
Spectrum on Facebook and see all the good things going
on, and it puts a smile on my face. I'm thinking I might
come back to Burlington for the Thanksgiving/Christmas
holiday. If I make it up there I plan to stop by.*

She did come by. We had lunch together and I invited one of her
favorite Spectrum counselors. We reminisced, laughed, and then
she got in her car and began the drive to California, where her
Navy base was located. That was the last time I saw her. I'm really
proud of her.

BEN

Ben arrived at Spectrum at age eighteen. His parents divorced
when he was a child, and he had been raised by his mother. Ben
and his mother had trouble getting along, until it got to the point
where, as he put it, "I needed a break from her, and she needed a break from me." She must have heard about Spectrum and
brought him to us, where we accepted him into our residence on
Maple Street.

He told us he was receiving Supplemental Security Income (SSI),
which is the Social Security program for individuals who are disabled, either physically, mentally or emotionally. It guarantees a
monthly check from the federal government for the rest of your life.

But Ben didn't want to be receiving this check any longer.

"There's nothing wrong with me," he said. "I want to work and earn a living, not receive a government check."

That impressed me, that Ben had enough self-respect and initiative that he didn't want to receive government assistance, even if he had somehow formally qualified for it.

Our staff took him to the local Social Security office. He asked to be removed from the SSI rolls. The government workers there were flummoxed because no one had ever asked this before. "Everyone we know is trying to get on SSI," they said. "We've never had someone ask to be taken off of it. We don't even know how to do that."

It took months, and they had to get their instructions from the main Social Security office in Washington, D.C. but it eventually happened.

Ben lived at Spectrum for two years. At one point he had a job at a grocery store near where I live and he spotted me. He approached me and started complaining about something related to one of the rules in the house. I said I'd look into it, but the next day I received an email from him apologizing for bothering me during my personal time.

"Don't apologize," I told him. "You were advocating for yourself, which is an important life skill to learn. Good for you."

I began to chat with him during meals in Drop-In, and in one conversation, he made several references to "my church." I don't bring religion up with kids at Spectrum, but I was intrigued and asked him to which church he belonged. He responded that he had been taking instructions to become a Catholic at the University of Vermont Catholic Center and would be baptized at the upcoming Easter Vigil service at the Cathedral.

"Do you mind if I attend?" I asked. He smiled and said he did not mind at all.

I showed up that evening along with his Spectrum case manager, Ray Beaver. Ben's mother was there and I met her for the first time. She leaned over to Ray and me and whispered, "It means everything to Ben that you two are here."

Ben left Spectrum shortly after that and moved into his own

place less than a mile from Spectrum. He had a job, as he always did while with us at Spectrum, although it was always one that paid minimum wage, such as a convenience store, gas station, or fast food restaurant. I stayed in touch with him, getting together for lunch every few months.

About a year later, Marybeth and I were in our car on a Saturday afternoon, two days after having spent Thanksgiving on Long Island with family. I was driving and she was checking Facebook when she asked, "Do you know a Joan Z_____?"

"I know a young man who has that last name," I replied. "He used to live at Spectrum. Why?"

Marybeth read me this woman's post: "Hi. My son lives in Burlington, Vermont, and lost his wallet. I live five hours away, can someone there please help him?"

"I actually think I have his cell number," I said and dialed him.

Ben answered and when I said, "Hey, how are you?" he replied, "Not very good, I lost my wallet."

"Are you around tonight?" I asked.

"Yes, I'm working the late shift at the McDonald's in South Burlington," he said.

"I'll come by around ten and lend you some money. Liam has a soccer game, and then we're supposed to go out for pizza with his teammates and families. I'll swing by after that."

We got to the McDonald's later that night, and I went in, while Liam and Marybeth waited in the car. I spotted Ben behind the counter flipping burgers and making shakes. I waved to him and motioned that I'd be sitting at a table.

It took a few minutes before he could break from the counter and sit with me. I sat there looking around. It was depressing. One person who looked inebriated sat slumped over a table. Another man, who might have been homeless, was in another corner. And here was Ben, making minimum wage or a little higher, working the night shift; and he was one of Spectrum's success stories.

He came over, we chatted, and I gave him $120, telling him he could repay me whenever he wanted.

I left there thinking Ben could do better. I believed he had the

intelligence to go to college and the drive and work ethic to succeed on that level. I also knew he loved working on cars. He had
spent some time in Job Corps, in its auto mechanics program, but
to actually work at an auto shop or dealership, I knew he'd have
to return to school and obtain an associate's degree and mechanic's license.

We met for lunch at a Burlington restaurant two weeks later.
"Listen Ben, you're doing well," I told him, "but I think you can
do better than working the overnight shift at McDonald's making
little better than minimum wage. You will never get ahead that
way. I know you like fixing cars, and Vermont Technical College
has an auto program at its campus in Randolph. I know the president of the college. How about you and I go down there together
to meet him and see what it's like?"

He said he'd think about it. A week later he called and said
he'd go.

Vermont Tech is about an hour away from Burlington, so one
afternoon I picked Ben up, and we drove down there. We met the
college president, Dan Smith, toured the campus, saw the dorms,
had lunch in the cafeteria, and then went to the building where
the auto program was housed.

"How does this auto shop compare with the one at Job Corps?"
I asked Ben.

"No comparison," he replied. "This one is light years ahead."

We introduced ourselves to the man running the auto school
there. He and Ben started talking about engines, brake systems,
carburetors, catalytic converters. To me it was like observing two
people speaking a foreign language. I barely know how to put air
in the tires.

When there was a break in their technological conversation, I
asked, "What is the job placement rate for graduates from here?"

"One hundred percent," he replied. "There is a huge need for
certified mechanics in Vermont and throughout the country."

"What kind of salary are people earning when they leave here?"

"Twenty-five dollars an hour to start, depending on what part
of the state and in what kind of setting, but mostly around that."

Way more than any convenience store or fast food place will ever pay, I thought.

Ben and I shook his hand, thanked him for the time, and left. We talked the entire ride back, and I told him I thought he should apply to the college.

"I don't know," he said. "I'd be giving up my Section 8 apartment and the job I have."

I understood what he was saying. Kids like Ben don't have a safety net beneath them like I did at his age. If I took a chance on something and it didn't work out, I knew I had a family to take me in and take care of me. He did not. Most of the kids we work with at Spectrum do not.

But I encouraged him to think about it, that it was a great opportunity in which I believed he could succeed.

We arrived back in Burlington, and I pulled in front of his apartment house. As he exited from my car, Ben extended his hand and said, "Thanks Mark. I'm not used to people doing nice things like this for me."

That just blew me away. It really did. "I'm not used to people doing nice things like this for me"? I mean, really, what had I done? Taken an afternoon off to drive him to visit a college. My parents drove me up and down the East Coast to look at many colleges, and then did it four more times with my siblings. I also thought about all the people who had done nice things for me in my life. My parents. Grandparents. Aunts. Uncles. Siblings. Teachers I had. Coaches. Job supervisors. Right up to the present day. The good friends I have. Marybeth. My coworkers at Spectrum.

I am very used to having people do nice things for me.

But Ben wasn't used to that, and I suspect very few of the youth we work with at Spectrum are. They *are* used to witnessing domestic violence. They *are* used to being shuttled from home to home and school to school their entire lives. They *are* used to poverty. They *are* used to being hungry.

But they're *not* used to people doing nice things for them.

"You're welcome," was all I could muster in response.

A few weeks later Ben told me he was going to apply to

Vermont Tech.

"Fantastic," I replied. "A very good decision."

I emailed Sabina Haskell, a woman I knew at the Vermont Student Assistance Corporation, asking her to recommend "the best person there who can help this young man to not only apply to Vermont Tech but also for financial aid." Sabina referred me to Monica Sargent, so I went with Ben to meet with her and fill out everything. Monica did a masterful job finding every bit of financial aid for which Ben was eligible.

A few weeks later Ben was notified that he was accepted. I emailed my friend who was president of the college, asking him, "Can Vermont Tech provide even more financial aid, can you guarantee him a dorm room, and can you guarantee a campus job for Ben?" Dan Smith came through on all counts.

Then I found out that a student in the college's auto program is required to buy his own tools, and they cost several thousand dollars. "Spectrum will pick that up," I told Ben, and we were able to do this because one anonymous donor gives us funds for expenses like this that will allow kids to progress in their education.

Next was an internship, which he'd be required to do as part of his auto training. I called the woman I know who owns Girlington Garage, and she agreed to take him on.

Ben left his McDonald's job and gave up his apartment. And when the day came for him to move to the campus, I volunteered to help him pack the moving van. But I did one other thing: I phoned one of our Spectrum mentors, Bob Wheel, because he is a big strong guy with a big strong truck, to see if he could help us. Those tools we paid for weighed about four hundred pounds. Bob showed up just as I knew he would.

Ben's first year at Vermont Tech went very well. He made the Dean's List, although he told me he was upset that he had one B among all A's. The college asked him to become a resident advisor for the following year, which allowed him to be there completely rent-free. At the end of the first year, he had nowhere to live, so Marybeth and I welcomed him into our house for a few weeks.

His second year didn't go well at all. He got into a shoving match with another student, which led to his losing his RA job and the free housing. There were other problems, and it looked like he was going to drop out. I was really disappointed. He had seemed to make so much progress. So much was going his way. So many people had stepped up to help him, and now it seemed as if it had all been for naught.

But Ben surprised me. He figured out a place to live, passed all his classes, and in May of 2018, received his associate's degree diploma at the college graduation. I went, as well as another Spectrum staff member, along with a priest who knew Ben. We were the family for his graduation.

A few months later, Vermont Tech held its annual dinner to thank those individuals who have donated to the college. It was a completely filled room. Ben was the featured speaker. The college asked me to introduce him, and I could not have been prouder to do so. He gave a great speech and received a standing ovation.

He later obtained his bachelor's degree, in business, and was even selected to give the commencement speech. We still keep in contact on a regular basis.

I have no doubt he will succeed in whatever he pursues in his life.

SHEILA

Eighteen-year-old Sheila showed up at Spectrum looking for a place to live, and during the intake interview, showed our counselor bottles of Prozac, Risperidone, Effexor, and Depakote, which she had been prescribed. She said that she had a history of cutting herself. She also disclosed that she had just been discharged from a psychiatric hospital, and that they gave her those medications to take with her. She had tried to go back and live with her mother, whom she had last lived with when she was age eight, but her mother was still an alcoholic, so Sheila didn't think she could live there.

Even though we deal every day with young people who have emotional difficulties and are on medication, our staff were alarmed by the severity of this young woman's condition. But they decided to give her a chance, and she started living in our shelter.

She had been with us for a few months when she wrote this letter.

One of the most important days of my life was in August 2005. I got into the Spectrum shelter. It was such a relief to get into the shelter, it pretty much saved my life.

Before that, I had spent eight months in a program for mental health in Ohio. The program did not help me out, and I had nobody to tell what was going on who would actually believe me. The eight months I was there, my cutting progressively got worse. I was dealing with anorexia and got in many fights with other residents and staff. Toward the end I went to jail for assault against a staff member. When I turned 18, I was discharged and sent back to Vermont.

Everything hit me so hard, I was at a loss of what to do. I returned to my mother's, where I hadn't lived since I was eight, since I had spent ten years in foster homes, group homes, shelters, detention centers, and programs. And my mother's problem of alcoholism was still there.

When I was at my mother's I ended up in the mental hospital a week later for two suicide attempts. I just broke down. In June I decided to get involved with Spectrum, and started working on my GED. I got my GED in August and Spectrum threw a graduation party for me. As I did all this I pushed myself to do what was important. I didn't let my depression hold me back this time, because I had to prove to people what I was capable of.

I continuously went to the Spectrum Drop-In Center and talked to them, and told them that I would prove to them that I could turn things around and be safe. As a couple weeks went by, they saw me turning things around. I started going to counseling again, I got involved in the JOBS program at Spectrum, and agreed to go back to the mental health program in South Burlington, and actually complete it this time. They were very surprised at how fast I turned things around.

After five weeks at the Spectrum shelter, staff worked with me to get into the Maple Street house, which is also through Spectrum.

Maple Street has been a great experience, and everybody continues to help me out every day. Staff was really supportive the few times I relapsed and cut myself. Those few times, I was sent back to the shelter to make sure I would be okay. I also went back to the shelter about three weeks ago because I didn't have a job. I spent every day looking for a job and collecting applications. At first I looked at it as a punishment, because staff said I had to be looking for a job all day every day, but I then realized they were just trying to help me out. I ended up finding a great job at the hospital doing housekeeping. I'm a lot happier now since I have so much going for me. I have a good job, I'm going to school, and I think the class I'm taking (Dimensions of Learning) will help me out a lot with reading and my fear of talking in front of people. I'm also involved in the Chill program where I learn how to snowboard.

That one day where I got into the Spectrum shelter helped me out so much, because it led to so many other things. Spectrum worked with me to get a stable place to live, they helped me find a job, they supported me when I had some hard times, and helped me find healthy and positive hobbies. By being at Spectrum I have found happiness in myself, great people, a reason to keep going, and so many new experiences. Without Spectrum, I don't know where I would be today. They saved my life and helped me open my eyes and realize how much was out there for me.

Sheila continued to live at Maple Street and continued to improve. This is the letter she wrote as she was getting ready to leave.

When I first moved into Maple Street in 2005, I didn't think I would complete this program. I was still very hopeless of life. I didn't think things could get better. I was struggling with many things, and had a very negative outlook on life.

I remember moving into Maple Street and staying in my room for like two or three days, because I didn't want to talk to anyone. I told staff I would probably get kicked out because I got kicked out of everywhere else. I didn't really have a plan for my life, and I wasn't working anywhere. I didn't really care what happened any more.

I then slowly started to get things together, by getting a job, and taking a couple of classes at the Community College of Vermont. I worked at one job for about two months and walked out, then another one for two weeks and quit. Then I worked at a deli for two months, and left to work for the Vermont Youth Conservation Corps, where I found real happiness in life. I worked really hard that summer, and it really opened my eyes, and I realized how good life could be. My boss at the Corps helped me get my driver's license, and I bought my first car for my 20th birthday with all the money I saved. I got a job at a horse farm part-time after the Corps ended, and I still work there after eight months. About a month ago I got a second job at a car parts store as a delivery driver. Between both jobs I work 40 to 50 hours a week, and it feels great. In the last month and a half I've saved up $900. I'm about to move into my first apartment and buy a better car.

*I think I've changed tremendously in the last year and a
half. It's like one extreme to another. I feel like a new
person. This is the first program I've ever completed, and
I'm very proud of myself. It's amazing to see that I've
made it this far in life, after everything that has happened.*

Seven years later I was standing in line at the Department of Motor
Vehicles to get my license renewed, looked up, and who did I see
a few spots behind me but Sheila.

"Hey, Sheila!" I yelled.

She smiled, we hugged, and I asked her how she was doing.

"Really well," she said, and told me she still has the auto parts
job and the horse farm job.

"Someone told me you are married and have a child. Is that
true?"

"I am married," she said, "but I now have two children – boys."

"Do they get along?"

"Sometimes!" she replied.

"Well, that's pretty typical!" I said.

We chatted a few minutes more, mostly about Spectrum and
some of the staff we both knew, most of whom had left Spectrum
by then, and one or two who were still there. Then my number
was called, so I hugged her and said goodbye.

After I left the DMV, I reflected on that day she arrived at
Spectrum – how desperate she was and how dire the situation
seemed, compared to how she seems now. I give our staff so much
credit for giving her a chance and then hanging in there with her
through many, many challenges. And I credit her, as well, for not
giving up on herself, for doing the hard work of addressing her
issues, and for having the humility to ask for help.

MIKE STAMATIS

One of the programs we run at Spectrum helps teenagers who
are in the foster care system in Burlington and another city, St.
Albans. It's called the Youth Development Program and is for
young men and women, ages fourteen and up, who are living with

foster parents or relatives. The program helps them to acquire what's known as independent living skills, preparing them to go out on their own in the near future.

In 2010 the woman who ran it for us, Amanda Churchill, told me there was one foster youth she really wanted me to meet: Mike Stamatis. She told me he had spina bifida, was in a motorized wheelchair, and had incredible energy and spunk. He was also one of the leaders on the statewide Youth Development Committee.

When he was at Spectrum one day, I met him and thanked him for the volunteer work he was doing. He had a great smile and disposition; he also had on a Red Sox hat, so I joked with him about that, teasing him because I'm a life-long Mets fan.

I'd run into Mike every few months at Spectrum, and we'd always have a fun chat. Then that fall I received an email from Chris Bohjalian, the best-selling novelist who, at that time, also wrote a weekly column for the *Burlington Free Press*; he wanted to know if there was a Spectrum youth he could interview for a column. I immediately recommended Mike.

The column ran on December 12, 2010, entitled, "At last, stars smiling on Mike Stamatis." It was a beautiful piece. Chris interviewed Mike on his twentieth birthday, and in the opening paragraph, Mike said, "I'm enjoying my life more now than I ever have in the past. The best birthday gift I could have is to see my life continue on this course." He went on to talk about his earlier years, which were difficult, and as Chris put it, "Mike had lived a life that made Job look like a lottery winner." He had been in many foster homes, including one in which the foster father took his own life. When he finally arrived at the home of John and Mary Provost in Burlington, the latter told Mike, "This is the last foster home you'll have. We'll make this work."

Mike blossomed in Burlington. Amanda set him up with Vermont Adult Learning so he could finish his high school diploma, and he also started taking classes at the Community College of Vermont. She also got him going on a driver's permit so he could learn to drive in a specially equipped vehicle. She bought him a gym membership, and he learned to swim, and from there he joined a sled hockey team and played motorized soccer. As he told Chris, "Being a handicapped person shouldn't stop you from acting on your dreams. You just have to go for it."

Amanda told me that one of Mike's dreams was to become a sportscaster, so I called one of our biggest supporters at Spectrum, Pam MacKenzie, who was an executive at Comcast. I asked her if she had contacts at ESPN, and of course, she did. Pam set up a three-day excursion for Mike at the ESPN headquarters in Bristol, Connecticut, in which he spent time meeting the sportscasters, seeing what their job was like, getting some career advice. Amanda worked out the transportation and the hotel accommodations. Mike came back apparently thrilled, and I couldn't wait to ask him about it.

I never had the chance. A few days after returning, Mike was out in his wheelchair in Burlington and crossed a busy street against the light. A car clipped him, and he was taken to the hospital. They checked him out and sent him home. He died in his sleep that night.

I was home on a Sunday afternoon and got the call. I was stunned when I heard the news. Amanda and others, like Chris and Pam, were stricken when I told them. Everyone had liked and cared for Mike so much.

I went to the funeral home for the wake, and it was packed. Mike was laid out in a Red Sox shirt and hat, the coffin adorned with Red Sox pennants and paraphernalia. Mary Prevost gave a beautiful speech, and one of his sled hockey teammates took the mic while seated in his wheelchair and talked about how Mike had inspired all of them with his incredible intensity and attitude.

Person after person talked about how much Mike had changed since coming to Burlington, and that these last few years really were the best ones of his life. That made me feel better. As sad as I was, and even though it was still a tragedy, I felt good that we had done things with Mike that transformed his life from one of loneliness and isolation to one of happiness. Much of his early life had been sadness. But not his time with Mary and with us. That had gone well; very well. And for that I was grateful.

MARCY

Like a lot of the kids we work with at Spectrum, Marcy had a chaotic childhood. One of her earliest memories is going to visit her parents in a prison on Christmas day. "My parents have always struggled with substance abuse," she told us. "They were always in and out of correctional facilities. They just had a lot of their own problems, and they couldn't take care of us at the same time."

Fortunately, Marcy never became homeless. At age fifteen, she and her siblings were removed by the State from her parents and placed with a foster mother. That woman turned out to be a positive and supportive influence on Marcy, to the point that she graduated from high school on time and then enrolled in a local college.

That's when we got involved with Marcy, through our Youth Development Program. Our staff taught her about budgeting, writing a résumé, and applying for college scholarships. But they almost always do so much more than that, like the time Marcy's car broke down, and our staff member drove her to work so she wouldn't be late. Or the time Marcy's mother got hold of her three thousand dollars–worth of scholarship checks and cashed them herself. Our staff helped Marcy contact the authorities and recover the money.

Almost a thousand kids come in and out of Spectrum every year in some capacity, but Marcy's counselor here thought it was important that I meet her, which I did. I was impressed right away, especially with her work ethic. Even though she was taking a full load of college courses, she worked thirty hours a week at a grocery store. (I was told that Marcy even requested a shift on Thanksgiving so she could earn the extra dollar per hour.) She started every day at 5 a.m., studying for school.

Not long after I met Marcy, her counselor phoned me with bad news. We had recently helped Marcy to buy a used car, and she decided to drive to New Hampshire with a group of friends to go to a concert. When it was over they discovered that someone had broken into her car, stealing the contents. The counselor forwarded me the email Marcy had sent her. She was distraught.

It was bad enough that her clothing had been stolen, but even worse was that her MacBook Pro, with all her schoolwork on it, had been taken. She sounded absolutely panicked.

I asked her counselor and the other staff from our Youth Development Program to come to my office. When they showed up I told them, "I don't care what it takes, we're going to do everything we can to replace everything that Marcy lost." We divided up the tasks, including clothes shopping and repairing the broken car window.

"How about the Mac?" someone asked.

"Leave that to me," I replied.

I had lunch scheduled that day with Pam McKenzie, the Comcast executive who had been such a help to Mike Stamatis. When we sat down she asked, "How are things?"

"Generally good," I said, "but I'm upset right now because a kid we really like, who has done a stellar job in her life despite incredible odds, just had her car broken into and her MacBook stolen."

Without hesitation Pam replied, "Don't worry about the Mac-Book. I'm good for it."

Two days later, Marcy had her MacBook. Our wonderful staff came through with everything else.

A few days later, I received a card in the mail from Marcy.

Mark,
Thank you so much for going out of your way to help
me through my unlucky times. You are an everyday
Superhero! Never forget how great you are!

FRIDA

Frida was a young woman who came to Spectrum after she had completed a stay at rehab. She was eighteen, and a native Vermonter, but estranged from her family. She decided not to return to her family after rehab because, as she said in a radio interview, "It didn't seem like a safe environment as far as drugs and my family situation." She came to Burlington, but, she said, "I was really nervous because I had come from a small town, and now here I was in the big city of Burlington – although it's not that big but it seemed it at eighteen." She heard about Spectrum and asked if she could live in our shelter. We took her in.

She did well at the shelter, staying clean from drugs and finding a job. After three months, she transferred over to our Maple Street residence a few blocks away, where she would get her own room, be able to save money, continue with her education, and learn independent living skills, while still receiving counseling from one of our licensed substance abuse and mental health clinicians.

But she reconnected with her boyfriend, who lived in another part of the state, and she decided to join him there. Our staff tried to talk her out of it, since she was making so much progress with us, but she could not be dissuaded and left to be with him.

The two of them lived in a house with many other young adults and lots of drugs. She quickly relapsed and started using again. Then she became pregnant, and her boyfriend took off.

She came back to Spectrum. "I was a wreck," she said.

Then Frida had a miscarriage. "After I got out of the hospital, I was feeling completely alone and abandoned. I felt like my parents didn't want me, my boyfriend didn't want me, even the baby inside of me didn't want me. I was addicted to drugs. I was living in a homeless shelter. It was at a pretty low point. So one night I went back to the shelter, and I took a box of sleeping pills and some drugs I had gotten and a 40 [ounce] of beer."

This was on a Friday night, and her counselor was about to go to a restaurant with several other Spectrum staff. She had told the others that she'd meet them there, because she had bought a card for Frida and wanted to stop at the shelter first to give it to her.

When she arrived at the shelter and found Frida, she knew right away something was very wrong.

In Frida's words, "I was sitting outside of the shelter, and I remember my counselor came up. She had a card for me – a really nice card, by the way; it was inspirational. She went inside and called the ambulance. That was the bottom; that was the worst point in my life. I went to the hospital, and they ended up keeping me for a week. I remember Morgan, who was my case manager at Spectrum, came up to see me every day, sometimes twice a day."

Frida later told her counselor that she never thought Spectrum would take her back after that. But we did. When she was released from the hospital, we re-admitted her to our shelter, and from then on, she did exceptionally well. She lived in the shelter a few months, as she had the first time, then moved over to Maple Street, and instead of leaving after only a few weeks, she stayed for over a year, going to school, working, opening a savings account, and applying to college.

Frida was accepted into the Community College of Vermont and left our residence to move into her own apartment. She worked in a social services job, and after a year there, applied for a job in our shelter, in the very place where she had once tried to take her own life. We hired her. She turned out to be one of the best staff we have ever had at Spectrum. In fact, after a year, we promoted her. She was able to connect with our young people in a unique and powerful way.

Again from her radio interview:

What is kind of funny is that Spectrum becomes like a family, because it was more of a family to me. My personal family, things got hard, things were hard with me, and I was out the door – I was done and it was over – and even at my worst point, the staff at Spectrum tried to help – help pick up the pieces – and I am glad they did.

I wouldn't have been able to connect, without my counselor being the person she was. I mean, I have had counselors in the past. I just put up the wall and didn't even want to deal with them, or talk to them. But with her it was different. I felt like she was understanding. She didn't have that uptight attitude, that "I am only here because I am paid to be here." She had a really caring personality, nurturing, and that's what really made the difference for me.

I could say that counseling, and having a place to sleep, and the Drop-In Center were all beneficial, but it was the people at Spectrum who really made the difference for me. It's amazing. I can't believe I am in college. I am hopefully going to go for a master's in social work, something I have been interested in since I was young. Also, I was so inspired by Spectrum – the people who work there – and how much change they made in my life, given what I have gone through, and how much I could help other people, help them realize the change within themselves.

There are days I will be coming out of class and will be walking to my car, and I will catch a glimpse of myself in the storefront window, and it just amazes me even now, two years after the fact, I have come so far. I have a place to sleep, I have a job that I go to consistently, I have patched things up with most of my family, which is a really big thing for me. There is just no way that I would go back to where I was, there was no way I could. I have worked too hard. I feel like a completely different person, although I'm not, but I really do, there are so many aspects of me that have changed. I have grown and matured. I can't even thank Spectrum enough, and especially my counselor, because they gave me the foundation to be able to move and make changes and help myself. And without that I wouldn't have gotten this far. Only God knows where I would be right now.

MATTHEW

Frida wasn't the only person we helped at Spectrum and then hired as a staff member later on. Like Frida, Matthew grew up in Vermont. He was physically abused by his mentally ill and drug-addicted mother. In time he was adopted by a caring woman who turned out to be a very good parent. Matthew's life was on track at that point. He was part of the school chorus when he was in high school, and a member of a national touring musical program called Up With People. After graduating, he decided to hold off on going to college, and instead moved to Florida to take a job at Disney World running rides.

Matthew got fired from Disney for smoking a cigarette when he wasn't on break, so he took a series of jobs and bunked with various friends. One friend invited him to a party where Matthew experimented with drugs for the first time. He spiraled downward, using ecstasy, crystal meth, and a drug known on the street as Special K, which is actually a tranquilizer used on animals. Matthew became addicted to drugs and even overdosed one night while outside an Orlando nightclub where he was employed. He was rushed to a hospital and lived.

He knew he needed to get out of Orlando, and so did his adoptive family. They flew him back to Vermont and took him to Spectrum, where we accepted him into our shelter. He started off fine: followed all the rules, found a job, and saw one of our counselors weekly. He relapsed once: drank two full bottles of Robitussin within twenty-four hours and ended up in the hospital; but we never discharged him from the shelter, and in time he did well enough to move to our transitional living residence. He stayed for two years and then moved into his own apartment nearby.

I stayed in touch with Matthew even after he left us. He had a pretty responsible job at a local toy and hobby store, and one day he called and asked if we could have coffee. We did, and he said he knew he could stay there and probably get promoted and make more money, but what he really had his heart set on was working at Spectrum and helping kids with whom he could definitely identify. I told him that even though he lacked the formal training we usually look for when hiring someone, his life experience would be invaluable for our youth and that he should apply. He did and we hired him. I was right: He was excellent. Like Frida, when kids would say, "You don't know what it's like," he could reply, "Oh, yes, I do."

Two years later I received a phone call from the office of Senator Patrick Leahy. Senator Leahy had been a Spectrum board member back in the 1970s and had continued to advocate for the organization. His staffer explained to me that the Runaway and Homeless Youth Act was about to expire, and the senator wished to hold a hearing at the senate Judiciary Committee, which he chaired. They asked if I would testify, and would I also bring a young person who was presently receiving or had formerly received help from Spectrum. I said I would, and I knew immediately who I'd ask.

Matthew agreed without hesitation. We flew to Washington, D.C., and went to the senator's office, where we met with him, two other representatives from nonprofit organizations helping homeless teens, and the Hollywood actor Djimon Hounsou. Djimon was born in West Africa and moved to Paris when he was thirteen and homeless. Somehow he made his way into modeling and then acting, which was his passageway out of the streets. He had a major role in the movie *Blood Diamond*, which had just come out, and Senator Leahy was very interested in talking to him about that, since it involved serious issues about child soldiers, slavery, and the diamond trade. "I'm sorry, senator," I interrupted, "but I still think *Gladiator* is his best movie."

We walked with the senator through the underground tunnels of the Dirksen Senate Office Building that led to the senate Judiciary Committee's meeting room. The room was packed with reporters and photographers. CSPAN was even covering the hearing live. That wasn't for me, or for Matthew, but obviously, for the Hollywood actor. In the end, though, it was Matthew whose testimony played more of a role than anyone else's in terms of getting the Act renewed. He talked about what he'd been through, including the physical abuse as a child, and what was going through his mind as he lay clinging to life in the back of a speeding ambulance after he had overdosed, with paramedics fighting to restart his heart.

"I awoke in a hospital bed several hours later, alone, homeless, broke, and terrified," he said. "The only thing I possessed in that moment was the realization that I wouldn't be alive much longer if I didn't get help."

He found that help at Spectrum and ended his testimony with, "I can only hope that the youth that I work with, as well as thousands and thousands of homeless and runaway youth in this nation today, will be able to share their own success stories."

Senator Leahy had the final word at the hearing. Speaking about the upcoming vote on renewing the Runaway and Homeless Youth Act, he said, "This country cannot afford not to do this, or we lose part of our soul if we don't."

A few days later, the Senate voted, and the Runaway and Homeless Youth Act was renewed.

AMANDA

The third time we did the Spectrum Sleep Out, we actively tried to get school children to do it, and in my town, Essex, one part-time teacher loved the idea and recruited about twenty-five high school students to sleep out on the football field, in the cold, to raise funds for us. Besides being a teacher, she was also a swim instructor and, in fact, had been teaching swimming to my son Liam for years. A few days before the Sleep Out, she was teaching a group of six-year-old children, and while waiting for them to dry off, mentioned to Amanda, one of the mothers there, that she was organizing a Student Sleep Out to help Spectrum. Amanda replied, "Spectrum? Nine years ago, I had nowhere to go, and Spectrum helped me. You tell Mark Redmond my name, and I guarantee you he will remember me. We even had lunch together once." She gave her phone number to the swim instructor, who gave it to me the next day. I immediately remembered Amanda and called her right away, delighted to reconnect with her.

She told me she had been at Spectrum in 2005, and I asked her to remind me what circumstances led her to us. She said she had grown up in Essex in a very dysfunctional household. When the Department for Children and Families removed her from her mother at age eleven, she was put into the foster care system, but was eventually returned home. In her senior year of high school, when she was eighteen, she came home from school one October afternoon to discover that her mother had crammed all of her belongings into the back of her car. Her mother ordered her to leave the house, telling her she was now on her own.

Amanda's story is a familiar one. She told me she just couch-surfed from friend to friend, and soon had to drop out of high school because of the constant moving around, trying to survive. It was too much for her. Eventually a friend's basketball coach advised her to go to Burlington to seek help from Spectrum. Amanda said she hadn't even heard of Spectrum until then, "and I went there, and you were all complete strangers to me, but you took me in and gave me food, clothing, and so much more. It was so good that I had great Spectrum people who were there for me." She rattled off the names of staff members who had helped her. "This person helped me find my own apartment. I went to the health clinic at Spectrum for all my medical needs. When I became pregnant a few years later, another counselor at Spectrum helped get me baby supplies. Your counseling program helped me too." I told her I remembered she had worn a beautiful white graduation gown for her high school commencement. "Yes," she replied, "the Spectrum staff enrolled me in Burlington High School, I graduated from there, and then they helped me get into the Community College of Vermont."

Asked how she is doing now, she told me she is married to a wonderful man – a firefighter, an EMT, and a member of the Vermont National Guard. They have a two-year-old and a six-year-old and own their own home, where they have been living for five years. "I wake up every day and can't believe I actually own my own home. I am so proud," she told me. Amanda runs a day care out of her home, taking care of her own two children and others.

We finished our lunch, and a few days later, she showed up at the Sleep Out at Essex High School. It was about twenty degrees outside, but she wanted to go that night to tell the students there her story – of how she had to drop out of that very high school, how she was homeless, how Spectrum helped her, and what her life is like now.

I watched the students as she spoke. She *definitely* made an impact.

VIRGINIA

In the summer of 2015, I had a business meeting at a software firm with which Spectrum was thinking of doing business. As the members of the firm introduced themselves, one of the women turned to me and said, "I am the webmaster here, and I used to live in the shelter."

"You mean COTS?" I asked, referring to one of the adult shelters in Burlington.

"No," she said, "yours. The Spectrum shelter."

I was surprised, because I didn't remember her at all. I started mentioning the names of our staff members, many of whom she said she knew.

When the meeting ended, I told her that we had our annual Empty Bowl fundraising dinner coming up and asked if she'd be the keynote speaker. She agreed.

These were her remarks:

If you had told me five years ago, when I was homeless, that I would be working in a tech job as a webmaster for a business, I probably would have laughed and blown smoke in your face, as I was smoking a lot of cigarettes back then.

I don't smoke cigarettes any more. In fact I am trying to be healthy. I'm not great at it, though. My rabbits like lettuce, but I don't understand salad. I like yoga, though.

The health is new to me, because I've spent most of my life being bitter and self-destructive.

My life began in a trailer park in northern New York affectionately known as "Wiggle Town." Soon after, we moved to a house I would later realize was home to much of my childhood trauma.

At five my mother left my alcoholic, abusive father and

*became an unstable and high-strung single mother of a
spastic autistic son ... and me.*

*When I was ten, we moved to Mississippi to start our
lives over again. As it was, Mississippi was a bad place to
start over, because four years later we lost our house in
Hurricane Katrina.*

*I was just starting high school, so I only know an
adolescence as a Katrina Kid. That being said, my version
of teenage angst was looting abandoned buildings and
stealing flooded bottles of alcohol and packs of cigarettes
from the remnants of liquor stores and gas stations along
Highway 90.*

*Nonetheless, I graduated high school – with honors even.
Unfortunately this was also the year the economy collapsed.*

*The economy of Mississippi was, and still is, especially
bad. My mother kicked me out of the house as soon as I
turned eighteen, and I lived on a mattress at my friend's
house and worked at Hobby Lobby until I hitched a ride
with my high school sweetheart to Vermont to attend
Burlington College.*

*I moved to Vermont with two hundred dollars and opti-
mism but soon learned that would not be enough. So I contacted my biological father from across the lake, and visited
the house where I had spent the first five years of my life.*

*Now, I knew the first five years of my life were bad, but
I didn't realize how bad they were until I was in the
Fletcher Allen Hospital psychiatric ward for having a ten-
hour manic episode from listening to* The White Album.
*They kept me in the psych ward for a week, and by the
time I got out, I was on a plethora of sedatives and mood*

stabilizers, with a huge medical bill, and had been kicked out of my apartment.

There was nowhere for me to go but down, so I flew back down to Mississippi and got back into my bad habits until I saved up money from my diner job and got a one way ticket back to Vermont.

I am so thankful y'all raise nice children up here, because if it weren't for the kindness of some kids I had met previously in college, I wouldn't have made it. They picked me up at the airport and let me crash on their futon while I tried to get my life together.

One day I visited Burlington College and broke down crying in the financial aid office, admitting I was homeless, but I really wanted to go back to school. One of the faculty members brought me to Spectrum's Drop-In Center on Pearl Street, and I started living in their Emergency Shelter shortly after. I stayed in the shelter for six months until moving to the Maple Street house. Spectrum gave me a place to put my trash bags of clothes and a bed of my own. The shelter staff were really awesome. They gave me the guidance and support I always wanted from my parents but so rarely received.

During that time, I attended the Community College of Vermont and started working at COTS. I was living in one shelter and working in another. I saved my money while I was at Spectrum, and in June of 2012, I moved into my own apartment. I have not fallen into homelessness since.

I stayed working at COTS for two years, until it was too emotionally taxing for me. Then I started working part time at a local start-up. I started working only 15 hours a week, doing menial tasks on the computer, but as the company has grown, so has my position. I now work there full time in my first salary job. My bosses are very supportive and have even paid for me to take computer programming classes.

My life has never been so good – seriously – and my future has never been so bright. And I know, without a doubt, that this would not have been possible without the love and support I have received from Spectrum.

When she finished, she received a standing ovation.

· *twenty-three* ·

IN JUNE OF 2015, Marybeth, Liam, and I traveled to Washington, D.C., to attend a family wedding. Marybeth recommended we go a few days early to show our twelve-year-old son the sites and memorials, so that's what we did.

Our first night there, we went out to dinner with a relative. As we walked back to our Airbnb, it started to rain, but Liam asked if we could go see the Lincoln Memorial anyway. As exhausted as we all were, we took a taxi there, and I was glad we did. Seeing the Lincoln Memorial, reading the Gettysburg Address and Lincoln's Second Inaugural speech, all lit up at night, was very moving. We then walked over, in the dark and in a light rain, to the Vietnam Veterans Memorial, also very emotional in its own way.

We then pulled out a map of the city and noticed that, not far away, was the Martin Luther King, Jr., Memorial. We headed that direction and shortly came upon the recently installed statue of Dr. King, surrounded by a number of his quotations chiseled into stone.

It was an incredible sight, and my mind immediately shot back twenty years, to a teenage boy I knew when I worked at St. Christopher's in Dobbs Ferry. His name was Nafari, but he called himself Nafi and asked us all to do the same, which we obliged. He was fifteen, African American, and had grown up in a low-income section of New York City. I can't remember his family situation, but it was probably, like many of the youth at St. Christopher's, parents in prison, or addicted to drugs and alcohol, or missing.

Standing at the Memorial, I thought of Nafi, because every year on Martin Luther King Day at St. Christopher's, we made a special effort to celebrate the holiday, and one year, the person

MARTIN LUTHER KING, JR. MEMORIAL

who ran the cottage where Nafi lived had asked each young man to fill out a piece of paper on which there was a picture of Dr. King, with this sentence: "I have a dream that:_____." The assignment was for each of them to write in what his dream was.

They were posted on a wall, and I started reading them, until Nafi's stopped me in my tracks:

"I have a dream that: I will be more than a street person."

It still affects me all these years later. Nafi's dream, that he not end up living on the street, was, to me, incredibly sad and very telling. I have thought many times about what I might have written as a teenager in completing that sentence, and what my peers might have written. "I have a dream that I will be: an engineer ... a doctor ... a lawyer ... successful ... a sports star ... a business owner ... rich ... married." But for Nafi, his dream was that he not end up living on the street. And he likely wrote that because he grew up in a neighborhood where he saw many people in that condition. His greatest aspiration was that he not end up like them.

It's been more than two decades since I last saw Nafi, and I have no idea how he fared after leaving St. Christopher's, what he is doing now, or if his dream came true. I hope it did and that he has a good life; a happy life. He was a nice young man and deserved that.

We left the memorial, walked over to see the Franklin Delano Roosevelt Memorial, and then took a taxi back to where we were staying.

Before going to bed, I decided to quickly check the news on my iPhone, and I learned that, at the very moment we had been at the Martin Luther King, Jr, Memorial and I was thinking about Nafi, nine African Americans had been shot and killed in a church in Charleston, South Carolina.

The entire world would soon learn that the killer was a white supremacist.

· *twenty-four* ·

LIKE EVERY OTHER CATHOLIC DIOCESE in the United States, the diocese of Burlington has had its share of cases of child sexual abuse perpetrated by priests and covered up by bishops over the decades. Even though "Diocese of Burlington" indicates the city, it covers the entire state. The *Burlington Free Press* and other papers had all done stories covering several scandals that involved cover-ups, payoffs, nondisclosure agreements, and the frequent transfers of priests despite overwhelming evidence of their having committed child sexual abuse.

In 2015, Christopher Coyne was named the new bishop of the diocese. He had previously been an auxiliary bishop in Indianapolis, but before that, had been in Boston, where he was very involved in handling the child abuse scandals surrounding Cardinal Law. In the fall of 2018, Bishop Coyne announced that he would be forming a committee composed of lay people to produce a report that would list those priests who had been credibly accused of abusing children. Other dioceses had done this, and it was widely regarded as a necessary first step to confirm that the church was finally done with covering up its sins and trying to be as transparent as possible. When I read that he was doing this, I emailed him offering to serve on the committee. I reminded him that I had spent my entire career, almost forty years, in the field of child protection and safety. He emailed back, "Thank you, because I was going to ask you."

There were seven of us on the committee, including one survivor of abuse by a priest. At the first meeting, Bishop Coyne announced that this report was ours, and only ours, to write, and that he would not attend future meetings unless we invited him. He vowed not to change one name or even so much as a comma. He also promised us total and complete access to any file of any priest – living, deceased, retired, active, it did not matter. We could see them all at any time.

A lawyer, a retired state's attorney, was named head of the committee, but in short order, he had to take time off for medical reasons, and I was asked to take over. I wasn't thrilled by the prospect. I had a full-time job as it was, running Spectrum, and I had the feeling this project wasn't going to be quick; but Bishop Coyne had come through for me when we needed space for Spectrum's Warming Shelter, so I felt as if I owed him. I said yes, I'd be the new chair.

We started meeting in October and predicted to Bishop Coyne that our report would be complete by the end of the year. Once we started digging into the fifty-plus files, some of which dated back to the 1940s, we had to tell him we would need many more months. "Take the time that you need in order to get it right," was his response, which we all appreciated.

The first thing we had to establish was our definition of "credibly accused," because unfortunately, we learned there is no one universally accepted definition among Catholic dioceses. We reviewed reports already done by other dioceses and settled upon a definition that was used by the Diocese of Syracuse. Its standard is an allegation that, based upon the facts of the case, meets one or more of the following thresholds:

1. natural, reasonable, plausible, and probable;
2. corroborated with other evidence or another source; or
3. acknowledged/admitted to by the accused.

We then began the hard work of perusing the files, reading every tattered, yellowed, mimeographed page. As one reporter later asked me, "Are you saying that all seven of you read every single file?"

"Every single page of every single file," was my response.

There was a great deal of upsetting and horrifying information in the files; but the hardest part was determining who reached the bar of "credibly accused," and who did not. A certain segment of them were simple in that the priest admitted what he did and/ or had been convicted of and imprisoned, thereby "credibly accused." Another segment included allegations made by one person against a priest who could not have possibly been in the parish or location at the specified time period, and thus deemed by us as "not credibly accused."

But most cases fell in between, where we would have to carefully go over the facts, reading and rereading files, sometimes comparing them to other ones, sometimes asking the bishop for more files, which were always provided to us as promised. We all took it seriously, not only because it mattered to the survivors of clerical abuse, but because it also mattered to the reputations of the priests being accused, even if they were deceased.

In the end we came up with forty names on our list of those credibly accused, which came out to 10 percent of the total number of priests who had been in the diocese during that time period, which, we later learned, matched national statistics. Bishop Coyne held a press conference at which he released our report, and we were all in attendance.

The aftermath was interesting. I received several messages from people I knew along the lines of, "I can't believe Fr. X was on that list; he helped my family so much when my mother was dying."

"I'm sure he did," was my reply, "but you will have to take my word for it that there are other things he did that constitute child abuse."

Much more common, however, were messages from people thanking me for what I and the other committee members did. Most were from Catholic friends, but not all. They truly appreciated the grim task that we took on.

A reporter at the press conference asked me why I took part in this.

"Because the Church needs to be transparent in order to regain the trust of the people," I responded, "but just as important, I did this because I believe it will be healing for those who were abused."

And that turned out to be true. I and other members of the committee received many messages from those who were survivors of clerical sexual abuse, telling us how grateful they were, and that our report finally gave them some sense of comfort and relief from their suffering.

That, to me, is what mattered most. I know, from the work I have done with children and teenagers for so many years, that to suffer abuse of any sort is traumatic, but to be listened to and believed can be healing.

I think that is what we accomplished.

· twenty-five ·

I WROTE ABOUT TONY IN MY FIRST BOOK, *The Goodness Within:
Reaching Out to Troubled Teens with Love and Compassion*, but
it was published in 2004, and a lot more has happened between
Tony and me since then. He deserves another chapter in this book.

When I arrived in the Faith Community at Covenant House,
there were about a hundred and fifty homeless teenagers and
young adults staying there on any given night, with around forty
per floor. I was assigned to 2C, which was for males ages sixteen
to twenty-one.

There were always kids coming and going. Those who didn't
return for the night were designated as AWOL and could not
return for another thirty days, so it pretty quickly became a
revolving door of homeless teenagers on 2C.

There was one young man, though, whom I did get to know
pretty well – Tony Turner.

Tony was nineteen, African American, from Harlem, and from
a family with enough difficulties that he ended up homeless. This
was a pretty typical story we heard many times at Covenant House.
For some reason, Tony and I hit it off right away, even though we
had absolutely nothing in common. I was his counselor and would
help him look for jobs and talk to him about his problems and
goals. He was friendly and funny and had an amiable personality.

But the more experienced staff at Covenant House warned me
about him. "You do realize he's into some bad stuff out there," one
of the veteran female staff told me. "Be careful of him. He could
be dangerous."

I had no reason to doubt her, and in fact, shortly after that,
I arrived for my shift at 2C and found out that Tony had been
permanently discharged from Covenant House. The report stated

that he had come in high on a street drug by the name of "angel dust" the night before and turned over every piece of furniture in the place.

I can't say I was shocked, and I figured that was the last I'd see of Tony.

I would be wrong about that.

A few months later, I was walking through Times Square on my way to Covenant House for my shift, and as usual, there were young men standing in front of strip clubs handing out fliers, chanting, "Girls, girls, girls, come on in and see the pretty girls." The first time I ever heard this, I was shocked; but in time I just got used to it, which in retrospect, is really sad to say. On this particular occasion, I was standing in place on the street corner, waiting for the Don't Walk sign to change. I heard the usual chant, "Girls, girls, girls," and who then would push a flyer into my chest but … Tony.

Our eyes locked, and he looked absolutely mortified. He tried to hide the flyers behind his back, as if it had never happened, and he then attempted a regular conversation.

"Oh, hi, Mark, how are you man?"

I felt as awkward as he did, so we both tried our best to pretend we weren't in the situation we were in.

"I'm good Tony," I replied. "How are you?"

"I'm good, I'm good." He asked about some of the other staff at Covenant House: "How's Dudley? How's Patty?"

"They're good," I said.

"Well then tell them I said hello, okay?"

"Sure, Tony," I said. "I'll do that.

The Walk sign lit up; the others on the corner with me began to cross, and so did I. "Take care, Tony," I said as I turned and hustled out of there as fast as I could, anxious to quickly end this little interaction. And as I walked away, I could hear him again, "Girl, girls, girls."

I figured that was the last I'd see of Tony.

I'd be wrong about that too.

Five years later I was no longer at Covenant House and was,

instead, attending graduate school at New York University. I had been invited to a fundraising event in Greenwich Village that someone was holding for a soup kitchen. Many of my Covenant House friends were there too, and I was talking to one of them, Gerry Stuhlman, when I heard a loud voice boom out:

"Does anyone here know Tony Turner?"

I looked and saw it was Father Jim Joyce, a Jesuit priest who had said Mass for us at the Faith Community. Father Jim was a very large man, around three hundred pounds and six feet, four inches tall, so when he yelled, you heard him.

Gerry had also counseled Tony at Covenant House, so we both yelled over, "Yeah, we know him!" Father Jim lumbered over and said, "Well, I'm a chaplain at Rikers Island prison, and I met him, and he said no family members ever go to visit him, but that he used to live at Covenant House, and it would be nice if someone from there would go see him sometime."

Gerry and I looked at each and said, "We'll go."

Before I continue, please keep this in mind: There were fifteen thousand inmates at Rikers on any given day. What are the chances that this chaplain would meet Tony out of that mass of people? And that he'd then randomly call out his name at a party, and Gerry and I would hear it?

Infinitesimal, I'd say.

But it happened.

The following Saturday, Gerry and I traveled to Rikers, which is literally an island in the borough of Queens. This was an experience in and of itself, with several hours of bus rides, transfers to other buses, searches, paperwork, and more searches. Finally we were ushered into an enormous room with hundreds of other visitors and prisoners sitting around small round tables. After a few minutes, we spotted Tony coming in. I don't think that, at Rikers, they inform prisoners exactly who it is who's coming to see them, because Tony had this look on his face of, Who the heck is here to see me? We waved to him, he spotted us and he was just overjoyed. He kept thanking us over and over for coming to see him.

We talked for about an hour, reminiscing about Covenant House and all the staff and kids we knew there, and then I finally asked him, "What are you in for?"

"Selling drugs," he replied.

"How many of you are in here because of drugs?" I asked.

What he said next is something that has stayed with me for over thirty years.

Turning around, he motioned toward the hundreds of other prisoners in that room, and said, "We're all in here because of drugs."

I asked him how long his sentence was.

"It'll be for a few years. They'll send me upstate soon, to a facility there."

I handed him my card and said, "Here's my address. If you write to me, I'll write back."

A few months later I received a letter from Tony, from an upstate prison. Most of it was about how much he hated prison – about the times he was sent to solitary confinement (the hole in prison terminology) for breaking some rule; how, when he got out, he'd never go back again. And he had a request: "Please send me some Little Debby's cupcakes." I'd write back and send him those cupcakes. This went on, writing back and forth, for about two years, and when he was released, we got together in the city, at Ray's Famous Pizza on Eighth Avenue, a few blocks up from Covenant House. He proclaimed his absolute conviction to stay out of trouble and out of jail.

But he'd always go back. And it was always drug-related. In jail. Out of jail. We'd meet at Ray's Famous. In jail. Out of jail. He'd tell me that this time he was going straight. In jail. The letters continued back and forth. So did the Little Debbie's. I wish I had kept all the letters, but I have only one, from June 18, 1993.

Hi Mark,
How are you and your lovely family doing? Fine I hope!
Mark, I know I have not written to you in some time, so
I said to myself let me write you this letter today so you

would know I'm doing just fine for myself. Also, could you tell your son, my little man Aiden, I said What's up?

Mark, this letter is also to let you know I will not be calling you for some time because I have been calling you too much and I know your telephone bill is going up and not down. I'm saying this to you and your family because I do care about you all and I know you all care about me as well. (Smile) I also would like to say people in here be telling me I need people to write me more, about two or more times a week. If not maybe I will not make it out of here this time. So Mark, when you have the time maybe you can sit down and write me one time a week until I come home. Also, Mark I'm not going to tell you I'm not coming back to jail. Only God knows what is going to go on in my life. I just like to let you all know what is going on in my mind at this time. I'm intending to come home and work until I can get my own business. If this does not work out I'm going to do what I have been doing for some time. You do know what this is, so you can see what is going on in my mind at this time. You can also see I do need you and your lovely family in my life because my family is not looking out at all for me. Just one of them is doing something for me and I have not received any letters from my father in 19 months or more. I have written to him more than once without getting any reply. I can go on and on about him but I'm not going to do this to you or myself. I'm going to go on with my life and do what I need to do for myself. The way I see it, all the people who love me are not in my family and my boss's family. I have been in jail more than once as you know, so people do say if you can't see him or her get them out of your mind and I'm doing just that. People say I'm not the one to do something good for myself and my loved ones, because all I do is come back and forth to prison. As of right now I'm trying real hard to correct myself before getting released from prison this time around. I'm getting too old and too tired to keep on doing the things that lead me to prison. I must get my priorities in order, deciding what I value most. I've concluded that I value freedom more than anything else. Nothing is worth me deprioritizing my freedom for. The hardest part about being in prison is consistently being surrounded by folks whom you know real well could care less about you. I miss affection more than I miss sex. That's word! Just a note from a loved one means so much while being in this situation. It serves as a reminder that I am being thought about and loved by somebody.

Thoughts of you and yours continue on without end, along with my love for you all. Write back soon as you are able and please send me the Little Debbies I asked you for. I really got a craving for some of those. Until next time, take good care of you and yours.

Love Always,
Tony

The in-and-out of prison and letter-writing went on for years, but eventually Tony stopped getting arrested. We kept meeting a few times a year, always in the city, always at Ray's. I lived an hour away by then, so it was no small feat for me to fight traffic, get in there, and find a parking spot, sometimes taking my son Aiden with me. But I'd do it. Unfortunately, Tony would show up only about half of the time. And I knew why: Someone had offered him drugs, and he'd blow me off. It got to the point where I'd call him and say, "Okay, I am leaving my house right now, I will be there in an hour; you'll be there at Ray's?" He'd say yes, I'd get there, no Tony. And I'd drive back home thinking, this is it, no more, I've had it.

But a few months would go by, he'd call me and ask to get together, I'd say yes, and we'd go through the whole routine again. And the times he'd show, we would have a great time, eating pizza, taking in a movie, laughing. But that was only about half the time. Tony may not have been dealing drugs any longer, which is why he wasn't going to prison, but he was definitely still using. In fact, there was one time we met, had pizza, watched the movie Stargate in a Manhattan theater, had our picture taken together for five dollars by some guy with a camera on the street, and as I walked him to the subway, he turned to me and said, "This is the first time in years I've had fun without using drugs." That it was a revelation to him, that people could enjoy themselves without using substances, told me how immersed he was in the drug culture.

That went on for several years, and then Tony became much more consistent about showing up. One day in the fall of 1999, he called and asked me to meet him on a Thursday night, this time at a different location than usual. "Why not at Ray's?" I asked, and he responded, "I haven't told you, but I've been going to Narcotics Anonymous meetings, and I've been clean off of drugs. This will be my two-year anniversary, and I'd like you to be there."

I had no idea that Tony had been going to a Twelve Step program, but it now made sense why he had become so much more reliable the last few years in terms of actually showing up to meet me. I was really glad. I'm a believer in the Twelve Steps and have seen this approach work for many people over the years. Apparently it was now working for Tony.

I went to this new address on the appointed night, thirteen-year-old Aiden with me, and when we arrived I discovered that the location was a church. Tony stood outside.

"Follow me," he said, as he led us down into the basement.

If you've never been to a Twelve-Step meeting, please go. It's raw, it's honest, and all the masks we wear, mine included, come off in a moving display of companionship and courage. Every Twelve-Step meeting has certain rituals and recitations, and if there is enough time remaining at the end, those individuals celebrating anniversaries are asked to come up and speak. When Tony got up, he talked about his gratitude toward his sponsor and others from NA. He talked about the difficulties drugs had caused him in his life, his various efforts to get clean, and how grateful he was to have found NA.

He also said, "You know, when you're dealing drugs, you think your dealer friends are always going to be there for you, no matter what happens. But when you get busted and go to prison, they all forget about you. You never hear from them. But there's one person who never forgot me, who always remembered I was there, who visited me, who wrote to me, and who even sent me Little Debbie cupcakes.

"That man right there."

He pointed at me.

Shortly after that meeting, Tony told me his partner was pregnant and invited me to the baby shower.

"Sure," I said, "just give me the address and which apartment to go to."

It turned out the shower was in a high-rise project in a high-crime neighborhood of Harlem.

"I'll give you the address," he said, "but don't you dare go inside. Stay in front and call me. I'll come get you."

When we got upstairs to the apartment, I discovered it was not exactly a Jack and Jill shower. It was filled with African American women. We were the only two males. He went around and introduced me to each woman, saying, "This is Mark Redmond; he's my best friend."

It startled me when I heard that. I had no idea that's how Tony saw me, as his best friend, and it touched me deeply.

When I met Tony's partner that night, I said to her, "Wow, you look like you're going to give birth right now!" A few hours later she went into labor, and he told me that she turned to him between contractions and screamed, "Your best friend jinxed me!"

They had a baby girl, and when it was time for her to be baptized, Tony asked me to be her godfather. I considered that to be a true honor and happily obliged. And when I got re-married in 2001, to Marybeth, Tony came to our wedding, and he brought a gift. And when we had a baby boy a year after that, he sent a gift for him too.

Unfortunately, Tony's partner relapsed into addiction and tragically passed away quite young. He raised his daughter as a single parent. I flew down to New York City for her middle school graduation, and if I heard it once, I heard it twenty times from the mothers there: "Tony's a good father."

I was so proud of him each time I heard that, because, in my mind, it's hard to think of a better compliment.

I had always promised Tony that, when he hit his ten-year anniversary of sobriety, I would come back to New York City for the NA meeting. I was all set to go in 2007 when a massive snowstorm hit Vermont that closed the airport and made driving impossible.

"I'm sorry," I said, "but I promise I will be there for your twentieth."

So ten years later, in the fall of 2017, I texted him, "Isn't this your twentieth?"

"Yes it is," he answered. "December 9, in Harlem again."

"I'll be there," I said.

That Saturday morning, I drove from Vermont to Poughkeepsie, New York, in a snowstorm, took the train, and got off at the Harlem station, where he met me on the platform. I insisted we get a soul food dinner because "that kind of food is impossible to get in Vermont." He said he wasn't hungry, so I ate and he talked.

Eventually it was time to go to the meeting, not at a church this time, but at a job training site called Ready Willing and Able for people coming out of prison. We had to first pass through a metal detector to go inside. There were about two hundred people in there, mostly men, all people of color except for me and one woman. (She came up to me and said, "Congratulations on your twentieth anniversary of sobriety!" I pointed to Tony and said, "It's not me, it's him.")

The meeting started with the same Twelve Step rituals I had witnessed eighteen years earlier. Then people started telling their stories of recovery. Some people were celebrating seven years straight; some were celebrating seven days. It didn't matter. One theme was constant: They were grateful to be sober, and didn't

TONY AND MARK, JUNE 2019

ever get overconfident that, just because they've been clean a certain amount of time that they can stop going to meetings.

Speakers then came up to pay tribute to Tony. A number of them talked about Tony's daughter and the struggles he's had with her, and how they were able to help him through that, which brought home to me how NA is more than just a support group to stay off of drugs; it's a support for people to help them with all aspects of their lives.

Unlike eighteen years earlier, the meeting time elapsed and Tony did not get a chance to speak. To close the meeting out, every person there, including myself, linked shoulders with the person next to them in one big giant circle. It was so moving. The sense of solidarity and support for one another was visceral.

Afterward Tony's sponsor came up to me to introduce himself. When I told him I had traveled from Vermont for this, and that I had known Tony for thirty-six years, he couldn't believe it.

"When do I read the book about you two?" he asked.

Tony and I stepped outside, and I hailed a cab to head downtown to my cousin's apartment, where I was staying. I went to hug Tony goodbye, and he said, "I love you Mark," which I'd never heard him say.

"I love you too, Mr. T."

Tony phoned me the next day, while I was on the train home, to thank me for coming, and then sent me this Facebook message:

"One more time, thank you for being there, I can't tell you in words how much it meant to me to see you there. I thank God for you being my friend."

I love the movies, and there is a Japanese film, *Afterlife*, that is one of my all-time favorites. The plot is simple enough: When a person dies, there is an afterlife, but you are allowed to take only one memory from your entire life with you. All other memories will be scrubbed clean from your mind, and the one you choose to keep has to be something truly unique. It can't be the typical (the day my child was born; the day of our wedding). It's got to be something particular and meaningful to just you. And I've often thought that, if I had to choose just one memory from my life to take with me, it'd be that time in the basement of the Harlem church, with my son at my side, and Tony, pointing to me, saying, "There is one person who never forgot me … who sent me Little Debbie cupcakes … that man right there."

· *twenty-six* ·

I **LOVE STORIES.** I love listening to stories. I love telling stories.

I'm a ham. A college professor even told me so at Villanova. One of the last courses I took there was Public Speaking, and on the last day, he said, "Redmond, you're a ham."

Guilty as charged.

I think it's because I grew up in a big Irish Catholic story-telling family. Every holiday, every Baptism, First Holy Communion, Confirmation, graduations, Easter, Thanksgiving, Christmas, Fourth of July, would be a giant gathering of people and there would be stories told around the table. People weren't looking at their phones then; they were actually talking to one another.

No doubt about it, my father was Storyteller-in-Chief. He'd sit at the head of the table and tell one story after the other. We'd heard them all, and each time he'd tell a story, it would get bigger and more fantastic. To this day, if you gathered my siblings and me in one room, we could rattle off all of Dad's incredible stories.

He called me a few years ago and said, "Mark, you've really got this story-telling thing down."

"Well, I learned it from you, Dad," I said.

"Yeah," he replied, "but mine were mostly bullshit. Yours are actually true."

I laughed.

I really got into the storytelling scene, though, with "The Moth." It's a syndicated radio program that started in 1997 and now plays on more than two hundred public radio stations in the United States. "True stories, told live, no notes," is its tag line. It's just ordinary people getting up on stage in front of a microphone and telling an interesting story. That's the concept, simple but brilliant, because it just so happens that everyone on Planet Earth has at least one fascinating story to tell. Once in a while, The Moth will have a celebrity telling a story, but 99 percent of the time it's ordinary people standing up there, ignoring their stage fright, and filling strangers in about something that happened to them or something they did.

I started listening every Saturday afternoon on Vermont Public Radio after we moved up here, and became a faithful listener when The Moth became a weekly podcast that I could simply stream on my phone and listen to when I wanted, which was usually on the drive to or from Burlington.

I was recently telling a group of college students about The Moth and asked, "If you listen to The Moth like I do each week, they always say one thing at the end of the show. What is it?"

"They say, 'Have a story-worthy week,'" someone yelled out. Grrr.

"Yes, it's true, they do say that," I replied, "but that's not what I'm looking for. They also always say, 'If you have a good story to tell, call 1-800-THEMOTH and leave us a one-minute phone message. If we like what we hear, we may contact you to hear the full story and put you on stage someday.'"

And that's what I did. I left a one-minute phone message sometime in 2012 or 2013, I can't quite remember. I may have done it more than once. Again, I'm not sure. I do know I completely forgot about it and never really thought anything would come of it. That is, until I received the following email on July 22, 2013, from the organization's headquarters in New York City:

Hi Mark,
I'm writing regarding your pitch for The Moth, with the story about going to a high school and ending up with the belongings of a teenager that had passed away.

We're going to be in Burlington, Vermont in September and I would be very interested in getting on the phone with you to hear a longer version of your story. Is there a time this week that works for you?

Thanks so much and all the best,
Maggie Cino, Senior Producer, The Moth

Maggie Cino had the story half right. I had left a one-minute
message about the time I had gone to a local church, not a high
school, but even so, I was surprised to get this message and called
her right away. "The Moth has never been to Burlington," she
said. "This is our first time. We'll be at the Flynn Theatre for
what we call a Main Stage event. We are flying in three of our
best storytellers from around the country, and we would like to
have at least one Vermont storyteller up there. Please tell me your
story now."

Without any kind of preparation I launched into it, about going
to the megachurch and meeting the little girl whose brother had
died from a heroin overdose. I just told it and at the end Maggie
said, "Okay, you're in."

"I'm in?" I said.

"Yes, you will have ten minutes to tell this story on stage. You
and I will have a weekly call between now and the show date,
which is Saturday night, September 7."

I was pretty blown away – shocked really. I had left a one-
minute phone message months earlier, and after telling a story to
someone from The Moth over the phone, and I was now going to
be on stage in the largest theater in the state? Crazy.

Once a week Maggie and I would speak by phone. I'd tell her
the story and at the end she'd say, "Why did you react this way to
that?" Or, "What else happened?" "How did you feel when you
heard the adult next to you say that?"

Her feedback was extremely helpful. She made me think
about the entire experience at a deeper level. She took what was
probably a good story and made it a great story. At the same time,
it was always my story. She never pushed, she never demanded
any changes to it. She just kept offering helpful advice.

The night before the Main Stage show, I went to a rehearsal at a
Burlington hotel. I finally met Maggie and three other storytellers,
all of whom were Moth veterans, from places like Chicago, New

York City, and Milwaukee. And there was another Vermonter – aviator Charles Lindbergh's daughter, Reeve. We each told our stories and then went out to dinner. We were joined by the woman who'd be the host for the show, Ophira Eisenberg, the host of Ask Me Another, a popular NPR show.

The next morning, the day of the show, Maggie called and asked me to tell her the story one more time. By then I didn't think there was one single thing to add or subtract, but once again, she had advice that turned out to be spot-on. That evening I drove into Burlington and went down to the lower-level room where all of us were to meet. Maggie walked in, pointed at me, and said, "You're going first."

I was pretty surprised but also relieved. I preferred to get up there and tell my story before the others so that I could actually listen to theirs afterward rather than sitting there obsessing over mine. By show time, we all came up to our assigned seats in the first row, and I could see the theater was pretty well packed. Apparently people in Vermont loved The Moth, and this was their first chance to see it live.

Ophira took the stage, warmed up the audience, and introduced a violin player, who would be seated on stage for the entire show. "He has a stopwatch with him," she said, "and it's set for ten minutes. After that, he starts playing."

I had been told this ahead of time; we all had, but I wasn't worried. I had practiced my story a million times, with and without Maggie, and I knew it clocked in at around nine minutes and forty-five seconds. I had nothing to worry about.

There were some things, however, that I hadn't thought of. I took the stage after being introduced, and my heart was pounding. I started in and quickly calmed down. Telling a story, for me, is like playing competitive sports. I'm a wreck beforehand, but once I get going, I'm fine. I was about a third of the way into my story when I said something funny and the crowd started laughing.

I hadn't counted on laughing. Laughing takes time. The audience's laughing was eating away at my spare fifteen seconds.

Stop laughing, people; please stop laughing, I thought.

But I calmed myself down, thinking, That's okay, I had that extra time built in. I'll make it.

Then a few minutes later, I said something that people found inspiring. Someone started clapping. Others joined in. It spread.

Now I was in trouble.

I looked at that microphone and every instinct in me told me to step even closer to it and continue with my story, to speak over the noise of the applause because if I didn't, that violin guy was going to crash my story at the end.

But I didn't, I held back, I let the applause die down, gambling that I'd either somehow finish within the ten minutes or he'd be kind and let me go past for a bit.

It turned out to be the latter. I still owe that musician a debt of gratitude for letting me go over.

I finished my story, the crowd applauded in a way I would describe as "vigorously," and as I walked off, Ophira came up to me. I could tell by the smile on her face that she thought I had done a good job. Back at our seats, the other four storytellers gave me high-fives and slapped my back, all smiling. I turned around to Marybeth, seated behind me with Liam and Aiden.

"You nailed it," she said, a wide smile on her face.

Friends, and a lot of my coworkers from Spectrum, were in the audience. Later on I read some of their tweets, which they had posted while I was up on stage. They were really funny.

"Redmond's not going to make it on time."

"My money's on the violin guy."

I listened to the other four storytellers during the rest of that evening. All the stories were great. At a reception for all of us afterward, I asked my four new Moth friends, "When do you think our stories will be on the radio show and podcast?"

They laughed. Each had a similar response: "I've been telling stories for The Moth for years, none of mine have ever made it to the actual show. Moth events like this one tonight are taking place now all across the globe. It's a long shot to ever have one played."

But I got lucky. A year later, Maggie contacted me to tell me that my story would be on the radio show and podcast that coming December. It was, and it ended up playing again a few years later, which is a rarity for The Moth.

When my story hit the airwaves, it was incredible how many people I heard from, all around the country. Some even started donating to Spectrum. And I heard from many, many people who had lost a loved one to addiction. They were grateful for the story, especially hearing about how this young man's mother, out of her pain and suffering, reached out to try and help other young people who were in need. "That story was healing for me," was something I heard over and over.

A few months later, it was announced that The Moth was coming to Burlington once a month, for what was called a Story Slam. It was held at a local restaurant called The Skinny Pancake, and tickets were required to be bought in advance. The rules were simple: When you arrived, you put your name in a bag, and through the course of the evening, ten names would be pulled. Each Slam had a theme such as fathers, gratitude, celebration, challenges. If you were lucky enough to have your name pulled, you would go on stage and have six minutes to tell a story. There were three teams of judges in the audience, and each story would be scored and a winner declared at the end of the night.

I started going to these and loved it. They quickly became extremely popular, to the point that, if you didn't buy a ticket within the first twenty-four hours they were on sale, forget it. You were not getting in. They kept moving these to bigger locales, but they'd sell out in a day.

The first nine Slams I went to, I got very lucky and had my name pulled from the bag each time. One guy who always went said to me, "You should play the horses or the lottery; you have incredible luck." I would always finish second or third in the voting. Then three months in a row my name was not pulled, as the laws of statistics caught up to me. I stopped going, out of frustration, but six months later, decided to give it another try, had my name pulled, and actually won. That landed me back on the stage of the Flynn Theatre along with nine other previous Slam winners for what's called The Moth Grand Slam.

I didn't win that night, but as Josie Leavitt, a fellow storyteller, said to me, "It's not about winning, it's about telling that story you can't *not* tell." She's right.

So I kept trying to do that, telling the stories I could not *not* tell. I kept in touch with one of the people who had done the Main Stage with me that first night, Shannon Cason from Chicago. He told me about a number of other storytelling sites and podcasts and encouraged me to send them story pitches, just as I had done for The Moth a few years earlier.

I did, and I was invited by one called RISK! to be on stage for a performance in Brooklyn, back on my old home turf twenty-four years later. My performance prompted them to ask me to perform in Montreal, and later on in Burlington, when they swung by here. I contacted another podcast called The Lapse, which ran two stories I told on its podcast. I emailed a podcast in Los Angeles called Strangers, telling them about our involvement with the Somali family we had hosted when they arrived in America. "Sounds interesting," they replied, "we'll let you know if we want to follow up." Then a year later, Donald Trump was elected and the ban on Muslim immigration was enacted. "We're interested now," they emailed me, "and we're sending someone on a flight to Burlington in a few days to interview you, your wife and son, and as many of the Somali family who will speak to us."

The storytelling connections kept growing. Someone told me that TEDx was coming to Burlington on the theme of "parenting." (A TEDx event is a local gathering where live TED-like talks are performed; it's independent from the TED talks, with which we are all familiar.) I found out who was in charge and emailed, "I think you should have me on." I was. I connected with someone linked to WGBH-TV in Boston, one of the largest public television stations in the country, because I learned it was holding and televising a storytelling series based on different themes. When I saw that one was called Welcome to the Neighborhood, I wrote about my experience in Brooklyn, when the home for disabled adults was being protested by my neighbors. The station invited me to its state-of-the-art studio in Boston, put me on stage along with five others, with the caveat: "No guarantee that any of your stories will actually make it to our television show." But mine did and was played on hundreds of public television stations around the country.

It was not long after that when The Moth offered to actually pay me to tell my original Main Stage story at an event in Massachusetts. By this point, storytelling, and The Moth in particular, were so popular that corporations, trade associations, and universities were paying for storytelling performances at conferences and other events. In this case it was the University of Massachusetts, which was installing a new president at its Dartmouth campus and had hired The Moth to put on an evening of stories in the main conference hall. The person in charge of this at UMass had listened to a lot of Moth stories and selected four, one of which was mine.

I was happy to oblige, especially when I heard that Ophira was going to again be the host. I drove there a day before the show and met the other storytellers. After we rehearsed, we went out to dinner. I liked all of them, especially Danusia Trevino. I had previously heard her wonderful and moving story about being on jury duty in New York City. When we chatted during dinner, she asked me if I knew about the United Solo Festival. When I said no, she explained that it was the largest one-person-performance festival in the world. It takes place on Broadway, in a theater in Times Square, over the course of several weeks in the fall. Every performer is on stage alone. Some do comedy, some tell stories. People from all over the world apply. After she heard my story, she thought I had a good chance of being accepted.

I had been thinking for a while about doing my own one-person show. I remembered a famous storyteller, Spaulding Gray, who had several one-person shows of his own on Broadway back in the eighties. I Googled "one person shows" and discovered that actor John Leguziamo had done several of them on Broadway and had even received a special Tony Award. I pulled them up online and watched, figuring I could certainly learn from him.

A few months later, Danusia emailed me the link to apply to

United Solo. I knew the competition would be heavy, but every time I had done a Moth Slam performance, I had subsequently paid for the video of it, so I had these to include with my application. In the spring of 2019, I found out I had been selected. I'd be going to Broadway.

This became a very big deal in Vermont. I put something up on Facebook about it, and within twenty-four hours, the local weekly *Seven Days* ran a story. One of the local radio stations wanted to interview me. The show was still months away, in October, but Vermont was buzzing with the news that one of its own would soon be performing in New York City.

A few months earlier, I had met with the new director of the Flynn Theatre and the artistic director to talk about my possibly doing a one-person show. They seemed mildly interested. Once they found out that I was going to be on Broadway, they became very interested.

"We'd love to have you do your own show here," someone from the Flynn told me.

"How much do I have to pay to rent the theater?" I asked.

"You pay us?" she replied. "Oh, no, we'll pay you. We'll put you in the brochure that goes out to all theater members this summer. We're sure it will sell well."

After working at Spectrum all day, I worked hard in my spare time putting together my one-person Broadway show. I had done a prior one-hour version in front of a small live audience in Burlington a few months before and received some excellent feedback. I strung together a number of the Moth Slam stories I had told over the years, built a theme around it, and added music in between each story. So when I got to Broadway I wasn't starting from scratch; I had done my homework and put in the hours.

I also put great effort into selling tickets. Vermonters were not going to travel to New York City for this, but I still had a lot of family and college friends in the metropolitan area. I emailed people and did social media blasts. It worked. The show sold out weeks ahead to the point where I had relatives and friends asking me to pull strings to get them in.

The show was scheduled for Saturday night, October 19, 2019. I went the day before to see the theater. I had walked by this theater hundreds of times back when I was a volunteer at Covenant House thirty-eight years earlier. I had lived blocks away, and Covenant House was around the corner. How ironic that here I was, back where it all had started. The area had drastically changed, though; it had all been crack houses, strip clubs, and porn palaces back then. Now it was international hotels, national chain restaurants, and retail giants. I tried to visit the building where the Covenant House Faith Community had been when I was there; it was now an Italian restaurant.

The show went better than I could have imagined. My eighty-nine-year-old mother came in for it. One brother drove down from Boston, another flew in from North Carolina. Liam and Marybeth flew down. Several of my relatives attended and rugby pals from Villanova showed up, as well as old friends I had volunteered with at Covenant House. It was like a reunion. And Danusia was there.

But there is no doubt that the highlight of the night involved Tony. I had asked him months earlier if I could tell the story of our relationship and connection at my show, without using his last name, and he said fine. I told him I'd send him free tickets for him and his girlfriend. A week before the show, Marybeth said, "Tony will be there. Are you going to ask him if you can point him out to the audience?" I wasn't sure how Tony would feel about this, so I called him to ask.

"It's your show," he said, "so if you want me to stand up at it, I will do that, but only under one condition."

"What's that?" I asked.

"That you wear one of my shirts."

Tony and a friend of his had started a clothing line called 40-Plus. I guess he wanted free advertising.

"Deal," I said.

So I told the Tony story early in the performance, and at the end, said, "Now this wasn't in the original script, but the person

I've been talking about, Tony, is here in the audience. Tony Turner, are you here?"

The lights were blinding in my eyes, as they always are when up on stage, so I wasn't even positive he had made it.

"He sure is!" I heard Marybeth yell out.

I could just make out what I thought was the silhouette of Tony as he stood up. The audience cheered. I motioned for him to come up on stage and join me. As he walked toward me I could see he was crying.

MOTH MAIN STAGE, FLYNN THEATER, BURLINGTON

Everyone was crying. Even the guy playing music for me was crying.

He came up, I hugged him, and asked, "Now Tony, you said I could tell our story but only under one condition. What was it?"

He laughed and said, "That you wear one of my shirts."

"That's right," I said, "and you know I'm a man of my word."

I then began to unbutton the dress shirt I had on and said to the audience, "Don't be afraid folks, I'm not undressing, it's just that I have one of Tony's shirts on underneath this one."

And there it was, a red 40-Plus t-shirt.

"Listen everyone," I continued, "I want all of you to buy Tony's shirts. Every Father's Day that's what I ask my sons to buy for me. I wear them to the gym. They're super comfortable. You all know how to email me or PM me on Facebook. We all need to help Tony sell his shirts."

Tony went back to his seat, and I continued with the show. Afterward we all headed to an Irish pub a few blocks away to celebrate – Tony, his girlfriend, old friends from Covenant House, my siblings, their kids, Marybeth, Liam, and my mom included. It was just great.

Six days later I did an entirely different one-person show at the Flynn in Burlington. I again used my connections and social networks to sell tickets, but this time was easier. The night of the show, I came early for a sound check and walked past the Flynn box office, where I spotted a poster with my picture on it.

I walked in and said to the person selling tickets, "Hey, that's me up there. Can I take a picture of it?"

"Sure," he said, "and do you know your show is almost sold out? There's just a few tickets left."

That was a nice surprise, as it was, later, when I was in the Green Room waiting to go onstage, with literally three minutes to go, and received a text from the Flynn manager for the night.

"We issued you six complimentary tickets for whomever you wanted, and three are still here unclaimed, and there are people at the box office who want to go to your show. Can we sell those three?"

I had completely forgotten about the comp tickets, so I texted back, "Absolutely."

So I had two sold-out storytelling performances in one week. Pretty good considering all this started with a one-minute phone message I had left for The Moth six years earlier.

I ended the Flynn show with the same message I delivered at the end of the Broadway performance:

I tell these stories because I believe they give people hope
– hope that people can change, and they can change for
the better. People can overcome their addictions. They can
overcome their wounds. They can heal. But it just doesn't
happen by chance. It happens because of qualities like
perseverance, resilience, dedication, and courage. And it
takes something else: It takes other people who are willing
to leave their bubbles, to leave their comfort zones, and
reach out in a spirit of compassion, care, and love. And
when you have those two things in combination, that's
when amazing, incredible, miraculous things happen.
So if you leave here tonight with any message at all,
I hope it is that.

Someone asked me once, "Why are you so into The Moth and telling stories like you do?" I answered that I had thought about becoming a priest when I was a child and then again when I was in my twenties, and one of the principle attractions of that was being able to stand up in front of a gathering of people to encourage and inspire them. I didn't pursue that path, but I still feel very much called to that aspect of offering hope to others, giving them a reason to live and to approach life at a different and deeper level.

I view the call to tell stories as every bit as essential to my life as the call to help young people who are struggling and homeless.

· *afterword* ·

I AM STANDING IN FRONT of Spectrum's Drop-In Center, waiting for one of our donors to arrive. This is a man who has been giving to Spectrum for a few years, but I know he can give more, and I plan to ask him to do exactly that.

He is supposed to arrive at 10 a.m., and I am there a few minutes early. It's December, so it's cold outside, and a few kids are waiting beside me for our Drop-In to open at its scheduled time.

One of the young women standing there knows me, so she comes over with an excited look on her face.

"Hey Mark," she says, "you know what? I've been sober for eleven days! Can you believe that? Eleven days!"

"Good for you," I tell her. "Good for you. And tomorrow will be day twelve. One day at a time, right?"

"That's right," she says. "One day at a time."

And then she says, "You know, I don't know where I'd be without the staff at Spectrum. I really don't. I don't even think I'd even be alive if not for Spectrum." She says this over and over again.

A few seconds later she spots one of our female staff members pulling up in her car; they are apparently headed somewhere together, for what purpose she does not say, but I am guessing it's for a job interview or something related to school. This young woman and I both wave to this person, who is one of the kindest and most loving and compassionate people I have ever met.

She says goodbye to me and gets in the car. They drive away.

Two weeks later she sends me a hand-written Christmas card:

Dear Mark,
I wanted to write to you a letter explaining what Spectrum
and Drop-In mean to me, how utilizing Drop-In can help

me succeed, acknowledge mistakes I've made in the past, and my game plan moving forward... .

Drop-In means a lot to me. First and foremost it means support. Through Drop-In I receive case management. A point person, all the staff who laugh and joke with me, they do their best to cheer me up when I am sad, strive to keep me on a good path and help calm me down when I want to punch walls. It provides a full belly, community, clean and warm clothes, a place to stay sober, fun activities to keep me out of trouble, and stability. Essentially it's the home I NEVER HAD!

In the past I've struggled with Drop-In rules such as staying sober in the space, being respectful to staff and other clients, and controlling my emotions. So I want to apologize to you and all of Spectrum for my actions. I'm so sorry and realize now that I was a huge jerk. I took all of the love, support, and services for granted.

At the time I was in a ton of pain. I also felt untouchable. I thought experimenting with drugs and abusing alcohol was the only way to make things better. I didn't know how to accept the things I've been through and continue to go through. Sometimes I feel the weight of the world on my shoulders. As a result I didn't know what to do with the support Spectrum offered me.

Over the past six months I've made some changes to help better my life. I started going to counseling and consistently meeting with staff at Spectrum. I'm now 28 days sober, a big thanks to the Valley Vista drug rehab for helping me to detox. I spend less time downtown and at the park, and lastly I am respectful to Spectrum and follow the guidelines while on Pearl Street.

*My game plan moving forward is to continue working
with all my supports, to continue meeting with my
therapist to gain coping skills and emotional control.
I'll also be moving in with my Gram (temporarily) while
I continue my journey to sobriety.*

*I know I wouldn't be able to go through this alone, and
with Spectrum I don't have to. I'm so thankful to have
you all in my life. You Rock!*

HAVE A MERRY CHRISTMAS!

. .

A WOMAN WHO HAS KNOWN ME since my days at Domus in Connecticut
recently asked me, "What's your dream job?"

I thought for a second and then responded, "I think I'm in it."

It's true. I often feel like I am the most fortunate person in
the world, to be doing this kind of work, with kids such as this,
working alongside other people who are so dedicated and caring.
Does that mean I will stay at Spectrum forever? Maybe. I'm not
sure. Every morning I say this prayer: "This is the work I am
doing today Lord. Help me to do it well. If there's something
else you want me to be doing with my life, please let me know.
Otherwise I am staying the course."

That's it. A pretty straightforward request.

I look back at the past decades, and all the crazy twists and
turns: Guatemala, Covenant House, Epiphany, St. Christopher's,
Domus, Vermont, meeting Marybeth, The Moth, Tony, Broadway. None of it ever, ever could have been predicted, much less
planned out. Impossible. And yet I have to believe there was some
guiding hand in the midst of it all, that I was being led the entire
time. I call that guiding hand God. Others may call it The Universe,
Fate, or something else. But to me it's God.

I feel the same way about meeting Marybeth. When her
Granddad was alive he once told my parents, "Those two belong

together." We do. I have stated to many people, "My life improved dramatically when I met Marybeth and it improved even more when we moved to Vermont." (By the way, after stints as a college professor, then the creator of a writing program for women in prison, then a nonprofit administrator, Marybeth was recruited to run for political office and is now serving her second term in the Vermont State Legislature, fighting for the rights of low-income families, survivors of domestic violence and New Americans. Among other things!)

And I totally lucked out when it comes to my two sons. Aiden graduated from college, did a few different things for work, and at age 30 decided to go back to school to become a Registered Nurse. He now works in the state psychiatric hospital in New Hampshire. He is married to a wonderful woman, Audrey, and they have two beautiful boys of their own. They are awesome parents to great kids. I could not be prouder.

Liam at this moment is age 18 and applying to colleges. He works hard and does well in school, is president of the board of directors of a nonprofit which helps young children in our town, excels in soccer and regularly beats me in whichever sport I foolishly dare to challenge him. He is a fantastic kid.

I feel very fortunate and blessed. I sometimes think that if I was diagnosed tomorrow with some terminal illness, I would not have one regret. I'd feel like I did it all, that I had a great life here on Earth, and that I spent my time and my gifts well.

I was asked to speak about one of my rugby teammates who passed away a few years ago, at the reception after the funeral. "He left it all on the field, in both rugby and in life," I said, explaining, "He held nothing back. Every bit of energy and effort he had in him, he expended to the utmost, right to the end."

If someone says that about me, at my funeral, it'd be a fitting end.

And I'd be quite happy.

CPSIA information can be obtained
at www.ICGtesting.com
Printed in the USA
LVHW030959300621
691472LV00009B/1146